BY TEJU COLE

Known and
Strange Things

Known and
Strange Things

ESSAYS

Teju Cole

Random House
New York

A Random House Trade Paperback Original

Published in the United States by Random House, an imprint and division of Penguin Random House LLC, New York.

RANDOM HOUSE and the HOUSE colophon are registered trademarks of Penguin Random House LLC.

Art permission credits are located on pages 389–390.
Text permission credits are located on pages 391–393.

LIBRARY OF CONGRESS CATALOGING-IN-PUBLICATION DATA
Names: Cole, Teju.
Title: Known and strange things : essays / Teju Cole.
Description: New York : Random House, 2016. | Consists of various essays some previously published in various journals and periodicals on art, literature, and politics.
Identifiers: LCCN 2015042074 | ISBN 9780812989786 |
ISBN 9780812989793 (ebook)
Classification: LCC PR9387.9.C67 A6 2016 |
DDC 824'.92—dc23
LC record available at http://lccn.loc.gov/2015042074

Printed in the United States of America on acid-free paper

randomhousebooks.com

4689753

Book design by Simon M. Sullivan

For Michael, Amitava, and Siddhartha

Contents

SECTION III · BEING THERE

Contents · xi

SECTION IV · EPILOGUE

Preface

So. The Spear-Danes in days gone by
and the kings who ruled them had courage and greatness.
We have heard of those princes' heroic campaigns.

WHEN I AM trying out a new pen in a shop, I write out the first words of *Beowulf* as translated by Seamus Heaney. Years ago, I memorized that opening page. After a while, those were the words that came most readily to hand when I was testing the flow of ink. And, once, an attendant in a shop, reading over my shoulder, said: "Hey, that's real nice. Did you just make that up right now or . . . ?"

We are our habits in sum. If someone asks me to say something in Yoruba, almost without thinking about it, I recite a tongue-twister from childhood: "Opolopo opolo ni ko mo pe opolopo eniyan l'opolo l'opolopo." ("Many frogs do not know that many people are very intelligent.") During soundcheck at a speech or public event, to test the microphone, instead of singing scales or counting, I start telling Lucian Freud's favorite joke, a joke about bodily fluids that is also notable for not being particularly "Freudian" in the sense associated with Lucian's grandfather Sigmund.

The wife of an alcoholic man had finally reached the end of her patience and said to him, "Listen, I can't take this anymore.

If you come home drunk one more night, with drink on your breath and vomit all over your shirt, it's over. We're getting a divorce." He manages to stay out of trouble for a while, but soon he gets the itch to drink again, and his friends insist that he come out with them that weekend. Usually, by this point, the sound engineers tell me they've got what they need, and so the joke ends there.

I reiterate *Beowulf,* I recite my Yoruba tongue-twister, I tell Lucian Freud's joke: we are creatures of private convention. But we are also the ways in which we enlarge our coasts. This book tracks some of my most vital enthusiasms, and even the semi-alert reader will quickly determine which places and writers are my touchstones. But it also registers some first encounters, including encounters with certain things I now consider irreplaceable parts of my life.

The man says, "No, my wife has reached the end of her rope. I can't come home drunk anymore." And one of his mates says, "Listen, it's easy. Just put a twenty in your front pocket." "A twenty in my front pocket? What for?" "So that when you come home, in case you've thrown up on your shirt, you can tell her: 'I'm sober, but some fellow in the pub threw up on my shirt. He was very apologetic, and in fact, what's this'—you bring out the twenty—'he gave me a twenty to get the shirt cleaned.'"

I used to wonder what creative freedom would look like. If I could write about anything I wanted, what would I write about? It has been my immense good fortune to have exactly that opportunity. Through the work I was assigned at various papers and magazines, in response to various occasions and invitations, I was able to follow my nose and think through a wide variety of subjects. The area I returned to most often was photography. But literature, music, travel, and politics were also subjects in which I was deeply absorbed. Through the act of writing, I was able to find out what I knew about these things, what I was able to know, and where the limits of knowing lay.

So this guy thinks, That's a brilliant idea. That weekend, he goes out with the lads, and they get drunk out of their minds as usual. He staggers home. He's thrown up on himself. He's a mess. She's waited up, and immediately says, "Look at you, you're disgusting, you lack self-control, it's over." "Wait, wait," he sputters. At this point, the sound engineers reiterate that they definitely have enough, thanks very much.

This book takes a more flexible approach to "essays" than most books of its kind. But it is not a compendium of all the nonfiction I have in print over an eight-year period of almost constant writing. It is certainly not an attempt to give a systematic account of all my preoccupations. I have excluded a large number of smaller pieces, a few newspaper columns, and some essays that were too topical for inclusion. In the years covered by these essays, I thought a great deal about poetry, music, and painting, I traveled to dozens of countries, and I engaged with many interesting artists whom I did not write about, or did not write about to my satisfaction.

There is another possible book that contains all that is not in this one. In that book, other habits take center stage, other unfamiliar experiences are recorded, and the jokes are told all the way to the end. That book's disadvantage, though, would be its exclusion of what is published here. It would omit these gathered experiences in favor of others. That other book might have a different tenor: it might perhaps be more critical in tone, be more analytical in approach, contain more argumentative opinion. But this book, the one you hold in your hands, though it has all those elements, favors epiphany. I think of Mrs. Ramsay's words in *To the Lighthouse:* "Everything seemed possible. Everything seemed right. . . . Of such moments, she thought, the thing is made that endures."

This book contains what I have loved and witnessed, what has seemed right and what has brought joy, what I have been troubled and encouraged by, and what has fostered my sense of possibility and made me feel, as Seamus Heaney wrote, like "a hurry through which known and strange things pass."

TEJU COLE
Brooklyn, July 2016

SECTION I

Reading Things

Black Body

THEN THE BUS began driving into clouds, and between one cloud and the next we caught glimpses of the town below. It was suppertime and the town was a constellation of yellow points. We arrived thirty minutes after leaving that town, which was called Leuk. The train to Leuk had come in from Visp, the train from Visp had come from Bern, and the train before that was from Zürich, from which I had started out in the afternoon. Three trains, a bus, and a short stroll, all of it through beautiful country, and then we reached Leukerbad in darkness. So Leukerbad, not far in terms of absolute distance, was not all that easy to get to. August 2, 2014: it was James Baldwin's birthday. Were he alive, he would be turning ninety. He is one of those people just on the cusp of escaping the contemporary and slipping into the historical—John Coltrane would have turned eighty-eight in the same year; Martin Luther King, Jr., would have turned eighty-five—people who could still be with us but who feel, at times, very far away, as though they lived centuries ago.

James Baldwin left Paris and came to Leukerbad for the first time in 1951. His lover Lucien Happersberger's family had a chalet in a village up in the mountains. And so Baldwin, who was depressed and distracted at the time, went, and the village (which is also called Loèche-les-Bains) proved to be a refuge for him. His first trip was in the summer, and lasted two weeks. Then he returned, to his own surprise, for two more winters. His first novel, *Go Tell It on the Mountain,* found its final form here. He had struggled with the book for eight years, and he finally finished it in this unlikely retreat. He wrote something else, too, an essay called "Stranger in the Village"; it was this essay, even more than the novel, that brought me to Leukerbad.

"Stranger in the Village" first appeared in *Harper's Magazine* in 1953, and then in the essay collection *Notes of a Native Son* in 1955. It recounts the experience of being black in an all-white village. It begins with a sense of an extreme journey, like Charles Darwin's in the Galápagos or Tété-Michel Kpomassie's in Greenland. But then it opens out into other concerns and into a different voice, swiveling to look at the American racial situation in the 1950s. The part of the essay that focuses on the Swiss village is both bemused and sorrowful. Baldwin is alert to the absurdity of being a writer from New York who is considered in some way inferior by Swiss villagers, many of whom have never traveled. But, later in the essay, when he writes about race in America, he is not at all bemused. He is angry and prophetic, writing with a hard clarity and carried along by a precipitous eloquence.

I took a room at the Hotel Mercure Bristol the night I arrived. I opened the windows to a dark view in which nothing was visible, but I knew that in the darkness loomed the Daubenhorn mountain. I ran a hot bath and lay neck-deep in the water with my old paperback copy of *Notes of a Native Son.* The tinny sound from my laptop was Bessie Smith singing "I'm Wild About That Thing," a filthy blues number and a masterpiece of plausible deniability: "Don't hold it, baby, when I cry / Give me every bit of it, else I'll die." She could be singing about a trombone. And it was there in the bath, with his words and her voice, that I had my body-double moment: here I was in Leukerbad, with Bessie Smith singing across the years from 1929; and I am black like him; and I am slender; and have a gap in my front teeth; and am not especially tall (no, write it: short); and am cool on the page and animated in person, except when it is the other way around; and I was once a fervid teenage preacher (Baldwin: "Nothing that has happened to me since equals the power and the glory that I sometimes felt when, in the middle of a sermon, I knew that I was somehow, by some miracle, really carrying, as they said, 'the Word'——when the church and I were one"); and I, too, left the church; and I call New York home even when not living there; and feel myself in all places, from New York City to rural Switzerland, the custodian of a black body, and have to find the language for all of what that means to me and to the people who look at me. The ancestor had briefly taken possession of the descendant. It was a moment of identification. In that Swiss village in the days that followed, that moment guided me.

"From all available evidence no black man had ever set foot in this tiny Swiss village before I came," Baldwin wrote. But the village has grown considerably since his visits, more than sixty years ago. They've seen blacks now; I wasn't a remarkable sight. There were a few glances at the hotel when I was checking in, and in the fine restaurant just up the road; there are always glances. There are glances in Zürich, where I spent the summer, and there are glances in New York City, which has been my home for fourteen years. There are glances all over Europe and in India, and anywhere I go outside Africa. The test is how long the glances last, whether they become stares, with what intent they occur, whether they contain any degree of hostility or mockery, and to what extent connections, money, or mode of dress shield me in these situations. To be a stranger is to be looked at, but to be black is to be looked at especially. ("The children shout Neger! Neger! as I walk along the streets.") Leukerbad has changed, but in which way? There were, in fact, no bands of children on the street, and few children anywhere at all. Presumably the children of Leukerbad, like children the world over, were indoors, frowning over computer games, checking Facebook, or watching music videos. Perhaps some of the older folks I saw in the streets were once the very children who had been so surprised by the sight of Baldwin, and about whom, in the essay, he struggles to take a reasonable tone: "In all of this, in which it must be conceded that there was the charm of genuine wonder and in which there was certainly no element of intentional unkindness, there was yet no suggestion that I was human: I was simply a living wonder." But now the children or grandchildren of those children are connected to the world in a different way. Maybe some xenophobia or racism is part of their lives, but part of their lives, too, are Beyoncé, Drake, and Meek Mill, the music I hear pulsing from Swiss clubs on Friday nights.

Baldwin had to bring his records with him in the fifties, like a secret stash of medicine, and he had to haul his phonograph up to Leukerbad, so that the sound of the American blues could keep him connected to a Harlem of the spirit. I listened to some of the same music while I was there, as a way of being with him: Bessie Smith singing "I Need a Little Sugar in My Bowl" ("I need a little sugar in my bowl / I need a little hot dog on my roll"), Fats Waller singing "Your Feet's Too Big." I listened to my own playlist as well: Bettye Swann, Billie Holiday, Jean Wells, *Coltrane Plays the Blues,* the Physics, Childish Gambino. The music you travel with helps you to create your own internal weather. But the world participates, too: when I sat down to lunch at the Römerhof restaurant one afternoon—that day, all the customers and staff were white—the music playing overhead was Whitney Houston's "I Wanna Dance with Somebody." History is now and black America.

At dinner, at a pizzeria, a table of British tourists stared at me. But the waitress was part black, and at the hotel one of the staff members at the spa was an older black man. "People are trapped in history, and history is trapped in them," Baldwin wrote. But it is also true that the little pieces of history move around at tremendous speed, settling with a not-always-clear logic, and rarely settling for long. And perhaps more interesting than my not being the only black person in the village is the plain fact that many of the other people I saw were also foreigners. This was the biggest change of all. If, back then, the village had a pious and convalescent air about it, the feel of "a lesser Lourdes," it is much busier now, packed with visitors from other parts of Switzerland, and from Germany, France, Italy, and all over Europe, Asia, and the Americas. It has become the most popular thermal resort in the Alps. The municipal baths are full. There are hotels on every street, at every price point, and there are restaurants and luxury-goods shops. If you wish to buy an eye-wateringly costly watch at 4,600 feet above sea level, it is now possible to do so.

The better hotels have their own thermal pools. At the Hotel Mercure Bristol, I took an elevator down to the spa and sat in the dry sauna. A few minutes later, I slipped into the pool and floated outside in the warm water. Others were there, but not many. A light rain fell. We were ringed by mountains and held in the immortal blue.

In her brilliant *Harlem Is Nowhere,* Sharifa Rhodes-Pitts writes, "In almost every essay James Baldwin wrote about Harlem, there is a moment when he commits a literary sleight-of-hand so particular that, if he'd been an athlete, sportscasters would have codified the maneuver and named it 'the Jimmy.' I think of it in cinematic terms, because its effect reminds me of a technique wherein camera operators pan out by starting with a tight shot and then zoom out to a wide view while the lens remains focused on a point in the distance." This move Rhodes-Pitts describes, this sudden widening of focus, is present even in his essays that are not about Harlem. In "Stranger in the Village," there's a passage about seven pages in where one can feel the rhetoric revving up, as Baldwin prepares to leave behind the calm, fabular atmosphere of the opening section. Of the villagers, he writes:

These people cannot be, from the point of view of power, strangers anywhere in the world; they have made the modern world, in effect, even if they do not know it. The most illiterate among them is related, in a way I am not, to Dante, Shakespeare, Michelangelo, Aeschylus, Da Vinci, Rembrandt, and Racine; the cathedral at Chartres says something to them which it cannot say to me, as indeed would New York's Empire State Building, should anyone here ever see it. Out of their hymns and dances come Beethoven and Bach. Go back a few centuries and they are in their full glory—but I am in Africa, watching the conquerors arrive.

What is this list about? Does it truly bother Baldwin that the people of Leukerbad are related, through some faint familiarity, to Chartres? That some distant genetic thread links them to the Beethoven string quartets? After all, as he argues later in the essay, no one can deny the impact "the presence of the Negro has had on the American character." He understands the truth and the art in Bessie Smith's work. He does not, and cannot—I want to believe—rate the blues below Bach. But there was a certain narrowness in received ideas of black culture in the 1950s. In the time since then, there has been enough black cultural achievement from which to compile an all-star team: there's been Coltrane and Monk and Miles, and Ella and Billie and Aretha. Toni Morrison, Wole Soyinka, and Derek Walcott happened, as have Audre Lorde, and Chinua Achebe, and Bob Marley. The body was not abandoned for the mind's sake: Alvin Ailey, Arthur Ashe, and Michael Jordan happened, too. The source of jazz and the blues also gave the world hip-hop, Afrobeat, dancehall, and house. And, yes, by the time James Baldwin died, in 1987, he, too, was recognized as an all-star.

Thinking further about the cathedral at Chartres, about the greatness of that achievement and about how, in his view, it included blacks only in the negative, as devils, Baldwin writes that "the American Negro has arrived at his identity by virtue of the absoluteness of his estrangement from his past." But the distant African past has also become much more available than it was in 1953. It would not occur to me to think that, centuries ago, I was "in Africa, watching the conquerors arrive." But I suspect that for Baldwin this is, in part, a piece of oratory, a grim cadence on which to end a paragraph. In "A Question of Identity" (another essay collected in *Notes of a Native Son*), he writes, "The truth about that past is not that it is too brief, or too superficial, but only that we, having turned our faces so resolutely away from it, have never demanded from it what it has to give." The fourteenth-century court artists of Ife made bronze sculptures using a complicated casting process lost to Europe since antiquity, and which was not rediscovered there until the Renaissance. Ife sculptures are equal to the works of Ghiberti or Donatello. From their precision and formal sumptuousness we can extrapolate the contours of a great monarchy, a network of sophisticated ateliers, and a cosmopolitan world of trade and knowledge. And it was not only Ife. All of West Africa was a cultural ferment. From the egalitarian government of the Igbo to the goldwork of the Ashanti courts, the brass sculpture of Benin, the military achievement of the Mandinka Empire and the musical virtuosi who praised those war heroes, this was a region of the world too deeply invested in art and life to simply be reduced to a caricature of "watching the conquerors arrive." We know better now. We know it with a stack of corroborating scholarship and we know it implicitly, so that even making a list of the accomplishments feels faintly tedious, and is helpful mainly as a counter to Eurocentrism.

There's no world in which I would surrender the intimidating beauty of Yoruba-language poetry for, say, Shakespeare's sonnets, or one in which I'd prefer chamber orchestras playing baroque music to the koras of Mali. I'm happy to own all of it. This carefree confidence is, in part, the gift of time. It is a dividend of the struggle of people from earlier generations. I feel little alienation in museums, full though they are of other people's ancestors. But this question of filiation tormented Bald-

win. He was sensitive to what was great in world art, and
sensitive to his own sense of exclusion from it. He made a similar list in the title essay of *Notes of a Native Son* (one begins to
feel that lists like this had been flung at him during arguments):
"In some subtle way, in a really profound way, I brought to
Shakespeare, Bach, Rembrandt, to the Stones of Paris, to the
Cathedral at Chartres, and the Empire State Building a special
attitude. These were not really my creations, they did not contain my history; I might search them in vain forever for any reflection of myself. I was an interloper; this was not my heritage."
The lines throb with sadness. What he loves does not love him
in return.

This is where I part ways with Baldwin. I disagree not with
his particular sorrow but with the self-abnegation that pinned
him to it. Bach, so profoundly human, is my heritage. I am not
an interloper when I look at a Rembrandt portrait. I care for
them more than some white people do, just as some white people care more for aspects of African art than I do. I can oppose
white supremacy and still rejoice in Gothic architecture. In
this, I stand with Ralph Ellison: "The values of my own people
are neither 'white' nor 'black,' they are American. Nor can I see
how they could be anything else, since we are people who are
involved in the texture of the American experience." And yet I
(born in the United States more than half a century after Baldwin) continue to understand, because I have experienced in my
own body the undimmed fury he felt about racism. In his writing there is a hunger for life, for all of it, and a strong wish to
not be accounted nothing (a mere nigger, a mere *neger*) when he
knows himself to be so much. And this "so much" is neither a
matter of ego about his writing nor an anxiety about his fame in
New York or in Paris. It is about the incontestable fundamentals

of a person: pleasure, sorrow, love, humor, and grief, and the complexity of the interior landscape that sustains those feelings. Baldwin was astonished that anyone anywhere should question these fundamentals—thereby burdening him with the supreme waste of time that is racism—let alone so many people in so many places. This unflagging ability to be shocked rises like steam off his written pages. "The rage of the disesteemed is personally fruitless," he writes, "but it is also absolutely inevitable."

Leukerbad gave Baldwin a way to think about white supremacy from its first principles. It was as though he found it in its simplest form there. The men who suggested that he learn to ski so that they might mock him, the villagers who accused him behind his back of being a firewood thief, the ones who wished to touch his hair and suggested that he grow it out and make himself a winter coat, and the children who, "having been taught that the devil is a black man, scream[ed] in genuine anguish" as he approached: Baldwin saw these as prototypes (preserved like coelacanths) of attitudes that had evolved into the more intimate, intricate, familiar, and obscene American forms of white supremacy that he already knew so well.

It is a beautiful village. I liked the mountain air. But when I returned to my room from the thermal baths, or from strolling in the streets with my camera, I read the news online. There I found an unending sequence of crises: in the Middle East, in Africa, in Russia, and everywhere else, really. Pain was general. But within that larger distress was a set of linked stories, and thinking about "Stranger in the Village," thinking with its help, was like injecting a contrast dye into my encounter with the news. The American police continued shooting unarmed black men, or killing them in other ways. The protests that followed, in black communities, were countered with violence by a police force that is becoming indistinguishable from an invading army. People began to see a connection between the various events: the shootings, the fatal choke hold, the stories of who was not given lifesaving medication. And black communities were flooded with outrage and grief.

In all of this, a smaller, much less significant story (but one that nevertheless signified), caught my attention. The mayor of New York and his police chief have a public-policy obsession with cleaning, with cleansing, and they decided that arresting members of the dance troupes that perform in moving subway cars was one of the ways to clean up the city. I read the excuses for this becoming a priority: some people feared being seriously injured by an errant kick (it has not happened, but they sure feared it), some people considered the dancing a nuisance, some policymakers believed that going after misdemeanors is a way of preempting major crimes. And so, to combat this menace of dancers, the police moved in. They began chasing, and harassing, and handcuffing. The "problem" was dancers, and the dancers were, for the most part, black boys. The newspapers took the same tone as the government: a sniffy dismissal of the performers. And yet these same dancers are a bright spark in the day, a moment of unregulated beauty, artists with talents unimaginable to their audience. What kind of thinking would consider their abolition an improvement in city life? No one considers Halloween trick-or-treaters a public menace. There's no law enforcement against people selling Girl Scout cookies or against Jehovah's Witnesses. But the black body comes prejudged, and as a result it is placed in needless jeopardy. To be black is to bear the brunt of selective enforcement of the law, and to inhabit a psychic unsteadiness in which there is no guarantee of personal safety. You are a black body first, before you are a kid walking down the street or a Harvard professor who has misplaced his keys.

William Hazlitt, in an 1821 essay entitled "The Indian Jugglers," wrote words that I think of when I see a great athlete or dancer: "Man, thou art a wonderful animal, and thy ways past finding out! Thou canst do strange things, but thou turnest them to little account!—To conceive of this effort of extraordinary dexterity distracts the imagination and makes admiration breathless." In the presence of the admirable, some are breathless not with admiration but with rage. They object to the presence of the black body (an unarmed boy in a street, a man buying a toy, a dancer in the subway, a bystander) as much as they object to the presence of the black mind. And simultaneous with these erasures is the unending collection of profit from black labor and black innovation. Throughout the culture, there are imitations of the gait, bearing, and dress of the black body, a vampiric "everything but the burden" co-option of black life.

Leukerbad is ringed by mountains: the Daubenhorn, the Torrenthorn, the Rinderhorn. A high mountain pass called the Gemmi, another 2,800 feet above the village, connects the canton of Valais with the Bernese Oberland. Through this landscape—craggy, bare in places and verdant elsewhere, a textbook instance of the sublime—one moves as though through a dream. The Gemmipass is famous for good reason, and Goethe was once there, as were Byron, Twain, and Picasso. The pass is mentioned in a Sherlock Holmes adventure, when

Holmes crosses it on his way to the fateful meeting with Professor Moriarty at Reichenbach Falls. There was bad weather the day I went up, rain and fog, but that was good luck, as it meant I was alone on the trails. While there, I remembered a story that Lucien Happersberger told about Baldwin going out on a hike in these mountains. Baldwin had lost his footing during the ascent, and the situation was precarious for a moment. But Happersberger, who was an experienced climber, reached out a hand, and Baldwin was saved. It was out of this frightening moment, this appealingly biblical moment, that Baldwin got the title for the book he had been struggling to write: *Go Tell It on the Mountain*.

If Leukerbad was his mountain pulpit, the United States was his audience. The remote village gave him a sharper view of what things looked like back home. He was a stranger in Leukerbad, Baldwin wrote, but there was no possibility for blacks to be strangers in the United States, or for whites to achieve the fantasy of an all-white America purged of blacks. This fantasy about the disposability of black life is a constant in American history. It takes a while to understand that this disposability continues. It takes whites a while to understand it; it takes non-black people of color a while to understand it; and it takes some blacks, whether they've always lived in the United States or are latecomers like myself, weaned elsewhere on other struggles, a while to understand it. American racism has many moving parts, and has had enough centuries in which to evolve an impressive camouflage. It can hoard its malice in great stillness for a long time, all the while pretending to look the other way. Like misogyny, it is atmospheric. You don't see it at first. But understanding comes.

"People who shut their eyes to reality simply invite their own destruction, and anyone who insists on remaining in a state of innocence long after that innocence is dead turns himself into a monster." The news of the day (old news, but raw as a fresh wound) is that black American life is disposable from the point of view of policing, sentencing, economic policy, and countless terrifying forms of disregard. There is a vivid performance of innocence, but there's no actual innocence left. The moral ledger remains so far in the negative that we can't even get started on the question of reparations. Baldwin wrote "Stranger in the Village" more than sixty years ago. Now what?

Natives on the Boat

TWO YEARS AGO, I was invited to a dinner party in New York. It took place on the Upper East Side of Manhattan, in a penthouse apartment. Our host was not merely rich: she had a name that through long association with money had itself become a shorthand for wealth. The dinner was being held in honor of a writer, by now old and famous, on the publication of his latest and perhaps final book. And because the book was about Africa, and because as a man ages his thoughts circle around questions of legacy, the writer, who was not himself African, had requested, in lieu of a normal book launch, a quiet dinner with a group of young African writers. This was how I came to be invited.

I stood in the luxurious living room of the penthouse, glass in hand, surrounded by Morandi's paintings and Picasso's prints. To the sound of a small bell, from a private elevator the old writer and his middle-aged wife emerged. He was short and stout—a little fat, even, though you could see he hadn't always been so—and he walked across the marble floor unsteadily, with the aid of a walking stick, and with the aid of his wife, a dark-haired, dark-eyed woman, taller than he, glamorous in her pashmina. My agent, who was also the old writer's agent, introduced us. "Teju, meet Vidia Naipaul."

The faint hiss of champagne being poured. The clink of glasses. Far below us was the obscurity of the East River and, beyond it, the borough of Queens, glimmering in the dark. In all that darkness was an infinity of information, invisible under the cloak of night. Vidia—please call me Vidia, he had said—whom the agent had told about my work on Lagos and New York, said, "Have you written about Tutuola?" I said no, I hadn't. "It would be interesting," he said. I demurred, and said I found the work odd, minor. There was something in Tutuola's ghosts and forests and unidiomatic English that confirmed the prejudices of a European audience. "That's what would be interesting about it," he said. "A reconsideration. You would be able to say something about it, something of value."

"There's a marvelous view from the roof," our host said. "Vidia's afraid of heights. He gets vertigo," said Nadira, Lady Naipaul. And when the women had moved away, because I was nervous, because I wanted to show off a little for the master, I said: "Maybe we don't all need the thrill of physical heights. Frank O'Connor writes somewhere that reading is another form of height, and a more perilous one." "Oh?" Vidia said. "That's very good." And we were called in to dinner.

I write these words in London. August has ended. I am sitting on the enclosed upper deck of a kind of boat. The boat is an architectural folly that has been placed on top of the Queen Elizabeth Hall, as though it has been stranded after a flood. The sky is crisp and white, the sky that has returned to page one as it does each morning. Below, the busy little people begin to go about their day, inscrutable to the one who watches and unknown to themselves. London, from this peculiar vantage point, is precise as an engraving. Toy red buses cross and recross

Waterloo Bridge as though maddened into repetition. St. Paul's Cathedral leads white, the buildings across the skyline follow, white on white. The stone of London is white and pale, the sky is white and pale and beginning to intimate blue. Laden barges bring news of the world in the form of goods. Above all this I sit on a boat stranded in time's river.

At dinner, in addition to Sir Vidia and Lady Naipaul, there was a well-known American actor and his third wife. There were Vidia's editor, our agent and his wife, our host, and three other young African writers. The host's family claret was served with dinner, served after a proud announcement of its provenance, and poured almost ritualistically. Such things are bound to disappoint, but this one was outstanding. And, buoyed by it, we began to toast V. S. Naipaul, who sat bunched up in his chair, serene but a little tired, nodding repeatedly, saying, "Thank you, thank you," with his characteristic *bis*, the repetition of language that was second nature to him. When three or four others had spoken, I gathered up my courage and said: "Vidia, I would like to join the others in celebrating your work"— though, in truth, the new book, called *The Masque of Africa,* ostensibly a study of African religion, was oddly narrow and stilted, not as good as his other voyages of inquiry, though still full of beautiful observation and language; but there is a time for literary criticism, and a time for toasts. I went on: "Your work, which has meant so much to an entire generation of postcolonial writers. I don't agree with all your views, and in fact there are many of them I strongly disagree with"—I said "strongly" with what I hoped was a menacing tone—"but from you I have learned how to be productively disagreeable in my own views. I and others have learned, from you, that it is fine to be independent, that it is fine to go your own way and go against the crowd. You went your own way no matter what it cost you. Thank you for that." I raised my glass, and everyone else raised theirs. A silence fell, and Vidia looked sober, almost chastened. But it was a soft look. "Thank you," he said. "I'm very moved. I'm very moved."

This boat of which I am temporary captain is named the *Roi des Belges*. In 1890 Joseph Conrad piloted a steamship down the Congo on a boat with the same name. That journey became his inspiration for *Heart of Darkness,* a puzzling novella with nested narrators who unfold a shadowed, strangled, brutal tale. He wrote and published it in the last year of the nineteenth century. So, this perch on which I sit above the Thames—the sky is blue now, the 180-degree view of it full of long stratus clouds—this perch in which the city is exposed to me but I am not to it, is an homage to Conrad's bitter vision. What might it mean when the native pilots the ship? What happens when the ones on the shore, numerous, unindividuated, are white?

Heart of Darkness was written when rapacious extraction of African resources by European adventure was gospel truth—as it still is. The book helped create the questions that occupy us till this day. What does it mean to write about others? Who are these others? More pressingly, who are the articulate "we"? In *Heart of Darkness,* the natives—the niggers, as they are called in the book, the word falling each time like a lance—speak only twice, once to express enthusiasm for cannibalism, then, later, to bring the barely articulate report "Mistah Kurtz, he dead." Otherwise, these niggers, these savages, are little more than shadows and violence, either pressed into dumb service on the boat, or launching dumb, grieved, uncomprehending, and deadly attacks on it from the shore. Not only is this primitive, subhuman Africa incoherent to any African, it is incoherent to any right-thinking non-African, too. A hundred years ago, it was taken as the commonplace truth; it wasn't outside the mainstream of European opinions about Africans. But we have all moved on. Those things are in the past, are they not?

"For the first four days it rained." Vidia's face crinkled with pleasure. "You like that?" "I do, very much. It's simple. It's promising." "I like it, too!" he said. What I had just quoted was the first line of *The Enigma of Arrival,* his intricate novel about life in rural England. I value Naipaul for his travel narratives, for his visits to the so-called dark places of the earth, the patient way he teases out complicated nonfictional stories from his various interlocutors in Iran, Indonesia, India, and elsewhere. I like *India: A Million Mutinies Now, Among the Believers,* and the long essay "The Crocodiles of Yamoussoukro," which, uncomfortable as they are in parts, also have the force of revelation. They are courageous not because they voice unpopular, and sometimes wrongheaded, opinion, but for the opposite reason: the books contain little opinion and are, rather, artful compressions of dozens of conversations. These are texts in which the natives, whoever they might be, speak for themselves and give an account, sometimes inadvertently, of their contradictory beliefs and ways of life, but also of their deep humanity. But it was *The Enigma of Arrival,* tirelessly intense, its intelligence fastened to the world of humans and of nature, that most influenced my own work, my own ear. I adore, still, its language, its inner music.

For the first four days it rained. I could hardly see where I was. Then it stopped raining and beyond the lawn and outbuildings in front of my cottage I saw fields with stripped trees on the boundaries of each field; and far away, depending on the light, glints of a little river, glints which sometimes appeared, oddly, to be above the level of the land.

In no small part, Vidia's writing held my interest because he, too, after all, was one of the natives. He, too, was thought savage and, in his cruel term, half-made. He was a contradiction like no other.

Dinner was over. We were in conversation, Vidia, our host, and me. He was in a good mood, flattered by the attention. Our host brought some rare books from her collection to show us. They were special editions of Mark Twain's works, and on the flyleaf of each was an epigram written by Twain and, below each, his signature. The epigrams were typical Twain: ironic, dark. And so we leaned over the old volumes, and Vidia and I squinted and tried to make out the words from Twain's elegant but occasionally illegible hand. We were sitting side by side, and Vidia, unsteady, had placed a hand on my knee for support, unselfconsciously. I read: "By trying, we can easily learn to endure adversity. Another man's, I mean." Laughter. "To succeed in other trades, capacity must be shown; in the law, concealment of it will do." More laughter. Vidia began, "You know, these remind me very much of . . ." Ever the eager student, I blurted out, "La Rochefoucauld.""Yes!" he said. "Yes! La Rochefoucauld." And with wonder in his eyes, the weight from his hand and arm bearing down on me, he turned his head up to our host, who stood just behind, and said, "He's very good. He speaks so well, he speaks well." And, turning back to me, "You speak very well." In any other context, it would have felt like faint praise, or even like an insult. But we'd drunk claret, we were laughing along to long-dead Twain, and I had managed to surprise the wily old master.

Our host drifted away, and Vidia and I continued chatting about this and that. Swift judgments came down. The simplicity in Hemingway was "bogus" and nothing, Vidia said, like his own. *Things Fall Apart* was a fine book, but Achebe's refusal to write about his decades in America was disappointing. *Heart of Darkness* was good, but structurally a failure. I asked him about the biography by Patrick French, *The World Is What It Is,* which he had authorized. He stiffened. That book, which was extraordinarily well written, was also shocking in the extent to which it revealed a nasty, petty, and insecure man. "One gives away so much in trust," Vidia said. "One expects a certain discretion. It's painful, it's painful. But that's quite all right. Others will be written. The record will be corrected." He sounded like a boy being brave after gashing his thumb.

The party was ending. It was time to leave. I said, "This was not what I expected." "Oh?" he said, some new mischief in his eyes. "And what did you expect?" "I don't know. Not this. I thought you'd be surly, and that I'd be rude." He was pleased. "Very good, very good. So you must write about this. You must write it down, so that others know. That would be good for you, too." The combination of ego, tenderness, and sly provocation was typical.

Finally, after about twenty minutes, Nadira came for her husband. The hand, at long last, lifted itself from its resting place on my knee. This benevolent rheumy-eyed old soul: so fond of the word "nigger," so aggressive in his lack of sympathy toward Africa, so brutal in his treatment of women. He knew nothing about that. He knew only that he needed help standing up, needed help walking across the grand marble-floored foyer toward the private elevator.

The city below. At certain heights, you get vertigo, but you also see what you otherwise might not.

Housing Mr. Biswas

A HOUSE FOR MR. BISWAS, published in 1961, is one of the imperishable novels of the twentieth century. It is a novel of epic length, formal perfection, and two notable peculiarities: its setting, which, being domestic, is unusual for an epic; and its geographical location, Trinidad, an important island in the Caribbean but not a particularly influential one on the world stage. And yet, this severely delimited context gave Vidiadhar Surajprasad Naipaul an entire world of experience and feeling on which to draw. The novel is episodic and packed with conflict, and Mr. Biswas, the hero, subverts heroic convention: he is smart and funny, but also often petulant, mean, and unsympathetic. His enemies, most of them his relatives, are largely unlikable, but they also have their admirable moments. The narrative is propelled by a clear goal—the acquisition of the titular house—which, it becomes apparent, can only be achieved by the most exhaustively circuitous route.

From his birth until his untimely death forty-six years later, Mr. Biswas mostly lives in a series of houses that either do not belong to him or are houses unworthy of the name. Each of these houses is for Mr. Biswas an attempt at solving a problem, and each is a wrong answer in a different way. Mr. Biswas, like a figure out of myth—and indeed his birth is attended by negative portents and dour prophecies; he is declared to be "born in the wrong way"—seems doomed to live through each of these futile iterations before his destiny can be complete. The pointlessness and the wasted effort of these dead-end attempts give the novel a comic edge that links it both to picaresque and to the existentialist tradition. Futility is the way home. In the search, Mr. Biswas carries his meager possessions and his growing family along, from one unsuitable house to another, from Hanuman House to The Chase to Green Vale to Shorthills to a rental in Port of Spain. These residences are mere walls and roofs to Mr. Biswas. His tragedy is not only that none of them is a house *for* him, but that his awareness of the poor fit is acute and constant. Most of the houses belong to his despised in-laws, the Tulsis. A couple of them are built by Mr. Biswas himself, but these are swiftly undermined by their shoddiness and by elemental threat: one succumbs to flood, the other to fire. Even an expensive doll's house he buys for his daughter Savi quickly ends up a splintered wreck. Brutal ironies dog Mr. Biswas every step of the way on life's journey, the unfairness mounts intolerably; and yet it is a funny book, too, full of jagged capers, lively malice, clever talk.

The novel opens with relief: Mr. Biswas has found his house. How terrible it would have been, he thinks, to have failed in this quest, "to have lived without even attempting to lay claim to one's portion of the earth; to have lived and died as one had been born, unnecessary and unaccommodated." In the long search for this accommodation—the what and why having been answered in the prologue, the novel's course is about the how—Mr. Biswas finds various lesser stratagems in which he can be temporarily housed. It begins with his name: not the "Mohun Biswas" inscribed belatedly on his birth certificate by a solicitor, but the "Mr. Biswas" by which we know him, right from the cradle. Mr. Biswas faces many humiliations but is rarely shorn of the modicum of dignity the honorific guarantees. The retention of this proper form of address is both comic and tense, particularly in the early sections of the novel:

> In the days that followed [his birth] Mr. Biswas was treated with attention and respect. His brothers and sisters were slapped if they disturbed his sleep, and the flexibility of his limbs was regarded as a matter of importance.

A schoolboy, much less a babe in arms, is rarely singled out from his siblings and mates in this way. But the perpetual "Mr." proves a shelter for Mr. Biswas. On the rare occasions at which someone calls him by his first name, there's a slight shock to both Mr. Biswas and the reader, as though at a sudden solecism. For instance, at the office of the solicitor with his mother's sister Tara:

> "Name of boy?"
> "Mohun," Tara said.
> Mr. Biswas became shy. He passed his tongue above his upper lip and tried to make it touch the knobby tip of his nose.

It is as though, even at a preschool age, Mr. Biswas knows that the "Mr." is a precious possession of which he should not be casually deprived.

Literature is a second form of protection. Most important are Marcus Aurelius and Epictetus, whom Mr. Biswas brandishes apotropaically. Were he to actually adopt their stoic precepts, his experience of life would be different. As it is, they serve him as defensive consolation, a carapace for his irredeemably querulous nature. Mr. Biswas himself nurtures the dream of literature. He writes, assembling the dream of writing from its basic building blocks, converting form into imagination. Schoolboy calligraphy becomes sign writing. Sign writing becomes journalism. Journalism edges toward something more lasting.

And Mr. Biswas buys things, he acquires things, his wife Shama owns things of her own. Hemmed in by dissent and discord, given to complaint, Mr. Biswas marvels at "the endurance and uncomplainingness of inanimate objects"; and these many objects, which he houses, house him, too. Gradually, they increase in number and presence, and, at several points in the novel, the reader is given an updated inventory of what has been acquired and by what logic. These inventories, which may bring to mind the catalogue of ships in the *Iliad* or the many descriptions of rooms by Dickens, are markers of Mr. Biswas's modest progress. Moving from The Chase, Mr. Biswas and Shama find that they cannot move out as they had moved in, with a donkey cart.

These disregarded years had been years of acquisition. . . . They had acquired a kitchen safe of white wood and netting. This too had been awkward to varnish and had been painted. One leg was shorter than the others and had to be propped up; now they knew without thinking that they must never lean on the safe or handle it with violence. They had acquired a hatrack, not because they possessed hats, but because it was a piece of furniture all but the very poor had. As a result, Mr. Biswas acquired a hat. And they had acquired, at Shama's insistence, a dressingtable, the work of a craftsman, french-polished, with a large, clear mirror.

Slowly, tentatively, with appalling setbacks, Mr. Biswas ceases to be one of the very poor. Later there's a rockingchair, then a cherished Slumberking bed. (The adjective-noun compounds are a special feature of Mr. Biswas's furnishings, as though to intensify the particularity of each item.) Then comes a delicate glass cabinet, which immediately loses one of its glass doors. The final time the family moves, to the house *for* Mr. Biswas on Sikkim Street in Port of Spain, the number of things has become impressive.

The gatherings of a lifetime: the kitchen safe (encrusted with varnish, layer after layer of it, and paint of various colours, the wire-netting broken and clogged), the yellow kitchen table, the hatrack with the futile glass and broken hooks, the rockingchair, the fourposter (dismantled and unnoticeable), Shama's dressingtable (standing against the cab, without its mirror, with all the drawers taken out, showing the unstained, unpolished wood inside, still, after all these years, so raw, so new), the bookcase and desk, Théophile's bookcase, the Slumberking (a pink, intimate rose on the headrest), the glass cabinet (rescued from Mrs. Tulsi's drawingroom), the destitute's diningtable (on its back, its legs roped around, loaded with drawers and boxes), the typewriter (still a brilliant yellow, on which Mr. Biswas was going to write articles for the English and American Press, on which he had written his articles for the Ideal School, the letter to the doctor): the gatherings of a lifetime for so long scattered and even unnoticed, now all together on the tray of the lorry.

These moments of inventory are among the most indelible passages in this masterwork of realism: one scarcely credits the idea that such meticulous and loving checklists could be invention. These things must have had these lives, and so they paradoxically underscore the veracity of Mr. Biswas's own experiences. But the realism of the human interactions throughout the novel is similarly irresistible. Here they all are: Mr. Biswas; his mother, Bipti; his brothers and sister; his aunt Tara and her husband, Ajodha; his wife, Shama; his children (Savi, Anand, Myna, Kamla, appearing one by one, becoming real before our eyes, and being themselves actively drawn into the contest of life); his aggravating in-laws: Mrs. Tulsi, Seth, Padma, the indulged sons of the family ("the gods"), the absurdly numerous daughters, their husbands, their children; and the cascade of secondary and tertiary characters, the innominate crowd. All are convincingly themselves, and yet all are contained in the arc of the novel, brought in to play their parts in the story of Mr. Biswas's life.

Incident, fight, rancor, subterfuge: this is Mr. Biswas's experience during the long years he lives with the Tulsis. His main foes are his mother-in-law, Mrs. Tulsi, and her brother-in-law Seth. They hold grudges against him, and he out-grudges them. He bickers, insults, mocks. His wife, Shama, no fool, plays both sides skillfully, siding with her husband sometimes, abandoning him at other times. Some of these battles of will Mr. Biswas wins, others he loses. Physical violence is commonplace: the frequent beatings the children in the extended household receive also spill over, rarely but astonishingly, into adult interaction. Pointless impasse is common. *A House for Mr. Biswas* hums along to the interweaving tunes of these several discords. But the book is also a patient, almost ecstatic, evocation of land-scape and social life in Trinidad in the first half of the twentieth century. And if the human interactions are characterized by agony, the times and places—the farms, the roads, the villages, the thrumming energy of the city, the mornings, afternoons, dusks, nights—are described with profound and vigilant affec-tion. Playing the angry and fast-moving currents of badinage against the dreamy swirl of memory, the novel's flow is one of full-bore local savvy. One finally reads or rereads *Mr. Biswas* for this balanced totality, this fecund complexity, for the way it brings to startling fruition in twentieth-century Trinidad the promise of the nineteenth-century European novel.

Great in macrocosm, the novel is also flawless in microcosm. It contains many perfect set pieces, strewn like jewels through the book, in which the prose gleams with a kind of secret knowledge. Many are the moments of imaginative sympathy that continue to bloom in the mind long after the page is turned. One such account, of the burning of poui sticks for the rough village sport of stick fighting, captures the way the scent of the sticks opens up in Mr. Biswas a sudden seam of memory. An-other, of Mr. Biswas working as a bus conductor in his youth, passing by a lone hut in the dusk, is a compressed little master-piece of longing:

In the gloom, a boy was leaning against the hut, his hands behind him, staring at the road. He wore a vest and noth-ing more. The vest glowed white. In an instant the bus went by, noisy in the dark, through bush and level sugar-cane fields. Mr. Biswas could not remember where the hut stood, but the picture remained: a boy leaning against an earth house that had no reason for being there, under the dark falling sky, a boy who didn't know where the road, and that bus, went.

Against that sad obscurity, against surrender, against darkness, *A House for Mr. Biswas* is a book for knowledge, for determination, for ragged unyielding life, a book that, over its great and complex length, shelters the one who reads it.

Tomas Tranströmer

Two truths approach each other. One comes from inside, the other
  from outside,
and where they meet we have a chance to catch sight of ourselves.
  —from "Preludes"

TOMAS TRANSTRÖMER HAS for years now been one of my ports of refuge. The books of his poetry on my shelves never remain unopened for long. I turn to him when I wish to come as close as possible to what cannot be said. The new century has been full of dark years, and I have returned again and again to poets. They kept watch over me, and, to adopt a phrase of Tranströmer's, I survived on milk stolen from their cosmos. I read Walcott, Bishop, Ondaatje, Szymborska, Bonta, and a dozen other marvelous writers, but above all I read Heaney and Tranströmer, who, in different ways, fused the biggest questions with personal experience.

To read Tranströmer—the best times are at night, in silence, and alone—is to surrender to the far-fetched. It is to climb out of bed and listen to what the house is saying, and to how the wind outside responds. Each of his readers reads him as a personal secret. For this reason it was strange, when he won the Nobel Prize in Literature in 2011, to see this master of solitude being celebrated in the streets or showing up as a trending topic on Twitter and a bestseller on Amazon. He usually dwells in quieter precincts.

Tranströmer's poems owe something to Japanese tradition, and early in his career he wrote haiku. Reading him, one is also reminded of American poets like Charles Simic (for his surrealism) and Jim Harrison, Gary Snyder, and W. S. Merwin (for their plain speech and koanlike wisdom). But Tranströmer casts a spell all his own, and in fact the strongest associations he brings to my mind are the music of Arvo Pärt and the photography of Saul Leiter.

> I swim out in a trance
> on the glittering dark water.
> A steady note of a tuba comes in.
> It's a friend's voice: "Take up your grave and walk."
> —from "Two Cities"

His poems contain a luminous simplicity that expands until it pushes your ego out of the nest, and there you are, alone with Truth. In a Tranströmer poem, you inhabit space differently; a body becomes a thing, a mind floats, things have lives, and even non-things, even concepts, are alive. There is much following in Tranströmer, much watching, from a distance and from close by, and the trees, pasts, houses, spaces, silences, and fields all take on invigilative personae. There are many dreams.

> I dreamt that I had sketched piano keys out
> on the kitchen table. I played on them, without a sound.
> Neighbors came by to listen.
> —from "Grief Gondola #2"

Tranströmer is well translated into English, and there are versions by May Swenson, Robin Fulton, Robin Robertson, and others. My favorite book of the poems is *The Half-Finished Heaven,* a selection translated by Robert Bly. Bly's translation is so clean and direct it seems to bypass language itself. This was the volume I turned to the most during the horrors of the Bush and Cheney years. Even though around the same time my own belief in God had faded away, I found that I needed to somehow retain belief in a cloud of witnesses. I had strayed away from religious dogma, but my hunger for miracle speech had not abated. Tranströmer's mysterious poems, hovering on the edge of the unsayable, met me right at this point of need.

> *I open the first door.*
> *It is a large sunlit room.*
> *A heavy car passes outside*
> *and makes the china quiver.*
>
> *I open door number two.*
> *Friends! You drank some darkness*
> *and became visible.*
>
> *Door number three. A narrow hotel room.*
> *View on an alley. One lamppost shines on the asphalt.*
> *Experience, its beautiful slag.*
>
> —from "Elegy"

And, from "The Scattered Congregation," which is in five short parts, these lines:

> *We got ready and showed our home.*
> *The visitor thought: you live well.*

The slum must be inside you.

. . .

Nicodemus the sleepwalker is on his way
to the Address. Who's got the Address?
Don't know. But that's where we're going.

There's a kind of helplessness in many of the poems, the sense of being pulled along by something irresistible and invisible. There are moments of tart social commentary, a sense of justice wounded ("The slum must be inside you"—for many years, Tranströmer worked as a psychologist at an institution for juvenile offenders). There is also in the poems a kind of motionlessness that is indistinguishable from terrific speed, in the same way Arvo Pärt's music can sound fast and slow at the same time. It's a good thing I'm unembarrassable about influence, because I realize now how many of Tranströmer's concepts I have hidden away in my own work. When I'm asked what my favorite thing about New York is, I often answer with a line lifted from "Schubertiana": "Outside New York, a high place where with one glance you take in the houses where eight million human beings live."

The images with which Tranströmer charges his poems bring to mind the concept of acheiropoieta, "making without hands"; in Byzantine art, acheiropoietic images were those believed to have come miraculously into being without a painter's intervention. The Shroud of Turin and the Veil of Veronica are the most famous examples. These were images registered by direct contact, and they were usually images of the Holy Face of Christ. (Albrecht Dürer, in his immodest way, was alluding to such images when he painted his deliriously detailed full-frontal self-portrait of 1500.) I feel Transtromer's use of imagery is like this, and like contact printing, in which a photograph is made directly from a film negative or film positive. There is little elaborate construction evident; rather, the sense is of the sudden arrival of what was already there, as when a whale comes up for air: massive, exhilarating, and evanescent.

The satisfaction, the pleasure, the comfort one takes in these poems comes from the way they seem to have preexisted us. Or perhaps, to put it another way, the magic lies in their ability to present aspects of our selves long buried under manners, culture, and language. The poems remember us and, if we are perfectly still, give us a chance to catch sight of ourselves.

Poetry of the Disregarded

THROUGHOUT HIS CAREER, W. G. Sebald wrote poems that were strikingly similar to his prose. His tone, in both genres, was always understated but possessed of a mournful grandeur. To this he added a willful blurring of literary boundaries, and, in fact, almost all his writing, and not just the poetry and prose, comprised history, memoir, biography, autobiography, art criticism, scholarly arcana, and invention. This expert mixing of forms owed a great deal to his reading of the seventeenth-century melancholics Robert Burton and Thomas Browne, and Sebald's looping sentences were an intentional homage to nineteenth-century German-language writers like Adalbert Stifter and Gottfried Keller. But so strongly has the style come to be associated with Sebald's own work that even books that preceded his, such as those by Robert Walser and Thomas Bernhard, can seem, from our perspective as readers of English translations, simply "Sebaldian."

Sebald's reputation rests on four novels—*Vertigo, The Emigrants, The Rings of Saturn,* and *Austerlitz*—all of them reflections on the history of violence in general, and on the legacy of the Holocaust in particular. Our sense of this achievement has been enriched by his other works: the ones published in his lifetime (the lectures *On the Natural History of Destruction* and the long poem *After Nature*), and those that were released posthumously (including the essay collection *Campo Santo* and the volumes of short poems *Unrecounted* and *For Years Now*). Sebald's shade, like Roberto Bolaño's, gives the illusion of being extraordinarily productive, and the publication now of *Across the Land and the Water*, billed as his *Selected Poems 1964–2001*, does not feel surprising. Ten years on, we are not quite prepared for him to put down his pen.

Across the Land and the Water is different from every other Sebald book in one important respect: it contains his early work. Because literary success came to him late (he was in his fifties when the first of his books was translated into English), the Sebald we know is the mature one. One of the pleasures of the present volume is the way it shows us the development of the author's poetic voice over more than three decades, beginning in the 1960s, when he was a student. A section in one of those early poems reads:

Glass in hand
They come and go
Stop still and expect
The metamorphosis of hawthorn
In the garden outside

Time measures
Nothing but itself.

Another poem, about Manchester, contains the lines "Bleston knows an hour / Between summer and winter / Which never passes and that / Is my plan for a time / Without beginning or end." Elsewhere, there are roses, garden paths, Victorian patterns. The guiding intelligence here, rather surprisingly, seems to be that of T. S. Eliot (an influence not so easily discernible in Sebald's later work), in particular the vatic and circumambulatory Eliot of the *Four Quartets*.

These early poems of Sebald's also contain the concerns that would later be seen as distinctively his. Trains feature prominently, as do borders, journeys, landscape, memories, and solitude. There is a debt to Hans Magnus Enzensberger, in the reportorial interrogation of vanished things, that would remain true of all of Sebald's work. But what is most notable is how clotted the poems are with references, untranslated fragments from different languages, and classical allusions (Horace and Virgil seem to be particular favorites); the assemblage, unlike in his later work, can seem hectic. Nevertheless, they are a pleasure to read, thanks to the translator Iain Galbraith's excellent endnotes, which guide the bewildered reader through the codes and secrets of the work. Without Galbraith's notes, some of the poems are dense almost to the point of opacity:

> . . . *Strasbourg Cathedral*
> *bien éclairée.—Between thresholds*
> *lines from Gregorius, the guote sündaere,*
> *from Au near Freiburg, rechtsrheinisch,*
> *not visible from Colmar—Haut Rhin.*
> *Early morning in Basel, printed on*
> *hand-made Rhine-washed lumpy paper*
> *under the supervision of Erasmus of Rotterdam*

The later poems are cleaner, clearer. Many of these helped lay the groundwork for the long poem *After Nature*, Sebald's first published book, either as sketches for ideas that would then be reworked or as pieces that were incorporated whole. Other poems were neglected once his prose-writing career took off; gathered here, they constitute a magnificent corpus. Some of these later poems are bracingly concise, a compression underscored by the way titles frequently also serve as first lines:

Somewhere

behind Türkenfeld
a spruce nursery
a pond in the
moor on which
the March ice
is slowly melting

It's a fine little idyllic lyric. We are looking at a small German town, perhaps, possibly as seen from a passing train. But the meaning of the poem darkens irrevocably when we read in the notes what is "behind Türkenfeld": it was the location of one of ninety-four subcamps linked to Dachau, and it was a station on the railway linking Dachau with the munitions towns of Kaufer-ing and Landsberg. Sebald leaves all this out of the poem, leaves out the fact that this railway was called the Blutbahn ("the blood track"), and that many thousands were transported along this very route to their deaths. As ever, he draws us into history's shadow in an indirect way.

But *Across the Land and the Water* is by no means a collection about the Holocaust. The material ranges widely, and among the most memorable poems it contains are those based on small incidents from the lives of historical personages. Some of these poems begin (as he began all four of his novels) with a precise date stamp. "On 9 June 1904" opens the one about Chekhov's last days, in which a small circle of mourners, likened to a "black velvet caterpillar," meet Chekhov's coffin at a train station and are overshadowed by the band assembled there to meet the coffin of a now forgotten general. "In the summer of 1836" is the beginning of the poem about Chopin's disappointed love for Maria Wodzinska, a great pain that he concealed for the rest of his life. A woman who did not respond to the aging Goethe's love is the subject of another poem; Daniel Paul Schreber, a German judge who suffered from psychosis and whose *Memoirs of My Nervous Illness* was analyzed by Freud, features in yet another. As Sebald once explained in an interview, "I do like to listen to people who have been sidelined for one reason or another." He is, among other things, a poet of the disregarded.

He had a feeling for the inanimate, too, for ruins and comminuted landscapes, places that have been reduced to their smallest units by the forces of nature and history. He is, in many of these poems, an adept of what Nabokov calls, in *Transparent Things*, "the iridescent dizziness of dream life." And he understood especially well the private life of objects. As he wrote in an essay in *Unrecounted*: "Things outlast us, they know more about us than we know about them: they carry the experience they have had with us inside them and are—in fact—the book of our history opened before us." Everywhere in *Across the Land and the Water* is a vigilance about the world of things. Greenhouses are "home-made crystal palaces," a power station is "a sick elephant / still just breathing / through its trunk," someone's "pigskin suitcase gapes," and the poem entitled "Room 645" describes, with deadpan humor, and with all the seriousness of an assistant janitor going through an inventory, the various objects in a garish hotel room in Hanover.

Sebald had a special love for paintings: they are half object, half window into another world. Recognizing that they served as self-contained Wunderkammers, he summoned their magic simply by close description of their contents. *The Rings of Saturn* ends with an evocation of Dutch landscape painting, and in *Across the Land and the Water* the last of the translated poems is "In the Paradise Landscape," a gently ekphrastic reading of a painting by Jan Brueghel the Younger: "goat & a few sheep / two polecats or martens / a wolf a horse / a peacock a turkey / & in the foreground / at the bottom edge / two spectacled / monkeys one of which / is gingerly plucking / strawberries from a little / shrub." A painting becomes, in Sebald's hands, a world of enumerated wonders.

Often, in describing the actual world, he paints it similarly, detail by detail, attentive always to effects of the light. In "Calm November Weather," he gives an account of a reading given by a Greenlandic poet that he'd attended:

> . . . *the*
> *sounds of her feathery*
> *language taavvi*
> *jjuaq she says the*
> *great darkness &*
> *lifting her arm*
> *qaavmaaq the*
> *shimmering light.*

What earns Sebald the gratitude and affection of readers, and makes this book a splendid addition to an already extraordinary oeuvre, is encapsulated in this fragment: the great darkness, the shimmering light. He was able to pin both down, time and again and with impeccable technique, onto the printed page. His are the books of our history opened before us.

Always Returning

ONE MORNING THIS past June, I played truant from a conference I was attending in Norwich, England, and called a taxi to take me out to the countryside. But the taxi was late, and I had to stand and wait awhile. When it finally arrived, shortly after nine, there was some confusion. Was this the taxi I had hired? Was I the person the driver had been sent to pick up? Had some other passenger, not yet waiting there at the circular drive at the heart of campus, called the dispatcher? We only had each other: I was going somewhere and he was prepared to take someone somewhere. I entered the car.

It was a gray morning, and visibility was poor. The high latitude and the date—it happened to be the summer solstice—meant the sun had been up since four-thirty, but fog persisted. I told the driver where I was going, and we drove in silence for a while through mild traffic and quiet streets, until the city began to thin out in the gray. And where exactly in Framingham Earl? the driver asked me. St. Andrew's Church, I said, reciting what I had written down: near Poringland, just off the Yelverton Road. He knew it.

I looked out the window, watching the landscape slip by, the houses, the hedges, the fields and farms, the strange-looking bales of hay bound in black plastic, the road signs with their unfamiliar East Anglian names, the heavy, threatening trucks that barreled down the busier roads. The driver broke the silence and became talkative, flitting from one subject to another in a laconic but unceasing way, not really caring much whether I was listening or interested.

I like the area and I like traveling in it, he said. There are many airfields around here, not just in Norfolk but also Suffolk and many other parts of the country. It's just something I do. I have a spare bit of time, yeah, I go down to an airfield, see an air show, or just visit a disused field, go down there, remember what it was like. Places like Greenham Common, down in Berkshire. You know about that, yeah? I said I didn't, but he could see now that I was making some notes, that he had captured my interest. He forged ahead.

Greenham Common's a major one. That's where your CND camp was, yeah, the women's peace camp, all that. Used to be cruise missiles and all sorts there through the eighties, until the nineties. I went down there, bit of runway left, but otherwise it's all gone. And right around here, in Norfolk, with all the airfields and bases and what have you, this was called Little America during the war. Whole area was full of American air bases. During the war, the Second World War, mind you, bomb groups were based here and they used to go out on flying missions from here in the evenings. We are near the coast, and they'd take off from here to bomb the German cities, from here and from Suffolk, too.

There is someone who would have loved to talk to you about this, I said, perhaps not loud enough for him to hear, and, as I said it, there was a sudden catch in my throat. Only then did the driver introduce himself, turning back for a moment with his hand on the wheel, his blue eyes a little bulbous, but the palest and most guileless of blues, tending almost toward gray. My name's Jason, he said. And, with the same laconic urgency as before, he continued talking. Bentwaters was another big Cold War air base, he said. That closed down in 1993, thereabouts, but many of the men just stayed here, you see. They'd been here so long, they were part of the life here, these American airmen. They married local girls. There's a museum down there in Bentwaters, that's in Suffolk, they've got some of the old airmen giving talks. Tell you what, I think the place belongs to a family now, they bought the airfield, if I've got that right. The Kemble family, it's theirs now. There's just the one plane flying from there now, a Spitfire, and it's flown by a lady called Carolyn Grace. She's nearing sixty now, but she still takes the plane out. Only lady that flies a Spitfire in this country, to the best of my knowledge. Strange to say, her Spitfire was flown in a mission over Normandy on the morning of the D Day landings. And there was another base in Woodbridge, close to the coast, and that one had an emergency landing field, with an airstrip three times your normal airstrip length. That's for your planes coming in from missions, maybe in distress or something.

Jason talked, and we drove on, through small country roads that were like a postcard idea of rural England, winding, narrow, sedate roads, which, at sudden intervals, became larger roads, fierce, fast, and dangerous roads, which seemed to have barely enough space for the heavy traffic that plied them. On one of these larger roads, just as I noticed a sign for a village called Dunston, a large trailer rumbled past us at speed, and, whether from the shock of that overtaking vehicle, or because I had eaten nothing that morning, or perhaps due to some uneasiness brought about by Jason's stories, I felt carsick for the first time in my life. And at that very moment, with a flickering photographic recall, as though someone had just switched on a slide projector, I remembered something W. G. Sebald had written. Looking it up now, I am surprised by how accurate my memory of it was, save for a few of the statistical details:

> His thoughts constantly revolved around the bombing raids then being launched on Germany from the sixty-seven airfields that were established in East Anglia after 1940. People nowadays hardly have any idea of the scale of the operation, said Hazel. In the course of one thousand and nine days, the eighth air fleet alone used a billion gallons of fuel, dropped seven hundred and thirty-two thousand tons of bombs, and lost almost nine thousand aircraft and fifty thousand men. Every evening I watched the bomber squadrons heading out over Somerleyton, and night after night, before I went to sleep, I pictured in my mind's eye the German cities going up in flames, the firestorms setting the heavens alight and the survivors rooting about in the ruins.

Are you all right? Jason said, glancing at the rearview mirror. I had rested my forehead on the window at the back and bunched myself up on the seat. I must have looked terrible. I feel ill, I said. I think I'd like to get something to eat, is there a small shop nearby where we could stop? Jason said there was a place right ahead, just past the Poringland Road, and within a few minutes we pulled in near a busy intersection. I went into the shop to buy a banana and a bottle of apple juice. It was about a mile away from where we were, in Framingham Pigot, in December 2001, that Sebald had had a heart attack while driving his Peugeot. The car had crashed and Sebald had died instantly.

His daughter, in the passenger seat, had been badly injured. As I thought about how close in space these events were, even though by now removed in time, I noticed from the backseat of the taxi the headlines of the *Eastern Daily News,* pasted in front of the shop: MAN JAILED FOR MURDER OF NORFOLK PENSIONER. It was another set of lives, another set of fates rising to the surface for a moment before falling into history.

Northwest of here is Swanton Morley, Jason said, when he saw that I had recovered somewhat, eager to resume his storytelling. I've been to that as well, there is another airfield there, they've got acrobatic displays. And just to tell you how a little bit of history opens things up, yeah, I noticed a small memorial when I was there, didn't recognize the name. But just from the name of the airfield, I was able to go home and on the computer find out who that was, what happened to him, why there's a memorial. With just a little bit of information your computer can tell you so much. Christopher Wilkins, that's the name, he was flying in an air show, in 1998, when his engines stalled and he went down. And while Jason was telling me this, I remembered one of Sebald's micropoems in *Unrecounted:*

> *On 8 May 1927*
> *the pilots Nungesser & Coli*
> *took off from Le Bourget*
> *& after that*
> *were never*
> *seen again.*

Jason said, as though he were commenting directly on my own silent thoughts: These people are worth remembering. It's nice to think that people will want to remember the past, because it shapes who we are, at the end of the day. I try to remember, you know. I've even been to some airfields in Germany. Well—his tone changed, and he stopped the car, bringing me out of my reverie—here we are. St. Andrew's Church. I'll just wait out here for you.

It was a quiet, shaded lane. The fog had lifted, but the day was not bright. There was not a soul around. I raised the slim iron latch of the wooden gate, which was overgrown with creepers, and went around the old Norman church with its characteristic East Anglian round tower. Round-tower churches are rare in England now, except in Norfolk and Suffolk. St. Andrew's is built of honey-colored stone, its churchyard full of old stones, old graves, well kept but arranged somewhat haphazardly. Flowers were in bloom all over, and there was in particular a profusion of foxgloves.

I searched. Finally, coming around the chancel, I saw Sebald's gravestone: a slab of dark marble, a slender marker shaded by a large green bush. There he is, I thought. The teacher I never knew, the friend I met only posthumously. Some water had trickled down the face of the slab, making the "S" of his name temporarily invisible, as well as the second "4" in "1944" and the "1" in "2001." The erasures put him into a peculiar timelessness. Along the top of the gravestone was a row of smooth small stones in different shades of brown and gray. There was a little space on the left. I picked up a stone from the ground and added it to the row. Then I knelt down.

How long was I there?

When I returned to the car, I asked Jason to drive me back to Norwich, to the Church of St. Peter Mancroft in the city center. Jason said: Just to satisfy my curiosity, this grave you came to see, he's a writer, yeah? What's his name, maybe I can find out more about him. I told him the name. He'd never heard it. He was a sort of local historian, I said, like you. Like you, he didn't want the past to be forgotten, especially the small and neglected stories. He lived in this area a long time, taught literature up at the university. Jason turned around, and from under his glasses I could see both a merriment and a melancholy. He was originally from Germany, I said. Germany? he said. Well, that's what you'd call ironic. And he wrote down the name.

At St. Peter Mancroft was the memorial to Sir Thomas Browne, the seventeenth-century physician and antiquarian whose weird and digressive texts *Urn Burial* and *Religio Medici* had meant much to me as a young would-be physician. I did not read Sebald until later, after I abandoned my medical studies. Only later still did I find out that he had been strongly influenced by Browne. That connection with Browne, and with others, like Nabokov and certain obscure historians of Northern Renaissance art, helped me to understand something of the uncanny feeling I had when I first read Sebald, and the feeling that I still have each time I read him: a feeling of return rather than of arrival.

That afternoon, thinking of Jason's eyes and the slight mischief in his serious mien, I was faintly aware of others traveling the same circuits, pulled by an unidentifiable gravitational force into certain habits of mind and psyche. In *The Rings of Saturn,* Sebald had written:

Across what distances in time do the elective affinities and correspondences connect? How is it that one perceives oneself in another human being, or, if not oneself, then one's own precursor?

I spent the rest of the afternoon wandering around the University of East Anglia, where he had taught for more than thirty years. A large magpie followed me around, disappearing for occasional spells, but always returning, a solitary bird, sharp black and white, bigger than I expected, and as starkly devoid of color as a woodcut. I am not superstitious, and thought nothing of it. But the bird was persistent. These things, as Sebald said in one of his last interviews, once you have seen them, have a habit of returning, and they want attention. He said this with regard to the interred past, but I think he possibly meant more.

Later, in the unending late afternoon of the longest day of the year, Sam, one of the conference organizers whom I had gotten to know that week, and who had come to Norwich just a few weeks before Sebald died, said—with no prompting from me—that it had been noticed at the university that Sebald always wore two watches, one on each wrist. Was it something to do with the mystical properties of different metals? Was it some strange sense of time that demanded simultaneous witness? Or was it simply Sebald's dry sense of humor? And were the watches even set to the same time zone, or was one testifying to past time, the way his writing did? Sam didn't know, but I found myself thinking again of the magpie, its talent for collecting this and that, and its eye for the sudden shards of brightness that enliven the ordinary. I said good night to Sam and, returning to my hotel in the last light, well past nine, saw the bird again, going from bush to bush in the uphill path ahead of me, little more than a shadow now.

A Better Quality of Agony

"SQUID MARINATED IN lemongrass and lime and chili flakes. Slices of salty haloumi cheese and lamb chops and sausages from Nicos, our local Greek Cypriot butcher. . . . We'd marinate a leg of lamb for two days in a mix of yogurt, almonds, pistachios, lots of spices, mint, and green chilies. . . . We'd buy greengages in August. Often they were perfect, not too yielding, but not unripe."

The book in which this passage appears contains other passages that speak of times in the garden, trips taken with family, children learning from their parents and vice versa, and moments of laughter and joy. In most books, these evocations of summertime ease and sweet familial conviviality would be a pleasure. In Sonali Deraniyagala's memoir, *Wave,* they are among the most difficult things I've ever read. The reason: *Wave* is about Deraniyagala's husband, her parents, and her two sons, aged seven and five, all of whom died in a single morning in December 2004, when a tsunami hit the resort where they were holidaying in Sri Lanka. Deraniyagala herself was found spinning around in circles and almost deranged in a swirl of mud after the water receded. *Wave* is her account of that day, and of the years that followed.

Wave is really two stories in one. The second story is about remembering the life of a family when they were happy. The first is about the stunned horror of a woman who lost, in one moment, her past, present, and future. Deraniyagala was raised in Sri Lanka, and trained as an economist at Cambridge and Oxford. She married her college sweetheart, the economist Stephen Lissenburgh, and together they had two preternaturally intelligent and happy boys. Her friend Orlantha, who was with them at Yala National Park in Sri Lanka, said to her that morning, "What you guys have is a dream." But the next thing Orlantha said was "Oh my God, the sea's coming in." The dream had become a nightmare so unspeakable, so incommensurate with typical human experience, that Deraniyagala would later wonder what she had done to doom herself to such a fate. Steve was dead, Ma and Da were dead, as were Vik and Malli. Orlantha, too: dead. "Why else have I become this shocking story, this wild statistical outlier?" Deraniyagala thinks to herself. "I speculated that I must have been a mass murderer in a previous life, I was paying for that now."

Sorrow flattens her. Then sorrow gives way to the amplitude of anger and to a suicidal fury. It takes a dedicated group of relatives and friends to lock away the knives and hide the pills and keep her from self-harm. There's a period of alcoholism, and for a while she harasses, with demonic inventiveness, a Dutch couple who have rented her parents' home. Grief is a frightening condition, and at its extreme is like the sun: impossible to look at directly. That Deraniyagala wrote down what happened is understandable. But why would some unconcerned individual, someone who has not been similarly shattered, wish to read this book? Yet read it we must, for it contains solemn and essential truths. I am reminded of what Anne Carson wrote in the introduction to *Grief Lessons,* her translation of four plays by Euripides:

> Grief and rage—you need to contain that, to put a frame around it, where it can play itself out without you or your kin having to die. There is a theory that watching unbearable stories about other people lost in grief and rage is good for you—may cleanse you of darkness. Do you want to go down to the pits of yourself all alone? Not much. What if an actor could do it for you? Isn't that why they are called actors? They act for you.

Carson is writing specifically about Greek tragedy, works of tragic fiction, and of course a book like *Wave* is only too real. There's nothing put on about Deraniyagala's suffering. But part of what Carson says applies. In witnessing something far-fetched, something brought out before us from the distant perimeter of human experience, we are in some way fortified for our own inevitable, if lesser, struggles.

Years pass. Deraniyagala revisits her old London home (she avoided it after the disaster) and begins to allow herself to recollect the lives of her boys, her husband, and her parents. The book gradually reveals itself to be about that greater thing on the other side of loss: love. She had avoided touching their things—the books, the clothes, the cricket equipment—she had avoided thinking about their little ways, their hobbies, their obsession with the natural world, their shared love of birds in particular. It was too hard to think about these things, and her grief was too raw. But then she found her way into it, and there's a lift when those pages arrive. They are difficult to read, but behind them is the generosity of the writer: to her family, to herself, and to her readers. Very few of us will ever experience loss on this scale, but, somehow, her having written about hers is a kind of preemptive consolation for us, too:

> Was that a dead pheasant on the side of the road? They are not here, they would have noticed it if they were. They would have said something. Yuk. Cool. When do you think it got killed, Dad? They are not here. But I do not want to emerge out of them. I want to hover inside our metallic blue Renault Mégane Scénic. Why am I allowing this? I will have to crawl back to reality soon, and that will be agony. . . .
>
> They are sitting quietly at the back, not kicking each other's shins for a change, no burping contests. Vik sees a gush of starlings wing the air, his eyes trail the whirr of gray filling the sky. But what he really wants to see is a sparrow hawk. Or, better still, a sparrow hawk sparring with a crow. Malli's nodding off, he always does this in the car, but it's too late to nap now. "Vik, talk to Malli and keep him awake, sweetheart. He won't sleep tonight if he dozes off now."

Readers who are looking for a neat story of loss and redemption, a simple narrative arc, catharsis on the cheap, will find no such thing here: the particularity of Deraniyagala's suffering, and the intensity with which she feels it, is immense. But something does shift in the course of the narrative. As Deraniyagala said in a recent interview, she found that "writing is a much better quality of agony than trying to forget." In accurately describing her family's life—and I'm drawn here to the root word "cura," care, from which we get "accurate"—she rescues her family from uncaring, careless fate. Losing them plunged her into darkness. Writing about what happened brings them back into the light, a little.

Derek Walcott

"WRITING POETRY IS an unnatural act," Elizabeth Bishop once wrote. "It takes skill to make it seem natural." The thought is kin to the one John Keats expressed in an 1818 letter to his friend John Taylor: "If Poetry comes not as naturally as the Leaves to a tree it had better not come at all." Bishop and Keats both evoked a double sense of "natural": that which is concerned with nature, with landscape, flora and fauna, and that which is unforced and fluent. In both senses, Derek Walcott is a natural poet.

Walcott was born in 1930 and began writing young. His first poem appeared in a local paper when he was fourteen, and his first volume, *25 Poems,* was self-published when he was eighteen. "Everyone wants a prodigy to fail," Rita Dove wrote. "It makes our mediocrity more bearable." Walcott did not fail. His early poems were expert, and, even though they bore traces of his apprenticeship to the English tradition (in particular W. H. Auden and Dylan Thomas), they were to prove thematically characteristic. Right from the beginning, he was keen to use European poetic form to testify to the Caribbean experience. This commitment made him a part of the boom in twentieth-century Caribbean literature, a gathering of talents that included Édouard Glissant, Patrick Chamoiseau, Aimé Césaire, and Maryse Condé on the French-speaking side; and Samuel Selvon, George Lamming, and C. L. R. James from the English-speaking islands, as well as V. S. Naipaul, with whom Walcott was one of the Caribbean's two Nobel Prize winners for literature.

The Poetry of Derek Walcott 1948–2013 does not contain all of Walcott's poems, nor is it the first edited selection from his oeuvre. *Collected Poems 1948–1984* was a midcareer reckoning. The three-hundred-page *Selected Poems* might have seemed, on its publication in 2007, a summation. The present volume doubles that page count. It includes many more of the earliest poems, a strong selection from *White Egrets,* Walcott's 2011 volume, and in general more poems from every phase of his sixty-five-year career. The notable exception is the epic poem "Omeros," which was presumably omitted to avoid having to break its narrative flow.

Walcott pays indefatigable attention to the look of things, and writes with a spendthrift approach to the word-hoard. These lines from "The Prodigal" are typical:

> *The ceaseless creasing of the morning sea,*
> *the fluttering gamboge cedar leaves allegro,*
> *the rods of the yawing branches trolling the breeze,*
> *the rusted meadows, the wind-whitened grass,*
> *the coos of the stone-colored ground doves on the road,*
> *the echo of benediction on a house—*

This is poetry written with a painterly hand, stroke by patient stroke. Walcott's early ambition was to paint, to inhabit the "virginal, unpainted world" of the Caribbean and take on, like some latter-day Adam, the "task of giving things their names." He learned the basics of watercolor painting, and it became his most serious pastime; his book jackets through the years have featured his gentle and competent paintings of tropical country scenes. But poetry was the deeper and more substantial practice. He brought the patient and accretive sensibility of a realist painter to his poems. They are great piles of intoxicating description, always alert to the demands of meter and form, often employing rhyme or slant rhyme, great layers of adjectives firming up the noun underpainting. He names painters as his exemplars more often than he names poets: Pissarro, Veronese, Cézanne, Manet, Gauguin, and Millet roll through the pages. And he embraces the observed particular as ardently as any Flemish painter might. As he wrote in the poem "Midsummer," only half jokingly, "The Dutch blood in me is drawn to detail."

From time to time, this love of description can strike false notes. "The Man Who Loved Islands," from the 1982 book *The Fortunate Traveller,* is marred by poor attempts at American vernacular. Early volumes like *The Castaway* and *The Gulf* would have benefited from some compression. But far more often, the writing leaves mere lyricism far behind to rise to the level of prophetic speech, as in the extraordinary poem "The Season of Phantasmal Peace." One inescapable conclusion from reading hundreds of pages of Walcott at once is the feeling that this is the lifework of an ecstatic. What if the descriptions do go on a bit? What else would one rather be doing?

Something of spiritual import did happen to the young Walcott, an experience he set down when he was older, in the seventh chapter (curiously omitted from the present book) of the autobiographical book-length poem *Another Life:*

About the August of my fourteenth year
I lost my self somewhere above a valley
owned by a spinster-farmer, my dead father's friend.
At the hill's edge there was a scarp
with bushes and boulders stuck in its side.
Afternoon light ripened the valley,
rifling smoke climbed from small labourers' houses,
and I dissolved into a trance.
I was seized by a pity more profound
than my young body could bear, I climbed
with the labouring smoke,
I drowned in labouring breakers of bright cloud,
then uncontrollably I began to weep,
inwardly, without tears, with a serene extinction
of all sense; I felt compelled to kneel,
I wept for nothing and for everything

The power of the passage is not only in its strong evocation of an instance of sublimity, but also in the modulation of the recollection: the Dantean opening, the apt but unexpected split of "my" from "self," and the uncontrolled syntax of "then uncontrollably I began to weep." Epiphany became Walcott's favored mode, his instinct, even as he struggled to satisfy each poem's competing demands of originality and necessity. In *White Egrets,* a supremely controlled collection dominated by an elegiac mood, a welcome epiphany intrudes, often heralded by the word "astonishment" or "astonished":

The perpetual ideal is astonishment.
The cool green lawn, the quiet trees, the forest

on the hill there, then, the white gasp of an egret sent
sailing into the frame then teetering to rest

Walcott has few equals in the use of metaphor. In his imagination, each thing seems to be linked to another by a special bond, unapparent until he points it out, permanently fresh once he does. Most of these metaphors he uses just once, brilliantly, discarding them in the onrush of description. The fine surprise in *White Egrets* of how "a hawk on the wrist / of a branch, soundlessly, like a falcon, / shoots into heaven . . ." is not easy to forget. Nor is this, from "Midsummer":

the lines of passengers at each trolley station
waiting to go underground, have the faces of actors
when a play must close . . .

Other metaphors he repeats with Homeric confidence through the years, and they are like irregular watermarks that place a subtle proprietary brand on his work: the night sky's similarity to a perforated roof, the coinlike glimmer of rivers or seas, the way city blocks bring paragraphs or stanzas to mind.

But best of all are those metaphors he grounds in the rudiments of his craft, in grammar and syntax: when "dragonflies drift like a hive of adjectives," when he imagines his late father pausing "in the parenthesis" of the stairs, or when "like commas / in a shop ledger gulls tick the lined waves."

The reader imagines Walcott, as he sets these striking images down, mentally shuttling between the fact of the world and the fact of the poem. Often, he is evoking the sea's activity, or the sky's, and making analogies with his own practice of describing it.

And so it is that in the last poem on the last page of this large-hearted and essential book, the two realities finally merge. The natural poet dissolves, astonished, into nature, "as a cloud slowly covers the page and it goes / white again and the book comes to a close."

Aciman's Alibis

WHEN, IN 2005 and 2006, a mysterious sweet smell wafted across Staten Island, Brooklyn, and Manhattan, it discomfited already jittery New Yorkers. The same thing happened again three years later. Finally, the smell was identified: fenugreek, carried on breezes from a New Jersey flavor and fragrance factory. The incident reminded me of a passage in André Aciman's fine 1995 memoir, *Out of Egypt,* in which he writes about the fragrance of hilba, fenugreek. Arab Egyptians drank it for its curative powers, and reeked afterward, but for many Alexandrian Jews who aspired to being European, nothing could be more déclassé than the smell of hilba. Aciman's father called it *une odeur d'arabe,* an Arab smell, and hated any trace of it in the house or on his clothes. But, Aciman points out, "all homes bear ethnic odors," and from the various smells of foods and perfumes the stories of communities and persons emerge. The opening chapter of *Alibis,* Aciman's beautiful new book of essays, is an extended aria on the sense of smell.

The fragrance in this case is lavender. Lavender, first encountered in his father's aftershave, and then used as a home cure for migraines, is the madeleine—Aciman's debt to Proust is deep and freely acknowledged—that opens up a cascade of memories. Memories of childhood, youth, marriage, and fatherhood are narrated in counterpoint with a dizzying tour of the varieties of lavender. The essay becomes a story about Aciman's discovery of different lavenders, lavenders associated with people, places, and half-forgotten encounters. His enthusiasm, expressed in meandering, enumerative sentences, is intense and catching:

> There were light, ethereal lavenders; some were mild and timid; others lush and overbearing; some tart, as if picked from the field and left to parch in large vats of vinegar; others were overwhelmingly sweet. Some lavenders ended up smelling like an herb garden; others, with hints of so many spices, were blended beyond recognition. I experimented with each one, purchased many bottles, not just because I wanted to collect them all or was searching for the ideal lavender—the hidden lavender, the ur-lavender that superseded all other lavenders—but because I was eager to either prove or disprove something I suspected all along: that the lavender I wanted was none other than the one I'd grown up with and would ultimately turn back to once I'd established that all the others were wrong for me.

After this prefatory inspiration, *Alibis* exhales into a pursuit of evanescence. Most of its chapters are travel essays, and Aciman is a spirited guide, sensitive to history but alive also to food, sunshine, art, and aimless wandering. The pleasure of reading him resides in the pleasure of his company. He knows a lot, and often gets carried away, but he also knows how to doubt himself. If his destinations seem conventional—Paris, Barcelona, Rome—his engagement with them is idiosyncratic. His mission is to "unlock memory's sluice gates," and it is a mission he accomplishes through the art of the essay itself: "You write not after you've thought things through; you write to think things through."

Aciman returns to memory obsessively, looking for the words that can help him understand it better, finding solace in the idea of being in one place while desiring another, not for the sake of being in that other place, but for the sake of desire itself. Visiting Egypt, he remembers how the smell from a certain falafel place in New York used to fill him with a deep longing for the small falafel establishments he had known in Egypt. But, in the course of this memory, he also realizes that the falafel place in New York matches his dream of Egyptian falafel more closely than can Egypt falafel itself. This displacement of desire is Aciman's favorite move, one he deploys in several of the essays in *Alibis*. The imbricated feelings owe something to the ironies of the seventeenth-century roman d'analyse. Aciman cites Madame de La Fayette's *Princesse de Clèves*, which was particularly dear to him; in it, a woman who wishes to regain her lover doesn't merely feign indifference but feigns an effort to mask her feigned indifference.

But there is something more than mere irony or dissimulation going on in Aciman's case. In one passage he writes: "What we missed was not just Egypt. What we missed was dreaming Europe in Egypt—what we missed was the Egypt where we'd dreamed of Europe." On revisiting an apartment building in Rome, he recalls: "At fifteen, I visited the life I wished to lead and the home I was going to make my own some day. Now, I was visiting the life I had dreamed of living." Of Cambridge, Massachusetts, he writes: "Here, at twenty-five, I had conjured the life I wished to live one day. Now, at fifty, I was revisiting the

life I'd dreamed of living." Writing of Monet's painting in Bor-
dighera, on the Riviera, he speculates that Monet "realized that
he liked painting this town more than he loved the town itself,
because what he loved was more in him than in the town itself,
though he needed the town to draw it out of him." And he describes his own experience as a young refugee in Rome thus:
"I'd grown to love old Rome, a Rome that seemed more in me
than it was out in Rome itself, because, in this very Rome I'd
grown to love, there was perhaps more of me in it than there
was of Rome."

What is one to make of this insistent ostinato? Certainly it
gives a picture of Aciman's mind: his love of recursion and contradiction, of being "elsewhere" (this is how he defines the "alibis" of the title), of cultivating shadow-selves and always feeling
out of place. And, certainly, memory is nothing if not repeti-
tive. But it is also evident that some of these repetitions are
simply due to the essays' having been written at different times
for different magazines and journals. This leads to some incon-
sistencies of tone, and some infelicities in the otherwise fine
text. For instance, having already written on Monet, Aciman
mentions, in the course of another essay, "the painter Claude
Monet," as though we had never heard of him; *La Princesse de
Clèves* is introduced twice; and a metaphor about old houses
leaning on each other for support, striking though it is, surely
wasn't intended to show up in an essay about Rome as well as
in one about Venice.

Nevertheless, Aciman's deep fidelity to the world of the
senses, and to the translation of those sensations into prose,
makes *Alibis* a delight. We enjoy, with him, the satisfactions of
coincidences, and (to put it as he might) of dreaming of pasts in
which we dreamed of the future from which we are now dream-

ing of the past. Aciman writes of Proust that "memory and wishful thinking are filters through which he registers, processes and understands present experience." The same has long been true of Aciman himself, and this fragrant book further bolsters his reputation as one of our best wishful thinkers.

Double Negative

S AUL AUERBACH, THE great fictional photographer at the heart of Ivan Vladislavić's *Double Negative,* is more meticulous than most. The unhurried processes and careful results of his photography, work made on the streets and in the homes of the people of Johannesburg, provide the calm pulse of the novel. Photography is a fast art now, except for those who are too old-fashioned to shoot digital. But for most of the art's history—until about fifteen years ago—most photographers had no choice but to be slow. Film had to be loaded into a camera, the shot had to be taken with some awareness of the cost of materials, the negative had to be developed, and the print had to be enlarged. A certain meticulousness was necessary for photographs, a certain irreducible calmness of temperament.

The narrator of *Double Negative* is Neville Lister, Nev to his friends and family, a smart young college dropout when we first meet him. He is anything but calm. Nev's life story, detailed in a discontinuous narrative from his youth to his middle age, is the main material of the novel, but it unfurls to the steady rhythm of Auerbach's photographs: Nev anticipating the photographs, witnessing the places and persons involved in their making, remembering the images years later, and remembering them years later still. Like every worthwhile first-person narrator, Nev has a suggestive and imprecise identification with his author. Meanwhile, the fictional Saul Auerbach has a real-life cognate in David Goldblatt, the celebrated photographer of ordinary life in South Africa during the last three decades of apartheid and the first two decades since its end. The temptation is to think that Nev and Auerbach are a pair of photographic positives printed from Vladislavić and his sometime collaborator Goldblatt. But this is a book that is obsessed with imperfect doublings, and it comes with its own caveat emptor: "Stratagems banged around the truth like moths around an oil lamp." Things are not what they seem, and this is not a roman à clef, though it has been expertly rigged to look like one.

With a language as fine-grained as a silver gelatin print, Vladislavić delivers something rarer and subtler than a novelization of experience: he gives us, in this soft, sly novel, "the seductive mysteries of things as they are." At heart, the novel is about an encounter between two intellects in an evil time. It is an account of a sentimental education, though there's a quickness to the narrative that allows it to elude such categorical confinement. The skeptical, hot-blooded, and quick-tongued younger man and the reticent, unsentimental, and deceptively stolid veteran navigate their way through a brutal time in a brutal place. Neither of them is politically certain—that rawness of response is outsourced in part to a visiting British journalist who goes on a shoot with them—but both are ethically engaged, and both realize how deeply perverse their present order (South Africa in the 1980s) is. "It could not be improved upon," Nev says of that time, looking back; "it had to be overthrown." This young Nev is direct but unsteady on his feet. We are reminded, subtly, that he is, as his name tells us, a Lister. He pitches forward. "I felt that I was swaying slightly, the way you do after a long journey when the bubble in an internal spirit level keeps rocking even though your body has come to rest." Vladislavić's prose is vibrant: it is alert to vibrations, movement, and feints, as though it were fitted with a secret accelerometer.

Double Negative is in three parts, dealing respectively with youth, a return from exile, and maturity. The plot is light: through the drift of vaguely connected incident, all set down as though remembered, Vladislavić draws the reader into a notion that this is a memoir. But these are invented stories about an invented self interacting with other invented persons. It is not recollection—but it is also not not recollection. It is a double negative. What sustains this enterprise, magnificently, is Vladislavić's narrative intelligence, which is nowhere more visible than in his language-work itself. We enter incidents in medias res—as though they were piano études—and exit them before we have overstayed our welcome.

Above all, there is in *Double Negative,* as in all Vladislavić's writing, an impressive facility with metaphor. Metaphors are the observational scaffolding on which the story is set. They also occasion much of Vladislavić's finest writing in this finely written book: someone has "three wooden clothes pegs with their teeth in the fabric of her dress and they moved with her like a shoal of fish"; "a window display of spectacles looked on like a faceless crowd"; barbershop clients "reclined with their necks in slotted basins like aristocrats on the scaffold"; somebody "faded into the background like a song on the radio"; and, impishly signaling his own technique, lenses on a pair of black-rimmed glasses are "as thick as metaphors."

In the 1980s, the scholars George Lakoff and Mark Johnson argued that metaphor is pervasive in the English language and that our penchant for metaphorical speech creates the structures of social interaction. But in Vladislavić's hands, the metaphor goes well beyond this quotidian utility and, refreshed, reconstructed, and revived, does a great deal more: it becomes a ferry for the uncanny, a deployment of images so exact that the ordinary becomes strange and the strange becomes familiar. Metaphors are at home in South Africa's strange and sad history, where many things are like many other things, but nothing is quite the same as anything else.

A metaphor is semantic. A double negative, on the other hand, is syntactical: two negations in their right places in a sentence usually lead to an affirmation (in the wrong places, they could be merely an intensified negation). A double negative, in the sense of two wrongs making a right, is a form of strategic long-windedness. To use two terms of negation, to say, for instance, that something is "not unlike" something else, is not the same as to say it is like that thing. Double negatives register instances of self-canceling misdirection. They are about doubt, the productive and counterproductive aspects of doubt, the pitching ground, the listing figure, and the little gap between intention and effect.

Beyond the grammatical sense of "double negative," Vladislavić wants us to think also of the photographic negative, upside down, its colors flipped, its habitation of the dark. Its double, the printed photograph, is the right side up, with a system of colors and shadows that resembles our world, and a form that invites viewing in the light. "A photograph is an odd little memorial that owes a lot to chance and intuition," Auerbach says. But a photograph is also a little machine of ironies that contains within it a number of oppositions: light and dark, memory and forgetting, ethics and injustice, permanence and evanescence.

Late in the novel, a grown-up Nev Lister talks to his wife, Leora, about someone who recently interviewed him:

> "She was being ironic, obviously," she said.
> "Yes."
> "And so are you."
> "I guess."
> "The whole thing is ironic."
> "Including the ironies."
> "Maybe they cancel one another out then," Leora said.
> "Like a double negative."

In Place of Thought

IN 1913 A compilation of Gustave Flaubert's satirical defini-
tions was posthumously published as *Le Dictionnaire des Idées
Reçues* (*The Dictionary of Received Ideas*). Flaubert hated cliché, a
hatred that expressed itself not only in the pristine prose of
Madame Bovary but also in his letters and in his notes on the
thoughtless platitudes of the day. *The Dictionary of Received Ideas*
is a complaint against automatic thinking. What galls Flaubert
most is the inevitability, given an action, of a certain standard
reaction. We could learn from his impatience: there are many
standard formulations in our language, which stand in place of
thought, but we proclaim them each time—due to laziness,
prejudice, or hypocrisy—as though they were fresh insight.

I let Flaubert's *Dictionary* inspire me, and I also opened myself up to the influence of Ambrose Bierce and his cynical *Devil's
Dictionary,* Samuel Johnson's mostly serious but occasionally
coruscating *Dictionary of the English Language,* and Gelett Bur-
gess's now-forgotten send-up of platitudes, *Are You a Bromide?*
What the entries in these books have in common, in addition to
compression and wit, is an intolerance of stupidity. As I wrote
my modern cognates, I was struck at how close some of them
came to the uninterrogated platitudes in my own head. Stupidity stalks us all.

AFRICA. A country. Poor but happy. Rising. ALMOND. All eyes are almond-shaped. AMERICAN. With the prefix "all," a blond. ARTICULATE. Say "You're very articulate" to young blacks, and then ask where they are from. ARTISAN. A carpenter, in Brooklyn. ATHEISM. Deranged cult of violent fanatics. AUSTRALIANS. Extremely fit. Immune to pain. If you meet one, say "Foster's." The whole country is nothing but beaches. BLUE. The color of purity. Countless mysterious ads are devoted to pads and liners that absorb blue liquid. BRAVE. Doomed. BREAST. No joking matter. One glimpse on television sufficient to destroy a childhood. (See CHILDREN.) BUDDHISM. The way of peace. CAESAR. "Veni, vidi, vici." Get into a conversation about the pronunciation. CARAMEL. Term used to describe black women's skin. No other meaning known. CHILDREN. The only justification for policy. Always say "our children." The childless have no interest in improving society. CHINESE. Wonder what they're thinking. CHOCOLATE. Term used to describe black women's skin. No other meaning known. CHRISTIANITY. Peace on earth. CLARIFICATION. Reversal. COAL. Clean. COFFEE. Declare that it is intolerable at Starbucks. Buy it at Starbucks. COMMUNITY. Preceded by "black." White people, lacking community, must make do with property. CRIME. Illegal activities involving smaller amounts of money. CRISIS. Mention that it is composed of the Chinese characters for opportunity and danger. DIVERSITY. Obviously desirable, within limits. Mention your service in the Peace Corps. EGGS. Always say "You can't make omelets without breaking eggs" whenever the subject of war comes up. EMIGRÉ. Jewish immigrant. EVOLUTION. Only a theory. FASCISM. Always preceded by "creeping." FEMINISTS. Wonderful, in theory. FISH. A vegetable. GERMANS. When watching football, "never rule out the Germans." HARVARD. Source of studies quoted on BBC. Never say "I went to Harvard." Say "I schooled in the Boston area." HAUTE COUTURE. Always declare that it is made by gay men for boyish girls. Wait hours to see fashion exhibits at the Met. HEAT. Antonym of "humidity." HILARIOUS. Never simply say "funny." HIP-HOP. Old-school hip-hop, i.e., whatever was popular when you were nineteen, is great. Everything since then is intolerable. HIPSTER. One who has an irrational hatred of hipsters. *ILIAD*. Declare a preference for the *Odyssey*. INDIA. Work your tolerance of or aversion to spicy food into the conversation as quickly as possible. "A land of contrasts." INTERNET. A waste of time. Have a long online argument with anyone who disagrees. ISLAM. Religion of peace. JAPAN. Mysterious. Always "the Japanese." Mention Murakami. JAZZ. America's classical music. The last album was released in 1965. LITERALLY. Swear you'd rather die than use "literally" as an intensifier. MAGISTERIAL. Large book, written by a man. MEN. Always say "All the good ones are gay or taken" within earshot of the straight single ones. MIGRANT. Mexican immigrant. MOCHA. Term used to describe black women's skin. No other meaning known. NEWSPAPERS. Bemoan their gradual disappearance. Don't actually buy any. NIETZSCHE. Say "Nietzsche says God is dead," but if someone says that first, say "God says Nietzsche is dead." *ODYSSEY*. Declare a preference for the *Iliad*. PARIS. Romantic, in spite of the rude waiters and Japanese tourists. Don't simply like it; "adore" it. POET. Always preceded by "published." Function unknown. PRETTY. On Facebook, to indicate an unattractive woman. PROUST. No one actually reads him. One rereads him, preferably on summer vacation. PUNS. Always say "No pun intended" to draw attention to the intended pun. RACISM. Obsolete term. Meaning unknown. REGGAE. Sadly, just one album exists in the genre. RUSHDIE. Have a strong opinion on *The Satanic Verses*. Under no circumstances actually read *The Satanic Verses*. SCANDAL. If governmental, express surprise that people are surprised. If sexual, declare it a distraction, but seek out the details. SEMINAL. Be sure to use in a review of a woman's work. Proclaim your innocence after. SMART. Any essay that confirms your prejudices. STRIKE. Always "surgical." (See EGGS.) SUNSET. Beautiful. Like a painting. Post on Instagram and hashtag #nofilter. TELEVISION. Much improved. Better than novels. If someone says *The Wire,* say *The Sopranos,* or vice versa. TOUR DE FORCE. A film longer than two and a half hours and not in English. VALUES. "We must do whatever it takes to preserve our values." Said as a prelude to destroying them. VIRGINITY. An obsession in Iran and in the olive oil industry. It can be lost, like a wallet. YEATS. Author of two quotations. ŽIŽEK. Observe he's made some good points, but.

A Conversation with
Aleksandar Hemon

―――――――

ONE DAY IN *early October 2011, I was waiting outside the hotel across from the New York Public Library when Teju Cole walked down the street. He advanced in long strides, like someone comfortable getting around the city. This was the first time we met, and it was to share a car ride to Scranton, Pennsylvania, to take part in Pages and Places, a literary festival dedicated to books and cities.*

The conversation in the backseat of the car started, I believe, with soccer—never a bad beginning—and then it went on for hours, touching on religion, Miles Davis, Sarajevo and Lagos, New York and Chicago, Sebald, soccer, writing, Hitchens and Dawkins, more soccer, faith, and many other things, including soccer. By the time we took part in the panel we were meant to share, there seemed nothing left to talk about. And then we talked some more, in a church with bad acoustics, and it seemed nobody could hear anything. By the end of the day, I felt I'd never talked so much in my life. But more importantly, I felt that I'd never listened so much ever before. We've been friends since.

Salinger's Holden Caulfield made a distinction between writers you would like to call on the phone and those you wouldn't care to talk to at all. Teju Cole belongs to the former group. I grab any occasion to talk to Teju Cole: in person, via Twitter, or, as in this case, by email.

—ALEKSANDAR HEMON

ALEKSANDAR HEMON: I've always found the insistent distinction between fiction and nonfiction in Anglo American writing very annoying, indeed troubling. For one thing, it implies that nonfiction is all the stuff outside of fiction, or the other way around, the yin and yang of writing. Another problem: it marks a text in terms of its relation to "truth," a category that is presumably self-evident and therefore stable. But narration cannot contain stable truth, because it unfolds, and it does so before the narrator in one way, and before the listener/reader in another way. Narration is creation of truth, which is to say that truth does not precede it.

In Bosnian, there are no words that are equivalent to "fiction" and "nonfiction," or that convey the distinction between them. This is not to say that there is no truth or falsehood. Rather, the stress is on storytelling. The closest translation of "nonfiction" would really be "true stories."

You declare *Every Day Is for the Thief* a work of fiction. Why?

TEJU COLE: I made a sideways move from art history into writing, and I think this, in part, is why I also find the stern distinction between fiction and nonfiction odd. It's not at all a natural way of splitting up narrated experience, just as we don't go around the museum looking for fictional or nonfictional paintings. Painters know that everything is a combination of what's observed, what's imagined, what's overheard, and what's been done before. Is Monet a nonfiction painter and Ingres a fiction painter? It's the least illuminating thing we could ask about their works. Some lean more heavily on what's seen, some more on what's imagined, but all draw on various sources.

Writers know this, too, but I think they knew it a lot better before the market took such a hold. Would Miguel de Cervantes have considered himself a writer of fiction? Would François Rabelais? Would Robert Burton consider his activity (let's telescope the eras here) essentially dissimilar to Rabelais's? They all pretty much understood themselves to be spinning narratives out of whatever was at hand. And let's not even get into Daniel Defoe, who played devious games with the emerging genres.

But these days, a work has to be clearly marked "fiction" or "nonfiction," and *Every Day Is for the Thief* is called a work of fiction because it has quite a number of things in it that are made-up. But when I'm reading Michael Ondaatje's *Running in the Family,* or W. G. Sebald's *The Rings of Saturn,* or those short stories by Lydia Davis, the last thing on my mind is whether they are literal records of reality. Who cares? All I want is to be dragged down into a space of narrative that I haven't been in before, into a place where, as you say, a truth is created. And let's be frank: even the most scrupulous *New Yorker* article is an act of authorial will and framing, and is not as strictly "nonfictional" as it suits us to think it is.

In any case, you are right, this is an Anglo American obsession. *The Rings of Saturn* was originally published in German as *Eine englische Wallfahrt (An English Pilgrimage).* Make of that what you will.

AH: Sebald is pertinent here, for a number of reasons. As far as I know, none of the books published while he was alive were labeled as fiction or nonfiction, novel or essays. And he made sure that storytelling was at the heart of it. In *Austerlitz,* for example, he does what I term (for personal use) "concentric narration" (he said that she said that he said . . .), whereby whatever comes from the past passes through people. The only way to have an organic connection with the past is by way of narration, while the knowledge of (as opposed to information about) history has to be shared in language. I always thought that Sebald used photographs in his books in order to expose their failure as documents. He places photos to interrupt the narration so as to show that they mean nothing unless they are inside storytelling. Photographs might be self-authenticating (as Roland Barthes thought), but their authentic truth is available only in language, as practiced in narration.

What prompted you to include photos in *Every Day Is for the Thief*? What kind of work do you want the pictures to do?

TC: For sure, Sebald was up to something sly with his photographs. His writing tested, much more than that of most other writers, the boundaries of what we consider fiction. I think the photos, many of which were found photos, and many of which were intentionally worn away through repeated photocopying, were there to create a mood. But they were also there to propose a dare. "Look, this is all testimonial," he seems to be saying. And we almost believe it—until we notice the slight fracture between the claim in the text and the photograph, or until we look so closely at the text that we realize there are elements in it that came into being because he had a certain photograph on hand for which he made up a story, and not the other way around. As you say, the pictures "mean nothing unless they are inside storytelling." So, I think of his photos as helping create the uncanny, destabilizing mood of his books: it must all be true, we think, but we know it can't all be true.

My interest in Sebald came late, only after I had written *Every Day Is for the Thief,* and some friends who read it said, "Hey, you should check out Sebald." My idea of putting photos in a book came from elsewhere: the fact that I happened to be interested in both photography and writing, the fact that I was a blogger. But, also, I had read Ondaatje (*The Collected Works of Billy the Kid*), Orhan Pamuk (*Istanbul: Memories and the City*), and Barthes (*Camera Lucida*)—the latter two of which are not fiction but use photos in a non-textbook way. And then, later on, in the time between the writing of *Every Day Is for the Thief* and its American publication, I became aware of other interesting uses of black-and-white photos. Many writers were using images in a way that had imprecise connections to the text: Julio Cortázar's *From the Observatory,* Catherine Taylor's *Apart,* Carole Maso's *The Art Lover,* and a certain Aleksandar Hemon's *The Lazarus Project.*

Add to all this the fact that I was being trained as an art historian, and that writing a paper and leaving out the images was unnatural to me: in a way, I was destined to put photos in *Every Day Is for the Thief.* And though I love Sebald to the point of tears, it's important to me to push back a little against the idea that there's this vacuum in which he alone ever put pictures in works of fiction. Also, I'm not completely sure of this, but I might be the most obsessive photographer of all the people I mentioned; I think almost everyone else is using other people's photos, found photos, or (in Sebald's case) sometimes snapshots. In my case, I have for sure spent more time in the past decade taking pictures than writing.

I know that your friend, the immensely talented Velibor

Božovic, did the photos for *The Lazarus Project*. Other than the sheer beauty of his pictures, why was it important for you to have images in that book?

AH: It started with two images of the dead Lazarus Averbuch sitting in a chair, being triumphantly offered by a blazingly white policeman to the American public. In 1908 these photos were supposed to show that his alleged anarchist proclivities were visible in his body and that the foreign life in said body was successfully terminated by law and order. I'd come upon the photos before I read Sebald and, more importantly, before the Abu Ghraib photos were released. When I saw the images from Abu Ghraib, they were instantly recognizable, because I'd seen and studied the Lazarus photos, which were structurally and ideologically identical to them.

In *The Lazarus Project,* I wanted to engage the reader into confronting the history as signified by the photos in the story. And I wanted to stretch the book between the (arbitrary) poles of subjectivity and objectivity (which some would equate with fiction and nonfiction), so I wanted the photos to cover the same range, too—but only to complicate readers' ideas and perceptions.

What always interests me—indeed obsesses me—is the way we engage in history. Except there is no "we." Americans do it differently and, often, irresponsibly and without particular interest. Abu Ghraib is long forgotten now; no lesson seems to have been learned. Specialist Lynndie England and ten others went to prison and are now out of it—with no officers among them, let alone anyone from Bush's court of sociopaths.

On the other hand, I (and the people like me, whoever they may be) engage with it perforce. There is no way to leave history. There is no other place to go. As a diasporic person I've learned that it's in fact really easy to leave your country. What is difficult is leaving its history, as it follows (or leads) you like a shadow. That kind of history is in your body (as it was in Lazarus's) and cannot be relegated to a museum or, as in America, to entertainment.

I loved the chapter in *Every Day Is for the Thief* in which the narrator visits the National Museum, which is nearly devoid of art, while the historical wing consists of a mention of slave trade and narratives of recent dictators. What is Nigeria to you? What does its history mean to you, as a writer, and as a citizen?

TC: Nigeria is an ideal for me in two ways. One, it's a space of possibility, an opportunity for its people to move beyond the pressures of tribe or ethnic group. This opportunity is often squandered. Two, it's a soccer team, one that could be one of the world's best—there's certainly enough talent to be, at least, on Uruguay's level. This opportunity, too, is often squandered. So, Nigeria haunts me in terms of being a space of unfinished histories. But my identity maps onto other things: being a Lagosian (Lagos is like a city-state), being a West African, being African, being a part of the Black Atlantic. I identify strongly with the historical network that connects New York, New Orleans, Rio de Janeiro, and Lagos. But, as a subject, Nigeria won't let go of me.

Like you, I am now in a country where people (convinced of their innocence) sleep well; and, like you, I'm still one of history's amnesiacs.

AH: Amnesiacs?

TC: I meant to write "insomniacs"! But the error is illuminating.

AH: You not only identify with but also write about—and in—cities. *Open City* is one of the great city books, it's also a great wandering book, as is *Every Day Is for the Thief*. It seems to me that it is impossible to write in a linear way about and in cities—they're necessarily nonlinear places. This is the case with a city like Lagos (though I've never been there) perhaps even more so than New York, with its orderly grids and spatial hierarchies. To my mind, the ultimate city-wandering book is *Ulysses*, radically devoid of linear narration and plot, built of fragments that exist simultaneously and often conflictually. What attracts you to cities? What connects the four cities in "the historical network"? Is it that cities are more conducive to nonlinear narratives, or is it that nonlinear narrators end up in cities?

TC: Thank you. Halfway through writing *Open City*, I thought to myself that I should learn some of New York history "properly." So I bought a stack of worthy books and started to read them. But, you know what? Doing that offended the sense of drift I relied on for my novel. The books were too systematic, too knowledgeable. So I just went back to my previous method: relying on the things I already knew, walking around aimlessly, and filling in facts and figures later as needed. The thing had to breathe, it had to drift, and it had to pretend not to know where it was going. (A dancer in mid-dance can't think too much about her legs.)

As for cities in general: I think they might be our greatest invention. They drive creativity, they help us manage resources, and they can be hives of tolerance. In a village, you can't stick out too much. In the city, if anyone judges you, you tell them to go to hell. So, there's that positive side. But the other side is that they are simply so congested with material history and the spiritual traces of those histories, including some very dark events. Your contemporary Chicago is haunted by the Chicago of the late nineteenth and early twentieth centuries, the Chicago of innovation and of systematic exclusions. Rural landscapes can give the double illusion of being eternal and newly born. Cities, on the other hand, are marked with specific architecture from specific dates, and this architecture, built by long-vanished others for their own uses, is the shell that we, like hermit crabs, climb into.

The four cities I listed—New York, New Orleans, Rio de Janeiro, and Lagos—are simply four that were important nodes in the transatlantic slave trade and in black life in the century following. They are the vertices of a sinister quadrilateral.

AH: Cities do offer spaces for uncontrollable exchanges, but then there is always controlled commerce, which not so long ago included slave markets. But cities also erase and reshape themselves in ways that are different in different places. American cities tend to erase their pasts, particularly the conflictual parts, just as they marginalize the inconvenient and unjust parts of the present—the killing and the greed are always elsewhere. Take the Bloombergian New York, the Vatican of entitlement, where glamour conceals the greed that drives (and destroys) it all.

Cities like Lagos, Sarajevo, Rio, or New Orleans do not project a harmonious version of themselves, because they cannot—

the conflict is ever present and indelible. Hence they're uncontainable, like language or literature—no experience or interpretation can be final, no delimiting or closure ever available.

Reading your books, I have a sense that, had you taken different routes in your wanderings, a different New York (in *Open City*) or Lagos (*Every Day Is for the Thief*) would've emerged. Or, to put it another way, there is no way to impose a self-sustaining narrative upon any city—only multiple, simultaneous plots/ stories are possible. Could it be that cities are therefore more conducive to poetry, which allows accumulation of fragments and does not require narrativization? You invoke Ondaatje a lot, a great poet and wrangler of fragments, as well as Tomas Tranströmer. What does poetry do for you? Do you write poetry?

TC: I rarely sit down to write a poem, not the kind you can submit to *Poetry* magazine or *The New Yorker*. But I think poetry and its way of thinking does infect a lot of my work. I certainly read a lot of it—there's a discipline and tightness in the language that very few prose writers can achieve. So, yes, people like Tranströmer and Ondaatje and Wisława Szymborska are touchstones for me. It's a long list: George Seferis, Anne Carson, Charles Simic, Sharon Olds, Seamus Heaney: anyone who has found a way to sidestep conventional syntax. And for this reason, I take pleasure in reading those writers whose prose also contains the elusive and far-fetched. I imagine in reading you, for instance, that you must make notes of the odd and remarkable ideas or moments in a way similar to a poet. Is poetry important to your reading?

AH: Actually, I don't make notes. I rely on memory and its failure. I do think in language and I imagine that is what poets do, except in tighter spaces, closer to the language, indeed inside it, wrangling its rhythms, uncovering its dormant possibilities. When I was coming up in Bosnia the most common distinction in literary discourse was between poetry and prose, and it was not unusual for writers to write both poetry and prose (stories/novels/essays). Consequently, if you were an invested reader, you would read poetry as well as prose. Whatever the reason for that, it foregrounded the notion of literature as made of language. The distinction was founded upon the different uses of language, and not, as in fiction versus nonfiction, upon the relation between representation and "truth." Poetry is, as far as I'm concerned, essential to the field of literature, it is its purest form. Sadly, I'm not good at writing it (I've tried), but I love reading poetry.

Now, you say you don't write poetry, but you're one of the great tweeters of our time. Is it fair to suggest that you exercise your poetic instincts in tweeting? And didn't much of *Every Day Is for the Thief* appear online first, in a blog? How do you see the future of literature? What are the possibilities in practicing literature in the context of social media? How are people going to read fifty years from now? What are they going to read? Will there be poetry?

TC: Now that's a real surprise: I could have sworn you were an inveterate note taker. It leaves me even more impressed with your writing then, because whenever I come across one of your intriguing turns of phrase, the little genie of writerly envy in my head says, "He must have been saving this one for a while." (First time I read *The Question of Bruno,* every couple of pages I would think, How the hell did he arrive at this phrase? He must have scribbled it down and saved it for this moment.)

Anyway, notes or not, I do get your sense of fascination and discomfort with language. The writers that interest me all have this wide-eyed amazement at what words can do. And since language is fresh in them, since they don't take it as a settled thing, they can deliver it with corresponding freshness on the page.

The Twitter thing is interesting. "Great tweeter" is a term that would have literally been gibberish to anyone but an ornithologist five years ago. Now, apparently, there is such a thing.

I'm not yet active on Instagram (though, in theory, it should be great for me), I couldn't connect with Vine, and I'm not sure I even know what Snapchat is. But Twitter has been a real part of my creativity these past couple of years. For sure, there's a poetic impulse there in me, perhaps not one disciplined enough to write finished poems, but still unwilling to let go of the intensely localized effect that poems can have. So, Twitter has been good for humor, for provocations, and for thinking about new ways to deliver the ideas that are important to me. Indeed, even new ways to find out which ideas are important to me. I should also mention that I've gotten more attention (maybe because of my more conventional published work) than lots of the other people who are doing seriously interesting work on Twitter. So, there's that element of luck and randomness as well.

Every Day Is for the Thief appeared online in January 2006, as a limited-edition experiment. I wrote one chapter each day. In effect, I was blogging on this weird project eight hours a day for an entire month. Months later, after I had erased the blog, a Nigerian publisher showed interest, and the project was edited and found a second life as a book. But, yes, I believe in life online, the way a person in 1910 might believe in aviation, or a person in 1455 might believe in movable type: with excitement and apprehension.

But who knows where it's going to go? For sure, some of the smartest and most interesting literary minds of our generation and the generations to come will work in areas that are not "books" as we currently think of them. That's a given. But I think some of these people will also write books. It's the way that, say, two hundred years ago, the most celebrated composers in Europe were all "classical" composers. Now some of the best composers are still writing so-called classical music, but others are writing rock, jazz, electronica, or other weird things. In writing, at the present moment, books have a near monopoly on the literary reward system (if not on actual literary production). I think that's going to change very fast. I'm not saying there will be a Nobel Prize for tweeting, but I expect that the rewards of literary production will inevitably include people whose work is embedded inside these newer technologies. The Lifetime Achievement Award for Distinguished Work in Snapchat. Whatever the hell Snapchat is.

AH: Yes, rationally, I agree with you. But it may be the function of my age that I increasingly find myself considering the possibility that the whole project of humanity is winding down and the end of it all is on the horizon of possibilities. For one thing, extinction of humans is one of the possible outcomes of climate change.

It is possible that we might have to rethink nearly everything in the light of the possibility that two hundred years from now there will be no one around to give a flying fuck about what we're doing at this time. Our ethical and philosophical underpinnings—to the extent that we share any of them—will have to be reevaluated against the ultimate failure of humanity to outlive individual human beings. If we cannot continue our individual humanity in the collective project of humanity, if we cannot imagine a world better than this—and not by means of some spiritual opiate—this world is over. In that case, literature, which is always sent to some reader in the future, will have to renegotiate its modes of participation in human experience. If we ever find ourselves writing only for the present—which would essentially mean that tweeting is all we can do—I would feel absolutely defeated as a human being and a writer.

I was particularly struck by the last chapter in *Every Day Is for the Thief,* taking place on the street of carpenters who make only coffins. There is a devotion to their work of packing people away into the void, never questioning the meaning of it all. That perhaps redeems all the other failures in Lagos, in the world, in literature. And the photo that ends the book not only is sublimely beautiful but suggests a transcendence that is beyond death, something that might be available to the carpenters/writers if they maintain their devotion for the work.

The questions: Where do you stand in relation to transcendence? Do you pursue it? Must we pursue it? Is that a way to imagine better worlds?

TC: Well, open up yourself to our new overlords, Sasha. But, yes, I'm with you, particularly on the cataclysmic climate change that's coming into view and that will cause so much needless suffering.

As for faith: I don't believe in the Christian god, or the Muslim one, or the Jewish one. I'm sentimentally attached to some of the Yoruba and Greek gods—the stories are too good, too insightful, for a wholesale rejection—though I don't ask them for favors.

What do I believe in? Imagination, gardens, science, poetry, love, and a variety of nonviolent consolations. I suspect that in aggregate all this isn't enough, but it's where I am for now.

SECTION II

Seeing Things

Unnamed Lake

O N T H E N I G H T of October 8, 2014, or, rather, early on the morning of October 9, I had trouble sleeping. I lay in bed, closed my eyes, and let my mind go blank. Hours passed. I was in something like sleep that wasn't sleep. Around two in the morning, a light that had been bothering me went out, a neighbor's lamp, perhaps, or one of the electronic devices in the next room (the door was ajar) that in these days keep watch over us at all hours. Now wrapped up dark, my thoughts, instead of dipping into the cool subconscious, began to churn and froth.

I paced inside my own mind like a tiger inside its cage, like the Tasmanian tiger going back and forth, maddened by the prospect of its coming doom. Where I had been pinned down in sleeplessness by one small glare, my eyelids now trembled with the flashes coming from within. So quick was the succession of images, each of which presented itself like a problem to be solved, that I could not at any instant remember what had gone before. It seemed to me instead that my consciousness had become like a narrow, high-walled corridor crammed with everything I had lately read or seen, every landscape I had recently passed through or touched on in my thoughts. The intensity and speed of these images—which had come to resemble a slide show played at absurd speed—became harder and harder to bear until I suddenly sat upright, shutting down the show, as it were, and got out of bed.

I went into the study, switched on a lamp, sat in a chair (not at the desk), and began to write notes (in a blank book, on my crossed knee). I wrote many pages. The room was peaceful like that, spotlit, silent. The shutters were drawn, the mountains in the distance invisible. I wrote for an hour or more with lucid ease, as though my hand were being guided by a benevolent spirit and there was no gap between the flow of my thoughts and the fluency of the ink. The next day, in daylight, I saw that the book was full of fevered scribbles, with only a clear word every now and again to hint at whatever it was I had hoped to set down in writing. I remembered only what I had watched on YouTube, what I had watched between having finished writing and not having yet returned to my bed.

For years now, when I cannot sleep, I rise from bed and watch Jacques Derrida talk. I watch what he said sometime in the late 1990s. Each time that I write something, he said, and it feels like I'm advancing into new territory (he demonstrates "advance" with his left hand), somewhere I haven't been before, and this type of advance often demands certain gestures that can be taken as aggressive with regard to other thinkers or colleagues—I am not someone who is by nature polemical but it's true that deconstructive gestures appear to destabilize or cause anxiety or even hurt others—so, every time that I make this type of gesture, there are moments of fear. (Derrida has proud white hair, and wears a red shirt, and at times he touches his thumb to his lip or lifts a hand to his face.)

The concerts were in honor of the Führer, who had been in power since 1933. The conductor was Wilhelm Furtwängler. The end of the first movement grinds and rumbles like the thick of battle. Never has it sounded so frightful: this is music March 1942: for the despair in Lodz, the internment of Japanese Americans, the horrific winter of the Red Army on the Eastern front, the heavy fighting in Malta. (Later that same year, Derrida is expelled from lycée for being Jewish.) But the adagio is clear and tender, played slower than usual, reaching an even greater ecstasy than usual. No one who heard it could have failed to be moved to human kindness. Could they? (In addition to Hitler, both Himmler and Goebbels are in the audience.)

The concerts took place on March 22 and 24, 1942, on a stage draped with Nazi flags. A recording patched together from these performances is considered the greatest recording of Beethoven's Ninth. The previous week, on March 17, a Nazi camp had begun operation in Belzec, southeastern Poland. For the first time, people were shepherded into "showers" and gassed to death. Not slave labor, not shootings, not gas vans: this was the beginning of the gas chambers. Belzec was designed for death and death alone. ("Is considered the greatest recording" by whom?)

This doesn't happen at the moments when I'm writing, Derrida said. Actually, when I write, there is a feeling of necessity, of something that is stronger than myself (here he gestures with both hands raised to his head), that demands that I must write as I write. I have never renounced anything I've written because I've been afraid of certain consequences. Nothing intimidates me when I write. I say what I think must be said. (A fierceness in his narrowed eyes here. He is tanned, and cannot be unaware that he is handsome.) That is to say, when I don't write, there is a very strange moment when I go to sleep.

Of the no fewer than 434,500 and as many as 500,000 who were eventually brought to Belzec, two survived. Karl Alfred Schluch of the SS was not at the Berlin concerts, for he was working with Christian Wirth ("Christian the Terrible") at Belzec. Schluch said, "My location in the tube was in the immediate vicinity of the undressing hut. Wirth had stationed me there because he thought me capable of having a calming effect on the Jews. After the Jews left the undressing hut I had to direct them to the gas chamber. I believe that I eased the way there for the Jews because they must have been convinced by my words or gestures that they really were going to be bathed."

A composer who loses his hearing can still compose. The real disaster for a composer would be to lose the ability to count.

In a small enclosure in Beaumaris Zoo in Hobart in 1933 (at the time Jacques Derrida is a three-year-old in Algiers) a Tasmanian tiger, or thylacine, paces. His name is Benjamin. He has a doglike head, and stripes on his back like a tiger. But he is neither canid nor felid; he is marsupial. He is also a carnivore, a hunting animal, though not an especially fast or particularly strong one. The thylacine was first described in 1806 by Tasmania's deputy surveyor-general George Harris. "Head very large, bearing a near resemblance to the wolf or hyaena. Eyes large and full, black with a nictitant membrane which gives the animal a savage & malicious appearance."

In mainland Australia, the thylacine may have survived until the 1830s, according to the oral history recorded by the Adnyamathanha people of the Flinders Ranges region to the east of

Lake Torrens. "Today *marrukurli* (thylacines) are known only as mammals of the Dreaming. That is, there is no one living who claims to have seen one. Both the Dreaming and other oral tradition, however, suggest the possibility of their bodily existence in the region in the not-too-distant past."

At moments, you may notice that what you are looking at contains both its own obliteration (the promise of death) and a curious quantity of eternity, like a single body possessed by two spirits. Survival and extinction are both indelibly there. There is a quality of listening in the dead of the night (the "dead" of the night) that is perhaps not conducive to writing or interpretation, but that heightens the possibilities of what can be heard, or that might lead one to believe that there is an unnamed lake underneath all reality, and that there are places where the ground, insufficiently firm, can suddenly plunge one through into the subterranean truth of things.

The thylacine is the quarry of a state bounty in Tasmania between 1888 and 1909. Many thylacines die in that crazed hunt. Then an epidemic finishes off most of the rest. In the year 1933, when he paces for the camera, Benjamin is the last of his species. And when he dies in September 1936, the thylacine goes extinct. There are sightings afterward, but none credible.

When I have a nap or something, Derrida said, and I fall asleep (these words in English, all of a sudden, and not in French; but only these words), at that moment, in a sort of half-sleep, all of a sudden I'm terrified by what I'm doing. And I tell myself: You're crazy to write this! You're crazy to attack such a thing! You're crazy to criticize such and such a person. You're crazy to contest such an authority, be it textual, institutional, or personal. (His gestures become more animated.) And there is a kind of panic in my subconscious, he said. As if . . . what can I compare it to?

Perhaps when people talk about liking a man in uniform, they are thinking of someone like Major Patrick Chukwuma Kaduna Nzeogwu, someone both confiding and confident. The interviewer is white. He asks about the events of January 15, 1966. "Did the Sardauna himself attempt to fight?" "No, we didn't see him until the time we actually shot him. He ran away from his house when we fired the first two rounds from the antitank guns into the building. The whole room was blown up and the place was set alight. Then we went to the rear of the house and started searching from room to room until we found him among the women and children, hiding himself." Nzeogwu says this part with faint but detectable mockery.

He is young, fit, not yet twenty-nine, the consummate professional in his officer's cap and short-sleeved uniform. He speaks with astonishing clarity. He is what will change Nigeria at last and for good, there can be no doubt about it. "So we took away the women and children and took him." By "took him," Nzeogwu means he himself shot the Sardauna of Sokoto, Sir Ahmadu Bello, who had been serving as the premier of Northern Nigeria. In the same coup on the same day, Nzeogwu's co-conspirators killed the prime minister of Nigeria, Sir Abubakar Tafawa Balewa; the premier of Western Nigeria, Samuel Akintola; the finance minister, Festus Okotie-Eboh; Brigadier General Samuel Ademulegun; and many others. Blood gushed.

What if the things that happened could be seen again as apparitions before us? And the people who did these things could speak as they spoke in life, and move about like the people you see in dreams?

Nzeogwu smiles as he gives his answers: the future is bright.

But within a year and a half, he will be killed in an ambush during the Biafran war. In the three years of the war, more than a million of his Biafran compatriots will be dead, too.

Imagine a child who does something horrible, Derrida said. Freud talks of childhood dreams where one dreams of being naked and terrified because everyone sees that they're naked. In any case, in this half-sleep, I have the impression that I've done something criminal, disgraceful, unavowable, that I shouldn't have done. And somebody is telling me: "But you're mad to have done that." And this is something I truly believe in my half-sleep. And the implied command in this is: Stop everything! Take it back! Burn your papers! What you're doing is inadmissible! But once I wake up, it's over.

On August 4, 2014, the MV Pinak-6 ferry, with more than 250 passengers, was crossing the Padma River near Mawa Ghat in Munshiganj, Bangladesh. It was high tide. The ferry was headed to Dhaka. It became inundated with water and capsized, sinking in a matter of minutes. A man on the audio track, presumably the same person recording the video from the shore, can be heard calling out God's name, in shock and in fear, and then reciting the shahada: Lā ilāha illā-llāhu, Muhammadur rasūlu-llāh. The ferry was approved for only eighty-five passengers. The death toll is well over a hundred. The event sinks into the handheld camera recording it, the amateur videographer calling out God's name.

What if the event were recorded on video, and could be summoned up out of the depths for helpless viewing again, and again, and again?

What this means, Derrida said, or how I interpret this, is that when I'm awake, conscious, working, in a certain way I am more unconscious than in my half-sleep. When I'm in that half-sleep there's a kind of vigilance that tells me the truth. First of all, it tells me that what I'm doing is very serious. But when I'm awake and working (he raises his hands and lifts his head, like a conductor about to give a downbeat), this vigilance is actually asleep. It's not the stronger of the two. And so, he said, I do what must be done. Jacques Derrida died on October 9, 2004, and I am watching the video in the wee hours on October 9, 2014; a good coincidence, but history has few dates into which to fit everything.

"I realize the tragic significance of the atomic bomb," said President Truman, after the first bomb had been dropped, but before the second. "It is an awful responsibility which has come to us. We thank God that it has come to us, instead of to our enemies; and we pray that He may guide us to use it in His ways and for His purposes."

The footage shows the island of Tinian in the Northern Mariana Islands on a sunny afternoon in August 1945. Men prepare a bomb—the second bomb, the pilot of the first having just returned to base—for deployment. They paint it, check its seals, and position it into place. Some of the men wear tan fatigues, others are shirtless. (Are they being exposed to radiation without even knowing it?) The atmosphere is cheerful and tropical. The bomb, bright yellow, looks like a school project. The large ovoid plutonium bomb is about the size of a small car. The president invokes God. I am half-asleep, and therefore more awake than if I were completely awake. The footage is in vivid color.

What if it were visible? What if you could rise from your restless bed and switch on a machine and see it all again?

Major Charles Sweeney pilots the plane, called Bockscar, from which the bomb, called "Fat Man," is dropped at 11:00

A.M. on August 9. Thirty-five thousand people below in the city of Nagasaki are killed instantly. They "took" them, brought whatever it is they had been, into instantaneous extinction. Another fifty thousand are to die later, in greater pain. But all that, and much else besides, is now in the time of the Dreaming.

Wangechi Mutu

W HEN WANGECHI MUTU first became aware of the sea mammal that coastal Kenyans call nguva, she knew she'd found the key to her next project. The nguva, or dugong, is a large mammal related to the manatee. It grazes on sea grass, and has a hippolike head and fishlike tail. This chimerical appearance was part of the attraction. An even stronger pull came from the way the nguva was conflated with mermaids in stories told about errant fishermen and what they'd seen at sea. So she began to think about this other sense of nguva: the sirens and their mysterious power.

"I am fascinated by these ocean-grown folks," she says. "On the coast, there's all this cross-pollination of ideas. Someone thinks they saw something. One person's madness is reiterated by another, and a story is born. The rumor becomes a substitute for news."

Since the mid-1990s, Mutu has been exploring what could be called in-betweenness. She was born and raised in Nairobi, before going to Wales and then the United States to study, going on to make work addressing feminism, ecology, metamorphosis, colonialism, and technology. She credits her American experience—particularly the exhausting task of attempting to evade foolish stereotypes—for how she finally found a way to incorporate African imagery in her work. Many Americans know little about African culture beyond images of Maasai warriors in *National Geographic*. This ignorance became fertile ground for Mutu's explorations. The resulting images are visually arresting, both easy and difficult to look at, seductive in their patterning, grotesque in their themes.

"To make things make sense, I have to make things up," says the artist, whose work is now held in major collections worldwide, including New York's MoMA and London's Tate. "I'm not a documentarian, I'm not a photojournalist." Early on, Mutu drew on her experiences in a girls' Catholic school in Nairobi and on a number of violent events in Africa's colonial and postcolonial history. Influenced by artists such as Hannah Hoch and Richard Hamilton, she made collages exploring how state violence shows up on people's bodies. The links between Belgian atrocities in the Congo, war crimes in Sierra Leone, and her many armless—or otherwise amputated—figures become obvious once they're pointed out.

As her work evolved, Mutu began to make collages out of ethnographic photography, nineteenth-century medical illustrations, and the pornography printed in magazines. She calls herself "an irresponsible anthropologist and irrational scientist." Her images underscore the way female bodies can act as measuring devices of any society's health. Her women respond to their environments with both intelligence and agony. Some are skinless, the rush of veins and colors alarmingly visible. Many are powerful, muscular, lithe, in heels, half-cyborg at times, often erotic, sometimes dangerous. Several are influenced by real women: Sarah Baartman (the so-called Hottentot Venus who was shown in European fairgrounds), Josephine Baker, Eartha Kitt, Grace Jones, and Tina Turner. It's an all-star lineup of black women who had fiercely ambiguous relationships with the racial and gender tropes imposed on them, women at war with history's impositions.

Mutu's work is sensual, delighting in the materiality of its media (paper, paint, mica, wool, Mylar). Seen in a gallery, the organic forms, hybrid anatomies, wild hair, machinelike forearms, delirious patterns, and compound eyes coalesce in a way that no digital reproduction can quite match. And what is true of the pictures is doubly true of the sculptures and installations, which also make use of smell and sound: dripping bottles, fermenting wine, rotting milk.

Nguva na Nyoka (*Sirens and Serpents*), made for an exhibition at London's Victoria Miro Gallery, comprises a video, a large sculpture, and about fifteen paintings. What's new is the focus on mermaids and their marine environment. Metamorphosis, one of Mutu's past concerns, is now foregrounded. "The ocean is the source of life," she says. "We all come from there. I think about these one-celled creatures and I think about the planet. It is related to my obsession with biology, even if it's only a layperson's obsession. The way I visualize what's at the bottom of the ocean is very much to do with how I feel when I'm swimming in the sea."

This surrender to both microcosm and macrocosm is visible in the waterworlds of the new images. There's an abundance of blue and purple, and the detailing is intricate and seductive, appropriate given the sirenic theme. There's also an abundance of tendrils, tentacles, and snakes. Forms swirl, curl, and proliferate, and seem to oscillate between the vegetal and the animal.

When I ask Mutu about this serpentine imagery, she tells me a story about living on the Swahili coast. She was just nineteen, but had become interested in the culture of her Mijikenda villager neighbors, finding in it "a social contract of belief" that was far removed from the skeptical thinking she was used to in Nairobi. She watched them kill a python. The snake's body, left out in the open, was unexpectedly gone by the next day: it had refused to die and had wriggled away. The villagers found it and they killed it a second time. Mutu asked them to skin it for her. "I don't know why," she says. "It just seemed like the thing to do. I wouldn't do it now." She hung the skin out to dry. But for weeks, the snake's skin stayed soft. It began to rot rather than dry: the snake had refused to cooperate. Something about this incident stayed with her. Years later, she has incorporated the stubborn and ungovernable form of the snake into her thinking about nguva: the power of women, the fear of the unknown, the possibilities of regeneration, the mysteries of coastal life.

On this last point, she notes the way exhausted fisherfolk out in their boats can hallucinate. Her images of nguva are themselves like hallucinations: female bodies, fish bones, porcupine spines, impossible anatomies, internal organs writhing like unkillable snakes. She draws a link between these Mijikenda stories, Chinese mermaids, and the waterwomen in Arab folklore, contrasting the intense and occasionally malevolent power of the nguva to the sanitized mermaid of popular European culture.

"Out there on the coast where I stayed, just outside Lamu, there are bats flying around, there's the sound of the ocean, and there's this magical atmosphere. This is the way the stories get under your skin."

Age, Actually

GEORGES AND ANNE, a Parisian couple in their eighties, are at breakfast, talking amicably. All of a sudden, Anne falls silent. For a few long moments, she seems to have vanished and left her body behind. Her husband, distraught but calm, tries everything to get a reaction from her: he waves his hand, questions her repeatedly, daubs water on her. Nothing. Only when he hurries off to change out of his pajamas and get help does she revive, just as suddenly as she blanked out. She has no memory of what happened and has to be convinced, in fact, that anything happened at all. This sequence occurs a few minutes into Michael Haneke's *Amour* and is a clue to the question at the heart of this masterful film: What does it mean when someone—particularly someone vital and beloved—becomes no one?

Haneke is rightly celebrated as one of the best filmmakers now at work. In film after film, he explores violence, prejudice, eroticism, loss, and fear in ways that seem to transcend cinema's limitations. He likes to shock, it's true, but his serious engagement with fundamental questions gives his work a bracing quality that links it less to the work of his contemporaries than to that of an earlier generation of auteurs. *Amour,* like Haneke's previous film, *The White Ribbon* (2009), won the Palme d'Or at

Cannes. Both were deserving of the accolade, but what is striking is how different they are. *The White Ribbon* is a polyphonic
historical drama shot in gorgeous black and white in a rural
German setting. It is a big film. *Amour,* on the other hand, is
small, and looks almost like the work of a different filmmaker.
Its action is confined almost entirely to a single Paris apartment, and its characters are few. Georges (played by Jean-Louis
Trintignant, who is eighty-two) and Anne (Emmanuelle Riva,
eighty-five) take up the bulk of the screen time, and their dia-
logue feels circumscribed, as though written for the stage.
Haneke's films tend to have a hectoring emotional intensity. An
atmosphere of menace, which can occasionally edge into sa-
dism, suffuses films like *Funny Games, Code: Unknown, The Piano
Teacher,* and *Caché*. This is much less true of *Amour,* which unfolds like a simple domestic drama. We see the lives and daily
rituals of a pair of retired piano teachers. One of them has had
a stroke, and the other cares for her. It is sad, but it isn't vicious
or unsettling. At moments, with its steady camera gaze, repeti-
tive domestic chores, and tiny kitchen, *Amour* evokes Chantal
Akermann's radical 1975 study of tedium, *Jeanne Dielman, 23
quai du Commerce, 1080 Bruxelles*. At other times, the tenderness
between Georges and Anne brings to mind tastefully made
films of decline like Sarah Polley's *Away from Her*. But this is
Haneke. We suspect and fear that he won't keep up either the
tastefulness or the tedium for very long.

"When we look at the image of our own future provided by
the old we do not believe it: an absurd inner voice whispers that
that will never happen to us—when that happens it will no
longer be ourselves that it happens to." Thus did Simone de
Beauvoir's *The Coming of Age* address the fundamental disbelief

with which we regard old age. It is something that happens, unquestionably, but it only happens to other people. In *Amour,* Haneke shows us that this disbelief remains even for those who are no longer young. One is intact to oneself, and the inevitability of one's radical diminishment is hard to credit.

Georges and Anne are distinguished by their acuity; Anne, in fact, is the sharper, more acid-tongued, and more attractive of the two. It is the contrast between this sharpness and its sudden vertiginous loss that frightens. Not long after her blank moment in the kitchen, she has an unsuccessful operation and becomes bedridden. Shortly after, dementia sets in. Georges insists on being her primary caretaker, and their lives become purely physical: eating, excreting, cleaning, sleeping. Anne often cries out in pain—helpless and wounded cries that Georges struggles to parse—and these are among the most harrowing sequences in the film. Cinema has its settled conventions about physical candor, most of them unrealistic. When, in one scene in *Amour,* we see Anne's aged body being bathed— the naked body of a woman in her eighties—it is a terrible and original moment, at once dignified and totally lacking in dignity. This is Haneke at his realistic and heartless best.

Georges and Anne's grown daughter, Eva (played by Isabelle Huppert), high-strung and selfish, cleverly distances herself from this day-to-day horror, but then demands her father tell her "what happens now." Georges says what we often think but seldom say in such situations: "What happens now is what has happened until now. Then it will go steadily downhill and it will be over." This plain truth is also a piece of misdirection. We are meant to suppose we know what "downhill" might mean; but we don't know, not really. Yet to come are further terrors, more loneliness, more pointless pain, all of which come in bursts, striking the family more or less harshly than expected. These are predictable things, but the suffering they cause is worsened because they happen in a wildly unpredictable sequence.

There are brief moments of diegetic music in the film, Schubert's impromptus and Beethoven's bagatelles, which, when they come, feel like small mercies, but mostly we are left in silence, and with the sounds of apartment life: chairs being moved, silverware clinking on plates, taps running, feet shuffling, unhappy human voices. "Every life is in many days, day after day," Joyce wrote in *Ulysses,* and Haneke shows how implacably difficult the last of those days can be. Even when the end is certain, the days must be lived, and little can be done to hurry things along. To express such things well in a film, to express them in a humane and unflinching way, to resist the temptation to entertain or soothe, to keep the film as arid as the material, as Haneke has done in *Amour,* is to provide some very small but indispensable comfort. This is not about the high tone of the work—the Schubert, the understated Parisian knowingness, the ironic repartee—for in a film as different from this one as Asghar Farhadi's *A Separation,* with a wholly different set of cultural codes, a similar kind of consolation exists. It is more a matter of a willingness to push past the clichés of representation into a zone of discomfort so specific that it achieves universality. The temptation for many filmmakers is to console too soon, or to console in the wrong ways; to encounter those who give us some fresh and necessarily unpretty version of "how it is" can be a tremendous relief.

The question then is whether *Amour* is one of those films that one urges everyone to see. I don't think so. It's difficult to place it as a product; it's too troubling and bruising to be a nice night out at the movies. You wouldn't want to watch it after dinner, nor would you want to go to dinner after watching it. But it is undoubtedly the kind of film that will find its viewers, and that will long continue to trouble them in the right ways. For hours after I saw it and, intermittently, for days afterward, I could not shake the world and truths it conveyed.

In a moment of tension and despair, Georges slaps Anne. The camera immediately cuts away from them and comes to rest on the paintings on the wall of the apartment. This goes on for slightly longer than we anticipate. We look at the indistinct details of figures in a landscape. The paintings are not remarkable, but they are a respite, showing us scenes where fate is settled, an Arcadian escape from the tyranny of time. It's a glimpse of what will happen when it's all over, which is to say: nothing.

Teju Cole, *Sasabe* (2011)

Wangechi Mutu, *Even* (2014)

Malick Sidibé, *Je veux être seule* (1979)

Alex Webb, *Bombardopolis, Haiti* (1986)

Roy DeCarava, *Mississippi Freedom Marcher, Washington, D.C., 1963* (1963)

Gueorgui Pinkhassov, *Parc des Buttes-Chaumont, Paris* (2012)

Richard Renaldi, *Nathan and Robyn, 2012, Provincetown, MA* (2012)

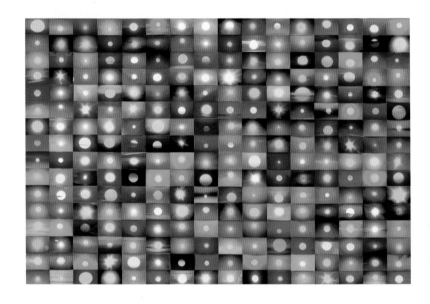

Penelope Umbrico, *541,795 Suns from Sunsets from Flickr (Partial) 1/26/06*
(2006–ongoing)

An African Caesar

W HEN *Julius Caesar* was performed at the Winter Garden Theatre in New York in 1864, the role of Mark Antony was played by John Wilkes Booth. His brother Edwin Booth played Brutus, and their brother Junius Brutus Booth, Jr., was Cassius. Five months later, John Wilkes Booth shot Abraham Lincoln with the cry "Sic semper tyrannis" ("Thus always to tyrants," words traditionally attributed to Brutus at Caesar's assassination). In the years following, Edwin Booth went on to one of the most distinguished theatrical careers of the nineteenth century. Between December 1871 and March 1872, he appeared in another run of *Julius Caesar* in New York City, playing, on different nights, Mark Antony, Brutus, and Cassius.

When I saw *Julius Caesar* in a production by the Royal Shakespeare Company at the Brooklyn Academy of Music, it happened to be on April 13, the Ides of April, and a day before the anniversary of Lincoln's death. The coincidence was theatrical in a literal sense, too: Lincoln died in Ford's Theatre in Washington, Caesar died in Pompey's Theatre in Rome, *Julius Caesar* was premièred at the Globe Theatre in London, and I watched it at the Harvey Theater, in Brooklyn. Shakespeare's love of superstition is rich soil for suggestible minds.

Julius Caesar bristles with augury, but hinges on a more terrestrial concern: Was Caesar a tyrant and thus deserving of tyrannicide? The Caesar of the play is imperious and inflexible, happy to compare himself to Mount Olympus and the North Star. But he also has "popularity" in the sixteenth-century sense of that word, as the scholar James Shapiro has written: his rule is a radical democracy that is the very opposite of tyranny. He might have escaped assassination had he read the note proffered him by Artemidorus as he entered the Senate on the Ides of March. That he waved it off with the self-promoting and self-abnegating line "What touches us ourself shall be last serv'd" is evidence of his popularity.

This finely balanced ambiguity is the material for the first half of the play; it is no surprise that Shakespeare's coinage "misgiving" should make its first appearance in English in this play of doubts. A tight conspiratorial knot leads up to the assassination, which is followed by the funeral orations by Brutus and Mark Antony. Shakespeare then takes us into the less interesting matter of the conspirators' fates, their various suicides and deaths by misadventure. The RSC players did their best with this later material, though they were hampered somewhat by a minimalist staging in which we got neither the sense of battle nor the tension of a battle camp.

The RSC production had an all-black cast and was directed by Gregory Doran. It was an African *Julius Caesar,* and the play contains many elements that aid this conceit: the soothsayer is a féticheur in body paint, Brutus has a silly houseboy, there's a lynching (of a poet who, by some ill luck, happens to share a name with one of the hunted conspirators). The assassination itself feels like a story from one of the newly independent African countries of the 1960s. Doran highlighted the political aspect of the play, and this was to the good, for it is still necessary to insist on Africa as a site of political and ideological contest, and not a static place mired in an unchanging anthropological past. Caesar, played with roguish charm and cold resolve by Jeffery Kissoon, is in the company of such manipulative despots as Idi Amin Dada, Mobutu Sese Seko, and Ibrahim Badamasi Babangida.

The alterations in the text were limited to a few compressions here and there, and to the occasional well-placed "ehen!" (one of the most frequent interjections in West African English, generally used as an affirmative, sometimes as a query). The most familiar lines—"The fault, dear Brutus, is not in our stars, but in ourselves," "Cowards die many times before their deaths," "The evil that men do lives after them; the good is oft interred with their bones"—were delivered as smoothly as proverbs. A small musical ensemble was on the stage in some scenes, playing highlife and Manding-influenced music, which added a beautiful aural texture to the proceedings. Before going, I had thought that a more precise identification of the play with a particular country—South Africa, say, or Nigeria—would be preferable, the better to avoid the pernicious notion that Africa is a country. But the performance persuaded me otherwise: Shakespeare's play is a gloss on an English translation of Plutarch's *Lives,* and its force is in the dramatic language. The general African setting unexpectedly illuminated that language. Had the setting been too narrow, it would have distracted the viewer from the delicate amalgam at hand: an ancient Rome in which Renaissance English is spoken by contemporary Africans.

The ensemble was extraordinary. Cyril Nri's Cassius and Joseph Mydell's Casca had such clear diction that I found myself wishing for more of Shakespeare's plays to be done in African-accented English. Kissoon's Caesar, Paterson Joseph's Brutus, and Ray Fearon's Mark Antony were less clear, their use of accents drifting at times into singsong. But the acting throughout was tense and vibrant. All commanded the stage, all had the broad shoulders, swagger, and calculated carelessness of African "big men." One of the pleasures on offer was the sight of these men strolling about, all coiled energy and purpose, in their dyed buba and sokoto, or in the white or earth-toned safari suits one sees on businessmen in Lagos, Dakar, or Kinshasa. Walking with authority is an art of which the leads in this *Julius Caesar* were virtuosi.

Shakespeare's rhetorical choices in *Julius Caesar* were intended to echo Roman public speech. He aimed, as W. H. Auden noted in his *Lectures on Shakespeare,* for a bleak, plainspoken style largely dependent on monosyllabic words. There's an added benefit to this: words written then sound much like they might now. Brutus, taking leave of Cassius in the first act, in the infancy of the conspiracy, says:

> For this time I will leave you.
> To-morrow, if you please to speak to me,
> I will come home to you; or if you will,
> Come home to me, and I will wait for you.

Mark Antony, manipulating the crowd during his "friends, Romans, countrymen" oration, is similarly straightforward. His reiteration of the word "honorable" emphasizes its unwieldy shape and ironic intent in what is otherwise a staccato pentameter:

Good friends, sweet friends, let me not stir you up
To such a sudden flood of mutiny.
They that have done this deed are honorable.
What private griefs they have, alas, I know not,
That made them do it. They are wise and honorable,
And will, no doubt, with reason answer you.

Later, Antony, in his arrogant way, tells Octavius, "I have seen more days than you"; later still, at the Battle of Philippi, he attempts to pull rank.

ANTONY: *Octavius, lead your battle softly on*
Upon the left hand of the even field.
OCTAVIUS: *Upon the right hand I. Keep thou the left.*
ANTONY: *Why do you cross me in this exigent?*
OCTAVIUS: *I do not cross you; but I will do so.*

It is an ominous bit of foreshadowing, and the lines were delivered well. But I missed a certain intensity that might have made this young Octavius (Ivanno Jeremiah) more convincing. This, after all, is the man who will transform himself into the emperor Augustus and will rule the world, and it is to him that Shakespeare gives the very last words of the play. I wished to see more evidence of that potential, in this play that is so much about how a fate only guessed at today can become a reality tomorrow.

In the spring or winter of 1865, sometime between the Booth brothers' *Julius Caesar* performance and Abraham Lincoln's death, Lincoln had a nightmare. He recounted it to his friend Ward Hill Lamon, who wrote it down. Lincoln had seen in his nightmare a mournful crowd in front of the White House and, on asking who had died, had been told it was the president, "killed by an assassin." The dream "annoyed" him for quite a while after, and then, presumably, he let the matter be. As in Shakespeare's play and Caesar's life, the portent proved exact.

Peter Sculthorpe

P ETER SCULTHORPE, AUSTRALIA's leading composer, died on
August 8, 2014, at the age of eighty-five. The news came as
a surprise to me, because by coincidence I had spent all of the
previous day listening to his music. (I hadn't known he was ill.)
I had also listened to a long radio interview that he gave to the
Australian Broadcasting Corporation in 1999. This was the first
time I'd heard his voice—a confiding, relaxed, thoughtful
voice—or the stories behind some of his best-known pieces. I
hadn't known that his somberly beautiful "Irkanda IV" was written after his father's death; now I understood the searching
grief of the solo violin. What I loved most in Sculthorpe's music
was the dry yet rich sound of the orchestral pieces and the
string quartets, so evocative of the Australian landscape, but I
hadn't known that Mahler's work, in particular the final movement of *Das Lied von der Erde,* had been a vital influence on him.
I didn't know that he was a child prodigy (his String Quartet
No. 1, composed when he was fourteen, is still performed
today), or that he'd been blamed, as a boy, for the accidental
death of a playmate.

Sculthorpe was born in Launceston, Tasmania, in 1929.
Apart from studying music at Oxford, he lived most of his life
in Australia, working as a professor at the University of Sydney.

I got to know his String Quartet No. 8 through a 1986 recording by the Kronos Quartet—the detail that struck me then was that three of its five movements were marked "con dolore"—but I only began to explore his other work after I visited Australia. When I traveled into the bush in Victoria, a few hours north of Melbourne, I had "Earth Cry" and "Small Town" in my ears. It was music that perfectly evoked the landscape of southeastern Australia—its vernacular architecture, beautiful stands of eucalyptus, red hills, dry grass, and sudden screaming flocks of lorikeets. The mental process by which one matches an orchestral texture to a physical landscape is mysterious and, of course, highly subjective. But, just as the soaring horns and massed strings of Sibelius are inseparable from the idea of the Scandinavian wilds, Sculthorpe's pizzicati and percussive effects sounded to me precisely as the Australian landscape looked. The ecstatic rhythms and the melody of a piece like "Kakadu" drew strong influence from northern Australian Aboriginal chant. And ever present in Sculthorpe's thinking was the question of Aboriginal land rights; he was one of the first Western-trained composers to write for the didgeridoo.

Sculthorpe's flowing and interesting soundscapes are brilliant in effect and in structure, and redolent of tone poems from the early twentieth century. Like his contemporaries John Adams and Einojuhani Rautavaara, he found a way to escape the strictures of post-Schoenbergian composition (Egon Wellesz, under whom he studied at Oxford, was a Schoenberg disciple, but not a dogmatic one) by bringing in a wide range of influences—not only Aboriginal music but also English pastoralism (Delius, in particular), minimalism, montage, and Japanese and Indonesian traditions. Sculthorpe said that it was important to him to consider Australia as part of the Asian world, and he had a profound personal engagement with Shinto. His music is intelligent and always gorgeous, like Mahler's was always gorgeous, but it is also imbued with warmth and gentleness. In a piece like "Small Town," for instance, a simple tune for the oboe is juxtaposed with a stately trumpet fanfare. With remarkable economy, Sculthorpe captures the bittersweet experience of small-town life, in which the Sunday picnic takes place in the shadow of the war memorial. It is a kind of antipodean double of Aaron Copland's "Quiet City."

No wonder, then, that Sculthorpe's music was so adored in Australia. That it was not better known internationally is evidence, yet again, of how poorly contemporary classical music, like contemporary poetry, travels. In the 1999 radio interview, Sculthorpe mentioned the particular honor he felt when, following the deaths of notable Australians, the obituary programs on television would feature fragments of his music. It made him feel like he had become part of the culture in some essential way. On the day before he died, I listened to Peter Sculthorpe all day. And on hearing the news, far from Australia, I did so again.

Red Shift

EW THINGS ARE more mysterious than someone else's favorite film. To hear it named is to be puzzled. You appreciate its merits but not how it can be preferable to all others. Perhaps your favorite film isn't the one that you like best but the one that likes you best. It confirms you on first encounter, and goes on to shape you in some irreversible way. Often, you first see it when you're young, but not too young, and on each subsequent viewing it is a home to which you return.

I first saw Krzysztof Kieślowski's *Red* in 1996, in the basement of a college library in Michigan. Valentine, a young woman in Geneva, played with austere grace by Irène Jacob, accidentally runs over a dog, loads the bloodied animal into her car, and seeks out its owner, a surly retired judge named Joseph (Jean-Louis Trintignant), who seems not to care about the dog, and who, Valentine discovers, passes his days listening in on his neighbors' telephone conversations. They are drawn into a relationship—not a romance but a series of tenderly exchanged confidences. In one scene, the judge, on his birthday, wonders if he made the right decisions during his career. There is another thread: Valentine's neighbor, a law student named Auguste (Jean-Pierre Lorit), whom she doesn't know but often passes in the street, is betrayed by his girlfriend. The three characters move through perfectly average days—unlocking an apartment door in time to catch a ringing phone, stopping at a kiosk to buy a newspaper—but their gestures seem to be part of a larger pattern.

The hushed intensity of the film, the sense of inner workings not fully grasped, stayed with me. I have since seen *Red* more than a dozen times: with my siblings during Thanksgiving in Alabama; alone in a crowd on the Museumsinsel in Berlin; in the middle of the night in a hotel room in Geneva; on a stalled Amtrak train somewhere near Poughkeepsie. Kieślowski uses the tiniest gestures to illuminate dilemmas: the camera lingering on Valentine's face as she tries to figure out where the dog, which she has adopted, has run off to; the twitch of Auguste's jaw when he realizes that his girlfriend has another lover.

Kieślowski explores the experiences of two people who live in the same city, visit the same places, touch the same doorknobs. Does their proximity have any meaning? Will they meet? He also looks at episodes from Joseph's life that are curiously reiterated in Auguste's: both drop a book, and it opens to a crucial page; both abandon their dogs. Kieślowski suggests that two separate lives can be enigmatically linked, displaced only in time. The search for one's double is like a bird's when looking for a branch. Color forms another set of links in the film: red streetlights, billboards, furniture, clothing seem interconnected in the same gentle and elusive way that the characters are. They create an alternative map of the city.

Kieślowski, who grew up under Communist rule, in Poland, was unembarrassed by big questions. What is the role of religion in modern life? Why does love so often force people into comical situations? *Red* was his last film, the final installment of a trilogy on which he worked with premonitory fervor before he died, at the age of fifty-four. *Blue,* a film about the confusions particular to grief, was followed by the picaresque romance *White.* Finally came *Red,* glowing and humane. At the end, two principal characters from each of the three films are brought together by chance on a sinking ferry, as though this were the fate they were being drawn toward all along.

I learned from Kieślowski how unforeseen encounters can subtly pile up and determine the course of a person's life. In any narrative, there is the material that moves the story forward. But the storyteller also includes objects or events that hint at a pattern of signification swirling above the surface, part of the story's logic but just out of reach.

In my novel *Open City,* as the narrator waits for an older friend at a restaurant, he watches the news on a TV with the volume muted. There's bad weather in the English Channel, and a ferry has capsized. Heavy rain is forecast for all of Europe. The bad weather, the sinking ferry, and the oneiric mood of this passage are an homage to *Red*. It wasn't until after the novel was published that I discovered I shared a birthday with Kieślowski. The bird had found its branch.

John Berger

I N THE SPRING of 2008, while sketching at the National Gallery in London, John Berger rested his satchel on an empty chair. A security guard approached Berger and asked him to remove it. Berger placed the bag between his feet, but the guard was not satisfied, and insisted that the bag be carried. Berger became obstinate and was thrown out of the museum.

There are three kinds of thought evident in Berger's *Bento's Sketchbook*. The first is his own text, consisting of the mixture of anecdote, essay, politics, reverie, and poetry that he has been exploring for more than half a century. Second, there are his drawings, most of them in ink, with a few splashes of color, some in charcoal or graphite. Third, there are fragments from the work of the freethinking philosopher Baruch Spinoza, nicknamed Bento, who died in the Netherlands in 1677.

Bento's Sketchbook is so named in homage to the sketchbook Spinoza was reputed to have carried around with him, but which was not found among his possessions after his death. The relationship between Berger's drawings and text in *Bento's Sketchbook* is intricate. In one instance, Berger presents a sketch of a dancer seated on the ground, and follows it with the story of his struggle to draw the dancer in question, his friend Maria

Muñoz. "The image in my head was often clearer than the one on the paper," he writes, but eventually he arrives at what he is after. "The effort of my corrections and the endurance of the paper have begun to resemble the resilience of Maria's own body." On the next page, in continuation of the argument begun by the drawing and the story, is a typically knotty quotation from Spinoza's *Ethics,* which reads, in part: "Although we do not remember that we existed before the body, we sense nevertheless that our mind in so far as it involves the essence of the body under a species of eternity is eternal and its existence cannot be defined by time or explained by duration."

This is the technique Berger employs for much of the book. With an unsteady but insistent line, he portrays the faces of friends and artists, a handful of quetsch plums, an old bicycle, a dead badger, and a host of other subjects; and with his clear, sinuous prose, he gives an account of how the contours of reality "harass" the act of drawing. "If the lines of a drawing don't convey this harassment the drawing remains a mere sign."

In some cases, the drawing the text discusses is not reproduced in the book. For his friend Marie-Claude he draws seven irises, an offering to be placed in her coffin the following day. Other drawings, like one of an angel by Luca della Robbia, or another of a dried fig split open, are depicted but not discussed. And certain aspects of the text, like Berger's digression into the management's fears of shoplifting at his local supermarket, or his musings about the cruelties of agribusiness, bear no obvious connection to drawing.

Nevertheless, the book coheres because Berger's is a humane and uniquely confiding voice, and this voice is co-extensive with his skill as a draftsman. The two attributes act in concert with Spinoza's enigmatic philosophical propositions. All three constitute a singular act of witness. One of the best drawings in *Bento's Sketchbook* is of the *Crucifixion* by Antonello da Messina. This drawing, we realize, was the modest but ineffable outcome of Berger's harassed afternoon at the National Gallery.

Portrait of a Lady

A PHOTOGRAPHER WORKING IN a commercial studio in West Africa in the twentieth century had a straightforward task: to please his clients. In that sense, the Malian photographer Seydou Keïta was—like his father, who worked as a blacksmith, carpenter, mechanic, and electrician, among other jobs— a craftsman. He was paid by the public to make pictures. But like his esteemed Malian compatriot Malick Sidibé, and like Mama Casset of Senegal and Joseph Moise Agbodjelou of Benin, he produced such fine work that we now consider him a great African artist. These master photographers gave us panoramas of life in Bamako, Dakar, and Porto-Novo, a vivid record of individual people, largely shorn of their names and stories but irrepressibly alive. Here are good clothes gracefully cut, glowing skin, beautifully coiffed hair, polished shoes: all the familiar markers of a person taking pride in his or her appearance. Here's someone who looks witty, here's another who looks querulous, another who's modest, or vain, or sweet. There we see a renegade bra strap slipping off a shoulder, there a large laughing man with a baby, a woman in a bathing suit, youths partying at night with their Afros, bell-bottoms, precious LPs, and endless reserves of cool.

These photographs are ripostes to the anthropological images of "natives" made by Europeans in the late nineteenth and early twentieth centuries. Those photographs, in which the subjects had no say in how they were seen, did much to shape the Western world's idea of Africans. Something changed when Africans began to take photographs of one another: you can see it in the way they look at the camera, in the poses, the attitude. The difference between the images taken by colonialists or white adventurers and those made for the sitter's personal use is especially striking in photographs of women. In the former, women are being looked at against their will, captive to a controlling gaze. In the latter, they look at themselves as in a mirror, an activity that always involves seriousness, levity, and an element of wonder.

A portrait of this kind is a visual soliloquy. Consider, for instance, one of Keïta's most famous pictures, now called the *Odalisque*. A woman reclines in a long dress with fine floral patterning on a bed with a checked bedspread. Her head scarf is polka-dotted. The bed is placed in front of a wall, which is draped with a paisley cloth. And even her face is marked with cicatrices. Then we notice, emerging from this swirling field— a profusion of pattern that brings to mind Matisse at his most inventive—her delicate hands and feet, dark but subtly shaded; the right arm, on which she rests her head; her narrowed eyes. Her look is self-possessed rather than seductive. She's looking ahead but not at the camera. It is the look of someone who is thinking about herself, simultaneously outward and inward. The image challenges and delights the viewer with its complicated two-dimensional game.

Keïta's and Sidibé's oeuvres make me think of August Sander's record of German people in their various occupations in the years between the World Wars, or of Mike Disfarmer's thousands of portraits taken in Heber Springs, Arkansas: faces peering out of the past, unknown to us but as expressive and intense as those we love. Keïta was not directly influenced by these photographers, or by any of the conventions of photography in the West. In an interview he gave the French gallerist André Magnin in the mid-nineties, he said: "I've heard that in your country you have old photographs that are like mine. Well, I've never met any foreign photographers, nor seen their photos." By his own account, he was an original. Looking at the body of his work, we become conscious of implied community, customs, and connections, a world that is perhaps now irretrievable.

Malick Sidibé—the younger of these two photographers—made many fine portraits as well, generally working with hipper, less formal poses than Keïta did and shooting more often at night and at parties. There's one portrait of Sidibé's in particular that I'm always drawn to. A woman stands alone in a sleeveless blouse and an ankle-length skirt. She has sandals on her feet, a pendulous earring in each ear, and hair woven close to her scalp. Her address to the camera is direct. No, she's not quite alone: a man's shoulder and arm are visible just to her left. We also see his right shoe and half of his right leg. But the rest of him has been dodged away in the printing of the picture.

On the brown paper border that frames the photograph are written the words: "Je veux être seule. 1979—Malick Sidibé." On the right border are Sidibé's signature and the date 2009. I suppose Sidibé signed this photograph in 2009 and wrote down what the woman told him thirty years earlier, before he had printed the photograph: "Je veux être seule" ("I want to be alone"). This young woman, like many others in Sidibé's work, has decided her own image. The photo's peculiarity is the mark of her authority.

I love the West African women in the photographs by Keïta and Sidibé, some of whom are of my mother's generation and the generation just before, women to whom a university education was widely available, and for whom working outside the home was a given. In West African photography of this period, there are many photographs of friendship among women, many photographs of women with their families, many of young women with their young men. And there are photos of women alone, some of whom perhaps might also have told the photographer, "Je veux être seule."

The confidence visible in photographs like Keïta's and Sidibé's can be evoked even when we don't see the sitters' faces. J. D. 'Okhai Ojeikere, who was born in Nigeria in 1930 and did most of his work there, understood the expressive possibilities of women's heads, particularly those crowned with the marvelous array of hairstyles common to many Nigerian ethnic groups. These photographs, made in the years following the country's independence from Britain in 1960, record evanescent sculptures that are both performance art and temporary body modification. Most of these heads are turned away from us. Has the back of a head ever been more evocative than in these photographs? Ojeikere made hundreds of them, and each head seems to convey an attitude, and even a glance. On the streets of Lagos today, such heads, necks, hairstyles, and elaborately constructed and tied head wraps can still be seen, tableaux vivants of assertive elegance.

Photographs by Keïta, Sidibé, Agbodjelou, and Ojeikere are united by the period in which they were made as well as by geographical and cultural proximity to one another. There seems to me a correspondence between the energy of these pictures and the optimism and determination of the West African independence movements of the fifties and sixties. The photographs' legacies have had a powerful effect on twenty-first-century African portraiture, but the contemporary work that most reminds me of them is from farther away on the continent, and made in very different circumstances. Zanele Muholi, one of the most prominent contemporary African photographers, who started working only a few years after the end of apartheid in South Africa in 1994, is in a sense a "post-independence" artist. She has tried to document a specific aspect of the country's new political, social, and economic terrain. One of Muholi's long-term projects, called *Faces and Phases,* focuses on the portraiture of black lesbian and transgender people, most of them in South Africa. Like her West African forebears, she shows people as they wish to be seen.

South Africa is one of the few countries whose constitution protects its citizens from discrimination on the basis of sexual orientation. But persistent prejudice remains a reality for many black South African lesbians and transgender people, many of whom have been raped and even murdered. Muholi's work is an answer to those who want to wish them away or intimidate them into invisibility. To look at their faces, in portrait after portrait, is to become newly aware of the power of portraiture in a gifted artist's hands. Muholi doesn't grant her sitters independence—they are independent—but she makes their independence visible. *Faces and Phases* is a complete world.

The work of Keïta and Sidibé, too, makes us aware of an entire world of experiences, one in which men are sometimes secondary. Keïta did well enough from his photo studio that, in the early 1950s, he was able to buy a Peugeot 203. Here is that car, used as a background prop for a group portrait made around 1956, featuring two women and a girl. The women's dark foreheads and cheekbones are echoed in the Peugeot's sinuous lines. And way off to the right, touching the hood of the car, is a man's hand. He has been sidelined, just as the man in *Je veux être seule* was. But a closer look reveals another man in the picture. He can be seen in the front wheel well of the car, in the gleam of its reflective curve. This second man, dressed in white, is stooped over something. He is the photographer, Seydou Keïta himself, in his limited role, collaborating with the true authors of the image: the women.

Object Lesson

I N NOVEMBER 2013, thousands of people gathered in Maidan
Nezalezhnosti, the central square in Kiev, to protest their government's refusal to ratify an agreement with the European
Union. The demonstrations went on for months; when brutal
attempts were made to stop them, they only became more popular. The crowds were enormous, containing, at times, more
than 100,000 people. Many of the photographs from the protests had the organized disorder of medieval battle scenes: spiky
barricades, rows of tents, patches of soil and ash, flashes of
color where flags were held aloft, sudden brightness from reflections and fires, a great swirl of angry humanity and dark-
helmeted riot police massed behind shields, all of it set against
backdrops of smoke, fog, or falling snow. So epic and cinematic
were the photographs from the Maidan that it took some effort
to remember that they were first and foremost news images,
unstaged depictions of real, ongoing human suffering.

In her 1977 collection of essays, *On Photography,* Susan Sontag identified a feeling of helpless voyeurism that comes over us
as we look at photographs of people in the midst of conflict. She
also wrote about how repeatedly seeing such images could
anesthetize the vision and deaden the conscience. Sontag understood photographs of conflict to be making a utilitarian

argument—that they could bring us into a state of productive shock—and she showed that they seldom did what they claimed, or hoped, to do. The more photographs shock, the more difficult it is for them to be pinned to their local context, and the more easily they are indexed to our mental library of generic images. What, then, are we to do with a thrilling photograph that is at the same time an image of pain?

In becoming part of a family of familiar cinematic images that includes *Throne of Blood* and *Alexander Nevsky,* but also *The Lord of the Rings* and *Star Wars,* the spectacular photos from Ukraine stopped doing what they were ostensibly made for. They supplied some aesthetic satisfaction, as well as a jolt of outrage, but they told us very little about the particular politics of the protests, much less what to think about it or do in response. Conflict photography comes with built-in risks for the photographers, who put themselves in harm's way to bring us news, but also, in a less visceral way, for us, the viewers. If it is done well, it can move us to think of art and pop culture ("it's just like a movie"), instead of the suffering it depicts. If it is not done well, if the images are not formally compelling, it might lose its claim on even our momentary attention.

There are other kinds of photographs, though, that can present particular crises without also giving us the feeling that it has all been seen before. There are photographic projects that document survivors long after war. Others use archival or found images to consider violence. Yet another approach is to take photographs that exclude humans: destroyed buildings, detritus-strewn battlefields, aerial photographs of damaged landscapes. An intriguing subset of that last category depicts domestic objects whose meaning has been altered in the aftermath of a calamity. The shock of the Ukrainian conflict is conveyed in one way by a photo of riot police dragging a protester through the snow, and in quite another way by an image of a ruined kitchen, like the one by the Ukrainian photographer Sergei Ilnitsky.

In Ilnitsky's photograph, taken in August 2013 in Donetsk, a major city in the eastern part of Ukraine, a length of white lace is swept to the left side. Like a theatrical curtain, it reveals a table with a teapot, a bowl full of tomatoes, a can, two mugs, and two paring knives on a little cutting board. It is a still life, but it is in utter disarray. Broken glass and dust are everywhere, and one of the mugs is shattered; to the right, across the lace curtain, the shards of glass, and the table, is a splatter of red color that could only be one thing. Domestic objects imply use, and Ilnitsky's photograph pulls our minds toward the now lost tranquillity of the people who owned these items. How many cups of coffee were made in that kitchen? Who bought those tomatoes? Were there children in this household who did their homework on this table? Whose blood is that? The absence of people in the photograph makes room for these questions.

No image stands alone; each is related in straightforward or convoluted ways to other pictures. Ilnitsky's photograph reads to me as a sad update of a famous one by Sam Abell taken in Moscow in 1983. Abell's picture also shows a diaphanous white lace curtain, but, in this case, it is not drawn aside. We see through the curtain a windowsill lined with seven pears, luminous in late-afternoon light, beyond which are visible the spires of Red Square. Abell had gone to Russia to shoot a story about the life of Tolstoy. For days he was shadowed by security forces who must have assumed he was a spy. Then, one Sunday, in his hotel room, he realized that the pears sitting on the windowsill might make an interesting picture. And so he worked on the composition for twelve hours, until a breeze lifted the curtain in just the right way. The resulting photograph evokes a private reverie in an atmosphere of Cold War paranoia. Andropov was the leader of the Soviet Union, Reagan was the president of the United States, and relations between the two countries were deteriorating. "People ask me why I worked on one composition so long," Abell wrote in response to my questions about this image. "My answer: for solace."

Another surprisingly quiet depiction of aftermath is Glenna Gordon's series on the things left behind by the Nigerian girls abducted by Boko Haram. Unlike Abell and Ilnitsky, Gordon did not take her photos in situ. She had the objects—schoolbooks, pens, dresses, shoes—sent from Chibok, where the girls lived, to Abuja, and she photographed them in a studio there. In Gordon's project, the human victims are themselves missing, not simply excluded. Their abduction could not be photographed, nor could their captivity; Gordon's photographs nevertheless bring us into close contact with the girls' lives. When we look at a blue blouse with the name written on its collar—"Hauwa Mutah"—we might reflect on the awful fate of this one particular girl among hundreds. It is like Gilles Peress's photograph of a stained infant bodysuit on the ground, taken just after the genocide in Rwanda, an image that persists in the memory longer than yet another horrific photograph of a corpse.

Gordon's notes tell us that Hauwa Mutah, the girl who owned the blue blouse, was the sixth-born of nine children. Her favorite subjects were English and geography, and she hoped to become a biochemist. Now, almost a year after the abduction, with the exception of a small number of the girls who escaped, there is no certainty as to whether they are alive or whether they will ever be found. The faint biographical traces left by this one girl activated my own memories and emotional responses. In my teens, my favorite subjects were English and geography. During the year I spent in a Nigerian boarding school, I wrote my name on my school uniform so that nothing would go missing in the communal wash. The blue blouse restores these fragments to me in a way a portrait of the girl might not have. Photographs of people's things reach us in this way even in the absence of such biographical coincidences because we recognize their things as being like ours. Our infants wear bodysuits, too. We have favorite coffee mugs, too. There's that lace curtain we have always liked, or have always meant to change.

Proust once wrote in a letter, "We think we no longer love the dead because we don't remember them, but if by chance we come across an old glove we burst into tears." Objects, sometimes more powerfully than faces, remind us of what was and no longer is; stillness, in photography, can be more affecting than action. This is in part because of the respectful distance that a photograph of objects can create between the one who looks, far from the place of trouble, and the one whose trouble those objects signify. But it is also because objects are reservoirs of specific personal experience, filled with the hours of some person's life. They have been touched, or worn through use. They have frayed, or been placed just so. Perhaps the kind of "object photography" made by Abell, Ilnitsky, Gordon, Peress, and many others in conflict zones cannot ever effect the political change we hope for from highly dramatic images. Perhaps their photographs don't make us think of the photographers' bravery, the way other conflict pictures do, or urge us to immediate action. We look at them anyway, for the change that they bring about elsewhere: in the core of the sympathetic self. We look at them for the way they cooperate with the imagination, the way they contain what cannot otherwise be accommodated, and the way they grant us, to however modest a degree, some kind of solace.

Saul Leiter

THE FIRST COMMERCIALLY available color photographic process, Autochrome, was introduced in the United States in 1907. Alfred Stieglitz and George Seeley soon began experimenting with it, but it was not until the 1950s that color photography began to come into its own as an artistic medium, in the work of Ernst Haas, Helen Levitt, and others. This was the generation of the photographer Saul Leiter, the Pittsburgh-born son of a Talmudic scholar, who photographed the streets of New York City for six decades and died in November 2013 at the age of eighty-nine.

Leiter was perhaps the most interesting of the fifties color photographers in his use of form. His bold chromaticism, off-center composition, and frequent use of vertical framing attracted attention—the work reminded people of Japanese painting and Abstract Expressionism—and he was included in *Always the Young Strangers,* an exhibition curated by Edward Steichen at the Museum of Modern Art in 1953. But Leiter didn't court fame, and, though he continued to work, his photographs almost vanished from public view. Then they came back to light in 2006, with *Saul Leiter: Early Color,* a monograph published by Steidl. The book brought him belated recognition, gallery representation, a stream of publications, and a new generation of fans.

Color is in the mainstream of photographic practice now. It is essential to the inspired street work of Harry Gruyaert and Joel Meyerowitz, the large-format portraits of Rineke Dijkstra, the architectural views of Candida Höfer, the personal journalism of Nan Goldin, and the stately landscapes of Andreas Gursky. But, for a long time, it was considered superficial and suspect. Henri Cartier-Bresson was firmly against it on the grounds that it interfered with formal priorities. John Szarkowski, the director of photography at the Museum of Modern Art, dismissed most color photography before he began championing William Eggleston's in the 1970s. This was the milieu—which, if not hostile, was not exactly encouraging—out of which Saul Leiter created a series of breathtaking, almost miraculous, photographs. He shot Kodachrome slides, and many of them were not printed until decades after they were exposed.

One of the most effective gestures in Leiter's work is to have great fields of undifferentiated dark or light, an overhanging canopy, say, or a snowdrift, interrupted by gashes of color. He returned again and again to a small constellation of subjects: mirrors and glass, shadows and silhouettes, reflection, blur, fog, rain, snow, doors, buses, cars, fedoras. He was a virtuoso of shallow depth of field: certain sections of some of the photographs look as if they have been applied with a quick brush. It will come as no surprise to a viewer of his work that Leiter was also a painter, that his heroes were Degas, Vuillard, and Bonnard, and that he knew the work of Rothko and de Kooning well. There are points of contact between his work and that of photographers like Louis Faurer and Robert Frank, the so-called New York School, but Leiter was an original. He loved beauty. To make a living, he photographed fashion spreads for *Harper's Bazaar* and *Vogue,* and the levity of his commercial work seeped into his personal work.

But the overriding emotion in his work is a stillness, tenderness, and grace that is at odds with the mad rush of New York street life. *In No Great Hurry,* the understated film made about Leiter by the filmmaker Tomas Leach, contains an exchange that gets to the core of Leiter's practice. Late in the film, Leiter says, "There are the things that are out in the open and then there are the things that are hidden, and life has more to do, the real world has more to do with what is hidden, maybe. You think?" I loved this confirmation of Leiter's loyalty to concealed realities, but loved even more his doubt, his interrogation of the hard-won insight. Leach, the filmmaker, replied off-camera, "That could be true." Leiter then asked him, "You think it's true?" "It could be," Leach said. "It could be very true," Leiter said, still not committing fully. "We like to pretend that what is public is what the real world is all about."

Leiter's best photographs lack all pretense, and are full of a productive doubt. When I heard the news of Leiter's death, I asked Leach what the experience of working on the film—over a period of three years—had been like. "He was funny, intelligent, and insightful," Leach wrote to me. "He was full of curiosity and mischief." The Magnum photographer Alex Webb, who is celebrated for the sophistication of his color work, said Leiter had "an uncanny ability to pull complex situations out of everyday life, images that echo the abstraction of painting and yet, simultaneously, clearly depict the world."

Undoubtedly, the charm of some of Leiter's pictures lies in

the fact that they depict fifties places, fifties cars, and fifties people (we rarely dress so well today), and that those analog reds and greens are more moving, somehow, than what our own digital cameras can offer up. But pictures such as *Through Boards* (1957), *Canopy* (1958), and *Walking with Soames* (1958) would be winners in any era. They are high points of lyric photography, which, once seen, become—like all the best pictures, poems, and paintings—a permanent part of our lives.

I asked the photographer Rebecca Norris Webb, whose own work is similarly concentrated and subtle, about Leiter. She praised his quietness, singling out the images taken through a window or some sort of glass: "some a delightful puzzle of reflections, and others softly aglow in the muted light of a storm, one of the few natural forces capable of slowing us New Yorkers down long enough to send us into a kind of reverie."

The content of Saul Leiter's photographs arrives on a sort of delay: it takes a moment after the first glance to know what the picture is about. You don't so much see the image as let it dissolve into your consciousness, like a tablet in a glass of water. One of the difficulties of photography is that it is much better at being explicit than at being reticent. Precisely how the hypnotic and dreamlike feeling is achieved in Leiter's works is a mystery, even to their creator. As he said in *In No Great Hurry*, laughing, "If I'd only known which ones would be very good and liked, I wouldn't have had to do all the thousands of others."

A True Picture of Black Skin

W HAT COMES TO mind when we think of photography and the civil rights movement? Direct, viscerally affecting images with familiar subjects: huge rallies, impassioned speakers, people carrying placards ("I Am a Man"), dogs and fire hoses turned on innocent protesters. These photos, as well as the portraits of national leaders like Martin Luther King, Jr., and Malcolm X, are explicit about the subject at hand. They tell us what is happening and make a case for why things must change. Our present moment, a time of vigorous demand for equal treatment, evokes those years of sadness and hope in black American life and renews the relevance of those photos. But there are other, less expected images from the civil rights years that are also worth thinking about: images that are forceful but less illustrative.

One such image left me short of breath the first time I saw it. It's of a young woman whose face is at once relaxed and intense. She is apparently in bright sunshine, but both her face and the rest of the picture give off a feeling of modulated darkness; we can see her beautiful features, but they are underlit somehow. Only later did I learn the picture's title, *Mississippi Freedom Marcher, Washington, D.C., 1963*, which helps explain the young woman's serene and resolute expression. It is an expression suitable for the event she's attending, the most famous civil rights march of them all. The title also confirms the sense that she's standing in a great crowd, even though we see only half of one other person's face (a boy's, indistinct in the foreground) and, behind the young woman, the barest suggestion of two other bodies.

The picture was taken by Roy DeCarava, one of the most intriguing and poetic of American photographers. The power of this picture is in the loveliness of its dark areas. His work was, in fact, an exploration of just how much could be seen in the shadowed parts of a photograph, or how much could be imagined into those shadows. He resisted being too explicit in his work, a reticence that expresses itself in his choice of subjects as well as in the way he presented them.

DeCarava, a lifelong New Yorker, came of age in the generation after the Harlem Renaissance and took part in a flowering in the visual arts that followed that largely literary movement. By the time he died in 2009, at eighty-nine, he was celebrated for his melancholy and understated scenes, most of which were shot in New York City: streets, subways, jazz clubs, the interiors of houses, the people who lived in them. His pictures all share a visual grammar of decorous mystery: a young woman in a white graduation dress in the empty valley of a lot, a pair of silhouetted dancers reading each other's bodies in a cavernous hall, a solitary hand and its cuff-linked wrist emerging from the midday gloom of a taxi window. DeCarava took photographs of white people tenderly but seldom. Black life was his greater love and steadier commitment. With his camera he tried to think through the peculiar challenge of shooting black subjects at a time when black appearance, in both senses (the way black people looked and the very presence of black people), was under question.

All technology arises out of specific social circumstances. In our time, as in previous generations, cameras and the mechanical tools of photography have rarely made it easy to photograph black skin. The dynamic range of film emulsions, for example, was generally calibrated for white skin and had limited sensitivity to brown, red, or yellow skin tones. Light meters had similar limitations, with a tendency to underexpose dark skin. And for many years, beginning in the mid-1940s, the smaller film-developing units manufactured by Kodak came with Shirley cards, so named after the white model who was featured on them and whose whiteness was marked on the cards as "normal." Some of these instruments improved with time. In the age of digital photography, for instance, Shirley cards are hardly used anymore. But even now, there are reminders that photographic technology is neither value-free nor ethnically neutral. In 2009 the face-recognition technology on HP webcams had difficulty recognizing black faces, suggesting, again, that the process of calibration had favored lighter skin.

An artist tries to elicit from unfriendly tools the best they can manage. A black photographer of black skin can adjust his or her light meters; or make the necessary exposure compensations while shooting; or correct the image at the printing stage. These small adjustments would have been necessary for most photographers who worked with black subjects, from James Van Der Zee at the beginning of the century to DeCarava's best-known contemporary, Gordon Parks, who was on the staff of *Life* magazine. Parks's work, like DeCarava's, was concerned with human dignity, specifically as it was expressed in black communities. Unlike DeCarava, and like most other photographers, Parks aimed for and achieved a certain clarity and technical finish in his photo essays. The highlights were high, the shadows were dark, the midtones well judged. This was work without exaggeration; perhaps for this reason it sometimes lacked a smoldering fire even though it was never less than soulful.

DeCarava, on the other hand, insisted on finding a way into the inner life of his scenes. He worked without assistants and did his own developing, and almost all his work bore the mark of his idiosyncrasies. The chiaroscuro effects came from technical choices: a combination of exposure manipulation, darkroom virtuosity, and occasionally printing on soft paper. And yet there's also a sense that he gave the pictures what they wanted, instead of imposing an agenda on them. In *Mississippi Freedom Marcher,* for example, even the whites of the shirts have been pulled down, into a range of soft, dreamy grays, so that the tonalities of the photograph agree with the young woman's strong, quiet expression. This exploration of the possibilities of dark gray would be interesting in any photographer, but De-Carava did it time and again specifically as a photographer of black skin. Instead of trying to brighten blackness, he went against expectation and darkened it further. What is dark is neither blank nor empty. It is in fact full of wise light, which, with patient seeing, can open out into glories.

This confidence in "playing in the dark" (to borrow a phrase of Toni Morrison's) intensified the emotional content of DeCarava's pictures. The viewer's eye might at first protest, seeking more conventional contrasts, wanting more obvious lighting. But, gradually, there comes an acceptance of the photograph and its subtle implications: that there's more there than we might think at first glance, but also that, when we are looking at others, we might come to the understanding that they don't have to give themselves up to us. They are allowed to stay in the shadows if they wish.

Thinking about DeCarava's work in this way reminds me of the philosopher Édouard Glissant, who was born in Martinique, educated at the Sorbonne, and profoundly involved in anticolonial movements of the fifties and sixties. One of Glissant's main projects was an exploration of the word "opacity." Glissant defined it as a right to not have to be understood on others' terms, a right to be misunderstood if need be. The argument was rooted in linguistic considerations: it was a stance against certain expectations of transparency embedded in the French language. Glissant sought to defend the opacity, obscurity, and inscrutability of Caribbean blacks and other marginalized peoples. External pressures insisted on everything being illuminated, simplified, and explained. Glissant's response: no. And this gentle refusal, this suggestion that there is another way, a deeper way, holds true for DeCarava, too.

DeCarava's thoughtfulness and grace influenced a whole generation of black photographers, though few of them went on to work as consistently in the shadows as he did. But when I see luxuriantly crepuscular images like Eli Reed's photograph of the Boys' Choir of Tallahassee (2004), or those in Carrie Mae Weems's *Kitchen Table Series* (1990), I see them as extensions of the DeCarava line. One of the most gifted cinematographers currently at work, Bradford Young, seems to have inherited DeCarava's approach even more directly. Young shot Dee Rees's

Pariah (2011) and Andrew Dosunmu's *Restless City* (2012) and *Mother of George* (2013), as well as Ava DuVernay's *Selma* (2014). He works in color, and with moving rather than still images, but his visual language is cognate with DeCarava's: both are keeping faith with the power of shadows.

The leading actors in the films Young has shot not only are black but also tend to be dark-skinned: Danai Gurira as Adenike in *Mother of George,* for instance, and David Oyelowo as Martin Luther King, Jr., in *Selma.* Under Young's lenses, they become darker yet and serve as the brooding centers of these over-whelmingly beautiful films. Black skin, full of unexpected gra-dations of blue, purple, or ocher, sets a tone for the narrative: Adenike lost in thought on her wedding day, King on an evening telephone call to his wife or in discussion in a jail cell with other civil rights leaders. In a larger culture that tends to value black people for their abilities to jump, dance, or otherwise enter-tain, these moments of inwardness open up a different space of encounter.

These images pose a challenge to another bias in mainstream culture: that to make something darker is to make it more dubi-ous. There have been instances when a black face was darkened on the cover of a magazine or in a political ad to cast a literal pall of suspicion over it, just as there have been times when a black face was lightened after a photo shoot with the apparent goal of making it more appealing. What could a response to this form of contempt look like? One answer is in Young's films, in which an intensified darkness makes the actors seem more pri-vate, more self-contained, and at the same time more dramatic. In *Selma,* the effect is strengthened by the many scenes in which King and the other protagonists are filmed from behind or turned away from us. We are tuned in to the eloquence of shoulders, and we hear what the hint of a profile or the fragment of a silhouette has to say.

I think of another photograph by Roy DeCarava that is similar to *Mississippi Freedom Marcher,* but this other photograph, *Five Men, 1964,* has quite a different mood. We see one man, on the left, who faces forward and takes up almost half the picture plane. His face is sober and tense, his expression that of someone whose mind is elsewhere. Behind him is a man in glasses. This second man's face is in three-quarter profile and almost wholly visible except for where the first man's shoulder covers his chin and jawline. Behind these are two others, whose faces are more than half concealed by the men in front of them. And finally there's a small segment of a head at the bottom right of the photograph. The men's varying heights could mean they are standing on steps. The heads are close together, and none seem to look in the same direction: the effect is like a sheet of studies made by a Renaissance master. In an interview DeCarava gave in 1990 in the magazine *Callaloo,* he said of this picture: "This moment occurred during a memorial service for the children killed in a church in Birmingham, Ala., in 1964. The photograph shows men coming out of the service at a church in Harlem." He went on to say that the "men were coming out of the church with faces so serious and so intense that I responded, and the image was made."

The adjectives that trail the work of DeCarava and Young as well as the philosophy of Glissant—opaque, dark, shadowed, obscure—are metaphorical when we apply them to language. But in photography, they are literal, and only after they are seen as physical facts do they become metaphorical again, visual stories about the hard-won, worth-keeping reticence of black life itself. These pictures make a case for how indirect images guarantee our sense of the human. It is as if the world, in its careless way, had been saying, "You people are simply too dark," and these artists, intent on obliterating this absurd way of thinking, had quietly responded, "But you have no idea how dark we yet may be, nor what that darkness may contain."

Gueorgui Pinkhassov

W E ARE NOT mayflies. We have known afternoons, and we
live day after day for a great many days. This long experience of how days turn—how afternoon becomes late afternoon
and late afternoon becomes night—informs any photographic
work we do with natural light. The time of day at which the
light is at its most glorious photographers call the golden hour:
you've seen them toting cameras on street corners and in abandoned lots, coming at 5:30 P.M. or 6:30 or later, depending on
the latitude and time of year. They wait for a certain intensity of
shadow, for the yellow sunlight to spill just so, before it dies
away into the night. But Gueorgui Pinkhassov (Russian, b.
1952, based in Paris) has done something more than wait: he
has detected the golden hour in unexpected hours. A low and
fractured light shimmers across his oeuvre. He has a fluency in
the language of the light at rest in all things, the light that is at
rest and invisible to most eyes.

Pinkhassov's work has come to the world in the usual way:
photojournalism, print magazines, exhibitions, a book (*Sight-
walk,* about Tokyo), and awards. He is a member of Magnum.
On his art he is elusive and insightful: "The power of our Muse
lies in her meaninglessness. Even the style can turn one into a
slave if one does not run away from it, and then one is doomed

to repeat oneself." Thus: he changes. New approaches, new subjects, new equipment; but always rescuing the small light in things.

The work approaches abstraction. There are Soviet precedents: the spiritual energy of Tarkovsky, for whose film *Stalker* he shot stills in 1979; the color of Savelev, intense and pained (Goethe: "Colors are the deeds and sufferings of light"); the deranged perspective of Rodchenko. Walker Evans and Friedlander, too, probably, in the deadpan patterning, and Leiter, in the playing off of painterly color against shallow depths of field. But he wouldn't be interesting if he weren't his own man; he is, and he is. And now, in addition to his "serious" work, he is posting photos on Instagram.

Digital photography and its children, Instagram among them, are causing arguments. There are studiedly old fogies like Danny Lyon, who insist that a machine that doesn't use film cannot be considered a camera. But this is no longer a common view: most photographers, professional or otherwise, either use digital or tacitly approve of it. Meanwhile, some serious photojournalists have reported wars and revolutions with the camera on a phone, and have won recognition for that work.

The statistics beggar belief: 380 billion photos were taken in 2011, and about 10 percent of all the photographs currently in existence were taken in 2012. Amateurs with Canon cameras and overpriced L lenses have something to do with this; even more culpable is the incessant and overwhelming production of camera-phone images by huge numbers of people. (By the way, why is it called a camera-phone rather than the more logical phone-camera?)

There are good reasons to be suspicious of this flood of images. What is the fate of art in the age of metastasized mechanical reproduction? These are cheap images; they are in fact less than cheap, for each image costs almost nothing. Postprocessing is easy and rampant: beautiful light is added after the fact, depth of field is manipulated, nostalgia is drizzled on in unctuous tints of orange and green. The result is briefly beguiling to the senses but ultimately annoying to the soul, like fake breasts or MSG-rich food. Matt Pearce, in his thoughtful polemic on this subject in the *New Inquiry,* wrote: "Never before have we so rampantly exercised the ability to capture the way the world really looks and then so gorgeously disfigured it."

But the problem with the new social photography isn't merely about postprocessing: after all, photographers have always manipulated their images in the darkroom. The filters that Hipstamatic and Instagram provide, the argument goes, are simply modern-day alternatives to the dodging and burning that have always been integral to making photographs. This argument is partially true. But the rise of social photography means that we are now seeing images all the time, millions of them, billions, many of which are manipulated with the same easy algorithms, the same tiresome vignetting, the same dank green wash. I remember the thrill I felt the first few times I saw Hipstamatic images, and I shot a few myself, buoyed by that thrill. The problem is not that images are being altered—it's that they're all being altered in the same way: high contrasts, dewy focus, oversaturation, a skewing of the RGB curve in fairly predictable ways. Correspondingly, the range of subjects is also peculiarly narrow: pets, pretty girlfriends, sunsets, lunch. In other words, the photographic function, which should properly be the domain of the eye and the mind, is being outsourced to the camera and to an algorithm.

All bad photos are alike, but each good photograph is good

in its own way. The bad photos have found their apotheosis on social media, where everybody is a photographer and where we have to suffer through each other's "photography" the way our forebears endured terrible recitations of poetry after dinner. Behind this dispiriting stream of empty images is what Russians call poshlost: fake emotion, unearned nostalgia. According to Nabokov, poshlost "is not only the obviously trashy but mainly the falsely important, the falsely beautiful, the falsely clever, the falsely attractive." He knows us too well.

There is of course nothing wrong with a photograph of your pug. But when you take that photograph without imagination and then put a "1977" filter on it—your pug wasn't born in 1977—you are reaching for an invented past that has no relevance to the subject at hand. You make the image "better" in an empty way, thus making it worse. Your adoring fans or friends can instantly see your pug or your ham sandwich on which you have bestowed the patina of age. This immortal sandwich of yours is seen by hundreds of people even before you've finished eating it.

I don't wish to begrudge anyone his or her pleasure: it's no bad thing that everyone is now a photographer. We can be the curators of our lives, and can record every banal moment if we wish. And indeed, why not? Nevertheless, in looking at a great photographic image from the past or the present, we know when blood is drawn. We know that some images, regardless of medium, still have the power to suddenly enliven us. And we know that these images are few. Not all 380 billion images per year, not 1 billion of them, not 100 million, not 1 million.

To my surprise, I joined Instagram. I did it only for Pinkhassov's sake. I wanted to see his new images, see what a really good photographer could do with an iPhone. I wanted also to give Instagram a chance against my objections. I love new technologies as much as I am skeptical of them (I went almost straight from rotary phone to iPhone; I tend to hold out, and then I plunge). I thought at first I'd post some of my own images as well, but I decided not to, in favor of just reading others' images.

Initially I also followed some other very good photographers—but I found that I was more content to be following Pinkhassov alone, at least for a while. Robert Frank said, "When people look at my pictures I want them to feel the way they do when they want to read a line of a poem twice." I'm drawn to this poetic notion of photography, and I think Frank's idea is what Pinkhassov, too, is after. He tries to foster the double take of seeing. Following only him on Instagram is a bit like having a house band: what you lose in variety, you gain in reliable quality.

It's possible to upload from your phone images taken with other cameras and saved in your image library, but Pinkhassov's Instagram photos, as far as I can tell, are taken with the iPhone; he has long valued simplicity and immediacy. Even his print work is done with a simple Canon SLR, which should be chastening news to all the gear obsessives: no fancy Leicas or Mark IIIs here.

On Instagram he does sometimes use a filter—the images are desaturated, the color field muted, with a slight degradation of image quality—but I'm not sure which filter it is. It doesn't matter; it's a fairly subtle one. What I like is that a visual language is being explored with new tools. He deploys Instagram's square format, which introduces new pressures to the organization of the picture plane. Verticality catches up with horizontality; diagonals gain new force. A peculiarity of Instagram I initially found frustrating, and that I still don't like, is that the program is written only for phones: you upload with the phone, you view on the phone. The "original" is on that small screen alone, not on a desktop or iPad (Instagram on iPad is, for now, an unpleasant adaptation of Instagram for iPhone, with no noticeable improvement in the viewing experience), and most images are too small as files to enlarge and print out nicely.

What kind of activity are we engaging in when we look at images in a gallery? Something of that activity is certainly about participating in "culture," about having good taste, and how good that makes us feel about ourselves. If the work exists nowhere but on the screen of an iPhone (in this case, on the screens of 2,307 iPhones—Pinkhassov's risibly small number of Instagram followers; compare this to Dmitry Medvedev's 55,000), then we have to adjust our expectations about the satisfactions a photograph can give. Squeezed in between images of sandwiches and sunsets, a Pinkhassov image (or any other image propelled by thought) must satisfy on its own merits. Thoughtfully made photographs, photographs that try to continue the conversation begun by Niépce and Atget, must somehow compete for attention among billions of other images presented in the same way. The images are not pre-credentialed by being hung on a wall at the International Center of Photography or the Leica Gallery.

We are left with optical discriminations and optical pleasures, and it is in this private space that the work regains its aura. In this sense, digital photography and social media, even though the tiny little screen can be irritating, are helping to introduce new criteria: there is no editioning, no signature, no date of printing. It will be a headache for curators in the future, but it's a pleasure for the pure lover of the image: while lying in bed in the morning, you can see the latest work from a photographer you find interesting. The image comes to you.

I'm looking at Pinkhassov's most recent photo on Instagram: *Parc des Buttes Chaumont.* So much delicious dark. I marvel at how well his use of depth of field evokes accommodation (the way we instinctively focus on only one area of the visual field at a time). Cameras and eyes behave differently, because cameras generally can take in more in an instant; it is sometimes interesting to have cameras behave as if they are eyes, and signal with selective blurring the eyes' imperfection. In this photo, the wine in the glasses—visible as such only on a second glance—threatens to return to the drops of blood we initially saw, just as the glass table is eager to get back to being a lake. I like scrolling through Pinkhassov's photos in part for this constant "Wait, what is this?" effect that comes off them, even from pictures I've already seen five times or ten times. I love the photos that are barely there, that almost resist parsing (usually due to fragmentation combined with some stubborn confusion of foreground and background). And I love the deeper mystery of why I should find these images moving, for there is very little journalism here, and hardly any narrative, but there is much emotion, none of which feels false or brushed on.

It is the emotion of moments defended by the camera's memory: the deposit of the experience of many afternoons and nights, of electric light and reflections, a catholicity of the visual, an inventory that includes legs, mirrors, fur, leaves, silhouettes, smoke, noses, trees, seas, windows, tiles, hair, steam, fronds, textiles. This last, the love of pattern, in particular the layering of one loudly patterned cloth against another, is a device exploited in both Keïta's studio photography and Matisse's Orientalist paintings. In Pinkhassov's use of it I find a similar sweet bewilderment ("Where does this end, where does that begin?") but also something feral, hyphenated, and slightly resistant to meaning. Pinkhassov's imagery is in this way like Hopkins's:

> *Glory be to God for dappled things—*
> *For skies of couple-colour as a brinded cow;*
> *For rose-moles all in stipple upon trout that swim;*
> *Fresh-firecoal chestnut-falls; finches' wings;*
> *Landscape plotted and pieced—fold, fallow, and plough;*
> *And áll trádes, their gear and tackle and trim.*
>
> *All things counter, original, spare, strange;*
> *Whatever is fickle, freckled (who knows how?)*
> *With swift, slow; sweet, sour; adazzle, dim;*
> *He fathers-forth whose beauty is past change:*
> *Praise him.*

Perfect and Unrehearsed

"I COULDN'T BELIEVE SUCH a thing could be caught with the camera. I said, 'Damn it,' took my camera and went out into the street." This was Henri Cartier-Bresson's dazzled and vexed reaction to Martin Munkácsi's photograph of boys running into the surf in Liberia. He saw it in 1932: the dark, sinuous bodies of three African boys—their rhyming legs at the place where sea meets land; their interweaving arms dialed to varying heights; their interlocking limbs creating abstract shapes; and the grace note, on the left side, of a single silhouetted arm. This image, Cartier-Bresson said, inspired his own approach, showing him that "photography could reach eternity through the moment."

Cartier-Bresson's *The Decisive Moment,* published in 1952, went on to become one of the most influential photography books ever made (a meticulous facsimile of the original was reissued in 2014 by Steidl). Here are Cartier-Bresson's best and most famous pictures: a cyclist zipping like a tangent past a spiral staircase in Hyères, children playing in a ruined precinct in Seville, Sunday picnickers on the banks of the Marne. Cartier-Bresson writes in the book's foreword that the goal of these pictures was "a precise organization of forms which give that event its proper expression." In that phrase "precise organization" there's a quality of intention that agrees with the English title, the idea of the decisive moment. But the book's original, French title was *Images à la sauvette,* images taken on the sly. It is not quite as catchy, but it suggests a different truth about Cartier-Bresson's work.

Alex Webb put it to me this way: "The humility of [*Images à la sauvette*]—which suggests the uncertainty and mystery of collaborating with the world as a street photographer—seems more in the spirit of Cartier-Bresson's photography. As he once said, 'It is the photo that takes you.' " To limit Cartier-Bresson's photos to just a single moment misses the point. Webb said Cartier-Bresson allowed him to see that there are "often multiple potential moments to discover in many situations—and that different photographers will find different moments."

There's no single right answer, just as there's no photographic formula. Each successful picture taken on the sly by Cartier-Bresson was one original solution to a set of circumstances he was encountering for the first time. Consider, for instance, a lesser-known photograph he made in Shanghai's Suzhou Creek in 1949. The piles of bundled wood, the fanned-out ends of the poles, the standing figures, the curved prows of the canoes: each element contributes to the kaleidoscopic coherence of the image. The long shafts of the poles create new rectangles inside the larger one that frames the picture. These smaller rectangles are close to square in their dimensions (squares tilted on their axes). Were a rectangle sketched around the pensive figure in the foreground, it, too, would approximate a square. The feeling of harmony in many photographs by Cartier-Bresson, this one included, comes in part from this ability to see and capture a scene's native repetitions of shape or gesture.

Cartier-Bresson's oeuvre, his reportorial as well as aesthetic achievements, laid the ground for future photojournalists. Maggie Steber, for instance, credits him with giving her a way to think about style, content, and construction. But then, as any mature artist must, she moved into her own visual language. In her photograph of a funeral in Port-au-Prince, Haiti, in 1987, an exquisitely balanced composition is further strengthened by the judicious color: light blue, dark blue, and brown. The main mourner's gesture, his powerful arms outstretched, echoes that of the figure of Christ on the cross behind him.

The picture's structure is sustained by intersecting lines. The man's head and left arm form a diagonal; a rectangle set off from this diagonal would contain the main action of the photograph. In the background are other crosses. Even the streetlamp is a half-finished cross. These crosses are like individual instruments taking up a musical theme. A roof at the left emphasizes the main diagonal and a glance from the second most prominent man in the picture, which parallels it. The pale-shirted shoulders from which the dark-suited mourner emerges form a radiating arrangement, and the bent elbows to the left and right are like parentheses around this group of helpers.

Beginning photographers are often tempted to reduce photography to rigid rules. The rule of thirds—thinking of the picture plane in terms of a grid made of three equal vertical and three equal horizontal divisions, with the points of interest placed at the intersections of these lines—is a common starting point. More sophisticated is the golden ratio (two quantities are said to be in a golden ratio if the ratio of the larger to the smaller is the same as the ratio of their sum to the larger). Imagine a triptych in which the center is about 0.618 as wide as each of the wings. Because this ratio is often found in nature, it is cred-

ited as the mathematical logic behind many efficient and visually pleasing phenomena: certain flower petals, or mollusk
shells, or spiral galaxies. These codes can be helpful for looking.
But the reality is that there is usually a much more improvisa-
tory and flexible mathematical order at play in a successful photograph.

A bright afternoon in 1986. Alex Webb is on the streets of
Bombardopolis, a town in northwestern Haiti. That afternoon
is long gone now, but a photograph Webb made that day remains. A woman stands in a blue frock and a red head scarf. An
enormous cigarette floating next to her face turns out to be in
the mouth of a man in deep shadow in the foreground. In the
middle distance are a donkey's ears, and little else of the donkey. Farther back is a boy, neatly contained in the frame created
by a bamboo pole on one side and a painted wall on the other.
He is in silhouette, and he appears to be looking at the photographer (and therefore at us, who share the photographer's
view). There are other people in the picture: a man in profile on
the left; another little boy, only his head visible, peeking just
below the silhouetted boy; a woman in a patterned red and blue
cloth standing in a doorway with her back to us. The plaster has
flaked off the wall on the right to reveal a shape as pointed and
angular as the donkey's ears.

In Steber's picture of the funeral, there is a miraculous unity
of action. She described to me how it came about: "Like an
orchestra playing a dramatic symphony, everything crescen-
doed at the same time. The dead woman's son, without warning, suddenly rose up in anguish in the painful last cry of a son
saying goodbye forever to his mother, and just as the last rays of
sun fell on his face." The opposite is true in Webb's picture.
There is no dramatic highlight; no one interacts with or even

looks at anyone else. The only communicative glance is from the two boys, outward, toward us. And yet the anomie of an afternoon in the 1980s in a small, hot Haitian town is given, in this photograph, uncanny, indelible, and exact form.

Webb's is perhaps not a picture Cartier-Bresson would have liked very much, as he was skeptical of color and strong shadows. But for Webb, everything is fair game: color, shadows, a silhouette, a rock, a wall, a cigarette, a donkey's ears, a saddle, a signboard, a hand here, a head there. Despite this freedom, everything is in its right place. Notice the repetition of an elongated rectangle: the door, the doorway, the vertical sections of wall, the lower edge of the window. Then there are the implied polygons around key figures: the silhouetted boy, the woman in the red scarf, the donkey's ears. The same elongated rectangle, or at least one related to it by ratio, appears in various sizes and in various disguises in free geometric play throughout the picture plane.

The success of certain pictures—pictures that make the viewer say, "Damn it," and wonder how such things are possible—comes from a combination of tutored intuition and good luck. Could Munkácsi, Cartier-Bresson, Steber, or Webb have considered some matters of pictorial complexity at the moment they made their pictures? No question about it. But could they have seen every element at the moment they pressed the shutter? Impossible. The photographer has to be there to begin with, tuned in and tuned up, active, asking a family for permission to attend a funeral in Port-au-Prince, following a man and a donkey down the road in Bombardopolis. The rest is fate.

Disappearing Shanghai

PHOTOGRAPHY DOES NOT share music's ability to be fully re-made each time it is presented. It does not have film's dura-tional quality, in which the illusion of a present continuous tense is conjured. A photograph shows what was, and is no more. It registers, in pixels or in print, the quality and variety of light entering an aperture during a specific length of time. There are no instantaneous photographs: each must be exposed for a length of time, no matter how brief: in this sense, every photograph is a time-lapse image, and photography is necessar-ily an archival art.

There are certain oeuvres within the history of photography in which this archival pressure is felt more intensely than in others. Eugène Atget's façades, architectural ornaments, and street corners depicted a Paris that was, even while his work was ongoing, already passing away from view. Atget's images have a sense of speaking out from a buried visual subconscious, a sense aided by but not wholly dependent on the depopulated views he preferred, and by the melancholia of the sepia tone bestowed by time. The other part of the charge of the images comes from what we know about the places they depict: chiefly that those places are gone.

A similar embedded charge can be felt in all the photographs presented in *Disappearing Shanghai,* a book of photographs by Howard French. French is a journalist of unusually broad expertise: he was bureau chief for *The New York Times* in several countries, and has had many years of experience reporting from Africa, the Caribbean, Central America, and Asia. His work as a photographer is less well known: the selection in *Disappearing Shanghai* marks the first appearance of that aspect of his work in book form.

It might be assumed that French is one of those dilettantes who, unwilling to leave well enough alone, insist on dabbling in areas beyond their specialization: a writer of well-received books and articles turning his attention to something less taxing, something easy, like the occasional snapshot. But there is much more going on in these images than hobbyism. They indicate intent, thought, order. They provoke questioning, demanding from us what all good photographs do, which is that they be placed in some relation to the wider practice of photography and to the ethics and possibilities of the form.

Disappearing Shanghai is a visual account of five years' worth of shooting in the rapidly changing back streets, homes, and alleys of China's largest city. The project originated during French's time living in Shanghai as a *Times* reporter, and developed side by side with that work. The instinct that brought these images to the surface (it seems natural to think of them as having been submerged) was that of a flâneur. Around the time that he began to learn Chinese, French also started to go on long walks in the less glitzy areas of the city: the older areas, the more traditional areas, precisely those parts of the city that were beginning to be effaced by the economic boom. He began to take photos of the people he met. Soon, he was invited into their homes.

The photos that resulted are notably different from what we might ordinarily think of as photojournalism: they are dynamic but are not the action-packed singles of the kind that win photojournalism prizes. There is something far more patient at work in them. We feel that the photographer has not so much captured a "decisive moment" as gained us admission into private moments of long duration. Many of the images project the longueurs that are, after all, a substantial part of regular life: unhurried, unharried, the part of life that isn't caught up in working for pay, the part of life that is a straight catalogue of the passing minutes.

Many of the photos in *Disappearing Shanghai* rescue a peaceful time of day—just before lamplight—from the heart of one of the world's brashest and fastest-growing conurbations. These Chinese faces and selves bring to mind the work of another archivist of the passing scene, August Sander. In the work Sander produced around and just following the First World War, he created a catalogue of images that stood in for an entire generation in Weimar Germany. Farmers, cooks, stevedores, teachers, priests, and manual laborers were all represented in their full dignity, and Sander achieved something like a double portraiture in each case, because each actual individual was at the same time a representative type.

This ability to be at once universal and yet ineluctably particular made John Berger ask, of Sander's images, just what it was the photographer told each of his subjects that made them all believe him in the same way. In a related fashion, the portraits of *Disappearing Shanghai* show people as their real and undisguised selves, so that one almost suspects that French has brought each subject into his confidence in the same way, so that each is unable to be before the camera other than he or she is in the absence of the camera. At the same time, these are also photographs of people in a story, players on a stage about which they might only be faintly aware, and the story they tell is of a world that is passing, and will soon be past.

The old man sitting down on the street and looking lost in front of a ruined building, a little boy sitting before a tricycle with his legs ostentatiously crossed, an infant unimpressed with the dinner his mother presents him. There are the moments in which French has been granted admission into small, cluttered apartments: an old lady with an image of her ancestor (or perhaps it is her deceased husband) on the wall behind her; a couple seated on bunks, between whom an enormous silence looms. They are all there in their entirety, even though we do not know their names or speak their language. The photographer's lens introduces them. They are intact, quiet, complex. They have all believed him in the same way.

Howard French came to photography early, shooting Olympus SLRs while he was still in high school, and already in those years was working in a darkroom built by his father. A signal event had occurred when he was a mere boy: he had seen a photograph someone had made of his younger brother. French recounts that he was astonished by this image, which seemed to contain not only his brother's appearance but also the entire context of sights, sounds, and emotions out of which the image was drawn: "It turned out to be one of the most revealing portraits I've seen, and even the summer heat, and Jamie's beading sweat, and an air of urgency, as if our mother had beckoned him to come home right away, or else, are all intensely palpable."

This description contains an honest love of the world of memories and experience (and strongly evokes one of Leonard Freed's photos of boys at play in the streets of New York). It is a sensibility at home in the layers of a moment, and in this early experience was sown the seed that would inspire French's later photography, which went on to span several countries, notably in Africa and in Asia. He learned a great deal from watching his photojournalist colleagues, but waywardness was to become his dominant note. His system is footloose and unsystematic, and the images that result are as in love with the world of surfaces, persons, and places as the writings of Walter Benjamin or Walt Whitman were. In a descriptive, inventorial passage that could have been lifted from Benjamin's memoir of Naples, French writes about the situations he encountered photographing Shanghai:

> . . . the songbirds and the crickets lovingly raised in their cages, the street markets and the foods, with their smells and colors that change so suddenly and so crisply according to the season, the eternal tending of laundry from long bamboo poles, the wildly screeching bicycle brakes, the lusty throat clearing, the world weary lounging about on beach chairs and in pajamas, the very appearance of the people's faces, weathered by a century of immense and often brutal change, like the old man in the faded Mao suit I saw on a street corner this afternoon looking for the life of him like an apparition lost amid the onrush of the new.

French's images are freed from the dramatic needs of a news report. With a quiet testimonial force, they bring us the deeper drama of mundane life. The cumulative effect of the images, all taken in the same half dozen neighborhoods of the city, is of how rich the substance of human experience is, and how reliably it is to be found side by side with an inevitable insubstantiality.

Touching Strangers

A PHOTOGRAPH IS NOTHING but surface. On this two-dimensional plane is presented, with areas of dark and light and sometimes color, an illusion of narrative depth. We know that abstraction is possible in photography, as is manipulative postprocessing, but in the case of most unaltered photos—landscapes, portraits, photojournalism—we rightly assume that the photograph's relationship with life is straightforward. We take it on trust that things are as they seem. These viewing habits, which serve us so well in most cases, make us tense and interested when we look at Richard Renaldi's photographs in *Touching Strangers*.

The portraits in the book all came about in a similar fashion. In a public place in one or another American city or town, Renaldi asked a stranger to allow his or her photograph to be taken. Another stranger was then asked to pose with the first stranger, and the pair were photographed together, not simply in terms of occupying the same frame, but in close physical proximity to each other. Often these strangers had to be cajoled by the photographer to hold each other, to embrace, to touch. The photos are not first takes. It took time to get the right closeness and an interesting-enough interaction between the strangers. Sometimes the number of subjects was three, or four. Some of the latter, the quadruple portraits, can only be described as "family photographs": we have no other vocabulary than the familial for images like those which show a man, a woman, and two children posed in a close group.

When we sit at a café or in a restaurant, we pretend to be wholly focused on our food and our companions, but we spend some of our time imagining the lives of the people around us all the time. Those two men holding hands a few tables over: How long have they been together? Why is the woman at that table over there crying quietly into her napkin? What will the suspiciously older man seated with her do about it? Is he her father or her lover? And the anxious woman who has been alone at the bar for a while now: What's happening with her? Has her date stood her up? Or is that her job, to wait until some generous stranger takes interest? We do this habitually, making up stories about other people, and, at the same time, they are certainly making up stories about us. Stories of these kinds—about love and about the uncertainties between people—are the kinds of stories suggested by the portraits in *Touching Strangers*.

"Fine photography is literature," Walker Evans wrote, "and it should be." The narrative force in Renaldi's fine pictures comes out of the way their calm surfaces suddenly open out to the most intense and troubling themes of contemporary life. It is possible to imagine this idea deployed in a less successful way: quick snapshots of strangers smiling together, a sentimental record of a walk down a crowded street, with no great insight or resonance in the resulting pictures. Something quite different happens in Renaldi's pictures. His subjects have been asked to briefly subvert their expectations about personal space and public propriety. In their bodies we read a large number of silent signals, often more than one present in each person: performance, tension, submission, affection, rigidity, unhappiness, comedy, sexuality, embarrassment, boredom, relief.

Any society is governed by the invisible perimeter fence of its taboos. Benign touch from a stranger is allowed when permission is granted and, usually, when some service is performed: at the doctor's office, at the barbershop, at the masseuse or the tailor. But intimate touch of the romantic kind is permitted not only by the mutual consent of adults but by laws and prejudices. We are still within living memory of the *Loving v. Virginia* case, when a black woman and her white husband had to fight the state for the legal right to be a married couple. In a historical sense, 1967 is not long ago.

In linguistic terms, "touching" is not uncomplicated. Earlier eras used it to mean "concerning," and this sense is present secondarily in Renaldi's title: it is a book concerning strangers and their interactions with each other. But the word is now also a euphemism for various forms of inappropriate contact: "touching children" is a crime, and "touching oneself" is not a subject for polite company. On the positive side of the ledger, we might think of the many stories of the healing touch: the power of the laying on of hands is a trope common to many religions. And science assents: monkeys that are touched and held in infancy do better, healthwise, than those that are deprived of maternal touch. Research on humans indicates that hugs release therapeutic endorphins and serotonin, increasing one's sense of well-being.

The portraits in Renaldi's book are situated in this terrain of taboos and consolation. In the silence between his subjects, there's a charge. How do we feel when we see two men of different sartorial instincts being tender with each other? What about a black man in hip-hop clothes getting up close and personal with a white woman in a wedding dress? We can quickly get past some of these—we prefer to believe that such unseemly bias is in other people, not in us. But why does the unease remain when we view an image like the one that shows Nathan, a policeman in full uniform, standing behind and embracing Robyn, a young woman in a tank top and short-shorts? How old is she? What is that look on her face? Is it apprehension, or is that just the way her face is? Why is this image even less comfortable to look at than the one of Lee and Lindsay, the nudists, who stand in a similar pose to that of Nathan and Robyn, and between whom there's an even greater age gap? There is also a cumulative effect of seeing the several pictures here in which people of different races touch or hold each other. The racial division in the United States remains stark, with most of the population practicing some form of "separate but equal." It is impossible to look at Renaldi's photographs without being a little sad at how rare it is to see, on the streets, in the diners, in the parks and public places of this country, some version of the invented narratives they illustrate. Their photographic fiction is a reminder of how shoddy reality can be in comparison to the imagination.

But *Touching Strangers,* even when it alerts us to society's hypocrisies, also does something more basic and more subtle: it brings us a reconsideration of the fundamental mystery of touch. Of the five traditional senses, touch is the only one that is reflexive: one can look without being seen, and hear without being heard, but to touch is to be touched. It is a sense that goes both ways: the sensitivity of one's skin responds to and is responded to by the sensitivity of other people's skin. This perhaps is why so many of these pictures project an air of gentleness, compassion, friendship, or care. There is something irreducible about the effect of touching another human being, or witnessing such contact. We see the results on the faces of the subjects of these photographs. The images play with the illusion of straightforwardness and testimony, and at the same time find their ways to precisely those values. Between the moment when a stranger is approached on the street and the moment when a print is made, some transformative magic takes place.

Renaldi's work is patient, done with a large-format camera, slow in the making, dependent on the cooperation of strangers. And yet, because these are strangers out in public, the element of unpredictability is ever present. Renaldi has shepherded chance and intuition into something both luminous and unreassuring. His photographs, once seen, are hard to put out of mind. The stories they evoke have a depth echoing beyond the brief encounters that occasioned them. A photograph is nothing but surface, but there are ineffable truths in the way things look; how things seem can be more startling than how they are. As Oscar Wilde wrote, "It is only shallow people who do not judge by appearances. The true mystery of the world is the visible, not the invisible."

Finders Keepers

WHEN HE VISITED the Plumbe National Daguerrian Gallery in Manhattan in 1846, Walt Whitman was astonished. "What a spectacle!" he wrote. "In whichever direction you turn your peering gaze, you see nought but human faces! There they stretch, from floor to ceiling—hundreds of them." In the seven years between the invention of the daguerreotype and Whitman's visit to Plumbe's, the medium had become popular enough to generate an impressive, and even hectic, stream of images. Now, toward the end of photography's second century, that stream has become torrential.

"Take lots of pictures!" is how our friends wish us a good trip, and we oblige them. Nearly one trillion photographs are taken each year, of everything at which a camera might be pointed: families, meals, landscapes, cars, toes, cats, toothpaste tubes, skies, traffic lights, atrocities, doorknobs, waterfalls, an unrestrained gallimaufry that not only indexes the world of visible things but also adds to its plenty. We are surrounded by just as many depictions of things as by things themselves.

The consequences are numerous and complicated: more instantaneous pleasure, more information, and a more cosmopolitan experience of life for huge numbers of people, but also constant exposure to illusion and an intimate knowledge of fakery. There is a photograph coming at you every few seconds, and hype is the lingua franca. It has become hard to stand still, wrapped in the glory of a single image, as the original viewers of old paintings used to do. The flood of images has increased our access to wonders and at the same time lessened our sense of wonder. We live in inescapable surfeit.

A number of artists are using this abundance as their starting point, setting their own cameras aside and turning to the horde—collecting and arranging photographs that they have found online. These artist-collectors, in placing one thing next to another, create a third thing—and this third thing, like a subatomic particle produced by a collision of two other particles, carries a charge.

A decent photograph of the sun looks similar to any other decent photograph of the sun: a pale circle with a livid red or blue sky around it. There are hundreds of thousands of such photographs online, and in the daily contest for "likes" they are close to a sure thing: easy to shoot, fun to look at, a reliable dose of awe. The American artist Penelope Umbrico downloads such photos of the sun from Flickr—she favors sunsets in particular—and then crops and prints them, assembling them into an enormous array. A typical installation may contain 2,500 photographs, organized into a rectangular mural. It is the same sun, photographed repeatedly in the same way, by a large cast of photographers, few of whom are individually remarkable as artists and none of whom are credited. But, with Umbrico's intervention, the cumulative effect of their images literally dazzles: the sun, the sun, the sun, the sun, in row upon brilliant row.

Optical brilliance is also the key to the American artist Eric Oglander's *Craigslist Mirrors* project, which is also based on found photographs. His biographical statement is deadpan: "I search Craigslist for compelling photos of mirrors." Oglander posts these pictures to his website, to Instagram, and to Tumblr. A surprising number of them are surreal or enjoyably weird, because of the crazy way a mirror interrupts the logic of whichever visual field it is placed in, and because of the unexpected things the reflection might include. Photographic work of this kind—radically dependent on context—can be unsettling for those who take "photograph" to have a straightforward meaning: an image made with a camera by a single author with a particular intention. This is where collector-artists come in: to confirm that curation and juxtaposition are basic artistic gestures.

The German artist Joachim Schmid, with a gleeful and indefatigable eye, gathers other people's photographs and organizes them into photo books. For his trouble, he has been called a thief and a fraud. Schmid initially used photographs found on the street and at sales, but more recently he has depended on digital images. His typological projects, like those in the ninety-six-book series *Other People's Photographs* (2008–2011), are alert to the mystery in artlessness. They are a mutant form, somewhere between the omnivorous vernacular of Stephen Shore's *American Surfaces* and the hypnotic minimalism of Bernd and Hilla Becher's water towers. Schmid brings the photographs out of one kind of flow, their image-life as part of one person's Flickr account, and into another, at rest among their visual cognates.

Each book in *Other People's Photographs* is a document of how amateur digital photography nudges us toward a common but unpremeditated language of appearances. Photography is easy now, and cheap, but this does not mean that everything is documented with the same frequency or that all possibilities are equally explored. As is true of every set of expressive tools, digital photography creates its own forms of emphasis and registers of style. Cellphone cameras are great in low light, and so we have many more nocturnal photos. Most of our tiny cameras are not easy to set on a tripod, and so there is a correspondingly smaller percentage of soberly symmetrical photographs of monuments; the dominant aesthetic of the age is handheld. A camera focused at waist level, as old Rolleiflexes were, is different from one held between the eyes and the chin, the optimal placement for a live digital display.

All selfies are alike as all daguerreotype portraits were alike: an image can be more conventionally an example of its genre than a memorable depiction of its subject. A plate of food, with its four or five items of varying texture corralled into a circle, is similar to countless other plates of food. But a book full of photographed meals, meals long consumed and forgotten, is not only poking gentle fun at our obsessive documentation of the quotidian. It is also marveling at how inexpensive photography has become. Things that would not have merited a second glance are now unquestioningly, almost automatically, recorded. The doors of our fridges, glimpses of cleavage, images of our birthday cakes, the setting sun: cheap photography makes visible the ways in which we are similar, and have for a long time been similar. Now we have proof, again, and again, and again.

The sheer mass of digital imagery was itself the subject of *24 Hrs of Photos,* a project by the Dutch artist Erik Kessels (first in 2011, and other times since). Kessels downloaded every photograph uploaded to Flickr in the course of a single day, about a million in all. He printed a fraction of them, around 350,000, which he then piled up in massive wavelike heaps in a gallery. Asked to explain the project, Kessels said: "I visualize the feeling of drowning in representations of other people's experiences." But that's not art! And yet the emotions that accompany such an installation—the exasperation, the sense of wonder or inundation, the glimpses of beauty—are true of art. The shoe fits, maddening as it is.

What are the rights of the original photographers, the "nonartists" whose works have been so unceremoniously reconfigured? And how can what is found be ordered, or put into a new disorder, and presented again to give it new resonance? And how long will that resonance itself last? The real trouble is rarely about whether something counts as art—if the question comes up, the answer is almost always yes—but whether the art in question is startling, moving, or productively discomfiting. Meeting those criteria is just as difficult for straight photography as it is for appropriation-based work. After all, images made of found images are images, too. They join the neverending cataract of images, what Whitman called the "immense Phantom concourse," and they are vulnerable, as all images are, to the dual threats of banality and oblivion—until someone shows up, says "Finders keepers," rethinks them, and, by that rethinking, brings them back to life.

Google's Macchia

"I DON'T KNOW WHAT they are up to. They just run around taking pictures of *things*." Her commitment was to ideas, or perhaps to something even more abstract than ideas. We were at a party. She was an avant-garde photographer. Photography, in her view, lived neither in the camera nor in the printed photograph, but in a more nebulous zone. Then came another round of cocktails, and she swirled away.

A dozen years from now we will enter photography's third century. We seem to be in the moment of its fullest bloom and diversity. More people than ever take photographs, and more photos than ever are being made. Geniuses, recognized or otherwise, stalk the earth. But the art is also in its moment of crisis. There's never been so much photography on view, and most of it is bad. There is curatorial uncertainty. The kinds of images celebrated by one set of institutions, say the Pulitzer Prize or the World Press Photo, are considered irrelevant and retrograde by the standards of another set of institutions, say the Deutsche Börse Prize or MoMA. Then there are those institutions that are able to contend with photography only in a nostalgic way. The scholarship of photography reflects these confusions.

This in part is a question of what presents itself as art, and what it attempts to say to its society. If photography is among the necessary forms of response to this present, photojournalism of the kind that wins awards seems increasingly inadequate to the task. A photograph of a funeral in the Middle East, a series on an austerity rally, a book of portraits of musicians: such images are important, but they rarely raise new questions. What, photographically speaking, addresses this new time, this age of clandestine assassination, torture, oppressive policing, economic immiseration, proliferating apartheids, and war without end? Or brings new light to the old questions of love, death, loneliness, beauty, and mystery? A number of photographers, only some of whom "run around taking pictures of things," make nonjournalistic responses to our current situation.

Among these are the various artists who have appropriated Google Maps' Street View and Google Earth, extending the practice of found imagery and the readymade to the images discovered on the computer screen. These Google-based photographic practices are forms of countersurveillance, and in part what they do is show that a photography of ideas can accommodate different kinds of images. There are images that torment visibility, and there are images that use clarity in an ambiguous way. The "neutral" and panoptic eye of Google itself becomes the camera, and, under these conditions, the photographer's task becomes curatorial.

Among the most interesting photographers who use Google in their work are Doug Rickard, Mishka Henner, Aaron Hobson, and Michael Wolf. Rickard's *A New American Picture* is a look at the collapse of certain cities: Detroit, Memphis, Oakland. The gaunt sun-stunned figures in these streets inhabit noonday nightmares, captured both by Google's car-mounted camera and by the brutal reality of American capitalism. Henner uses Google Earth to look at pixelated images of secret, usually military, locations in the Netherlands; it is a bracing update of the Dutch landscape tradition. In another project, made using Google StreetView and titled *No Man's Land,* he finds images of sex workers standing on the roadside in rural Italian locations, most of them alone, and most in broad daylight. The images are painful, poignant, but the real surprise is that there were so many to be found. Aaron Hobson, meanwhile, stitches together a number of screenshots to create ethereal panoramic photographs of unpeopled places, photos in their own way as desolate as Henner's, but more conventionally beautiful. And Michael Wolf curates vignettes out of StreetView by zooming in to find little visual poems (walking legs, high heels, people interacting with street signs) or thematic conceits (such as a series on people giving the finger to the Google camera).

Rickard, Henner, Hobson, and Wolf are not alone in their creative refashioning or subversion of Google Maps and Google Earth. Other artists are doing it, too, as are amateurs with the hours to spare and the desire to trawl for hours through virtual space in search of the inadvertent, the alluring, the bad, and the sad. Such conceptual artistic practices are only a tiny part of the use of Google. But the new forms of photography opened up by Google are indexical: they say something about what the company is up to, about its weird power, and about how we might elude its intentions.

Google is incessantly productive and very enthusiastic about itself. The company's bright-eyed but curiously unreassuring motto is "Don't Be Evil." In *The New Digital Age,* the recent book by executive chairman Eric Schmidt and the director of Google Ideas, Jared Cohen, we find the following words: "The best thing anyone can do to improve the quality of life around the world is to drive connectivity and technological opportunity." This might almost read as a Panglossian parody of technological optimism, were it not so earnestly meant. And so, Google grows, it makes new things, it makes the world more interesting, though not always to the good. Under the guidance of its founders and of guru-like software engineers like Jeff Dean and Sanjay Ghemawat, it brings abstractions and a whole new level of automation into computer science, and helps sustain our current age of frenzied information collection, massive computation, and feral capitalism.

Google tried to do everything. It proved itself the deepest and fastest of the search engines. It stomped the competition in email. It made a decent showing in image hosting, and a good one in chat. It stumbled on social, but utterly owned maps. It swallowed libraries whole and sent tremors across the copyright laws. It knows where you are right now, and what you're doing, and what you'll probably do next. It added an indelible, funny, loose-limbed, and exact verb into the vocabulary: to google. No one "bings" or "yahoos" anything. And it finishes your sen . . .

All of a sudden, one day, a few years ago, there was Google Image Search. Words typed into the search box could deliver pages of images arrayed in a grid. I remember the first time I saw this, and what I felt: fear. I knew then that the monster had taken over. I confessed it, too. "I'm afraid of Google," I said recently to an employee of the company. "I'm not afraid of Google," he replied. "Google has a committee that meets over privacy issues before we release any product. I'm afraid of Facebook, of what Facebook can do with what Google has found. We are in a new age of cyberbullying." I agreed with him about Facebook, but remained unreassured about Google. The Google privacy committee had given the thumbs-up to predictive text of all kinds, to data mining, and to the collection of location information. It had conciliatory relationships with bad governments at home and abroad, governments that might demand strategic pieces of stored information, or call for the heads of dissidents.

And all of a sudden, one day, much more recently, there was Google Search by Image (no prizes for whoever named it). Somewhere deep in the thousands of parallel machines running searches, an algorithm had emerged for matching an image to exact and inexact versions of itself across the Web. This makes it sound mystical, but in actuality there were precursors to Search by Image—sometimes called Reverse Image Search—at Google itself, and at TinEye. Research in the last decade into object recognition and into the matching of visual data (research done not only at Google but at other corporations and at universities; see, for example, the work of Abhinav Gupta and Abhinav Shrivastava) was brought to a point of refinement, incorporating findings about how to estimate the relative importance of different parts of a picture. And, in time, sophisticated code that made use of artificial intelligence was written, by a team led by Amit Singhal and Ben Gomes.

So, the science was straightforward (though not simple), but the result was mystical: faces and places and scenes were legible in a new way, shorn of their mute anonymity. A photograph—say the famous one of a child carrying bottles by Henri Cartier-Bresson (*Rue Mouffetard, 1954*), or a tourist's snapshot of her family in front of the Taj Mahal—could be pinned to the wider world of data in a precise way. If not, if it were a unique image of a situation or of an unremarkable location, it could be brought into the family of images. This latter, a more involved and more interesting technical feat than mere matching, was presented as pages of "visually similar images." This use of visual similarity had a formal and coloristic sophistication that took me aback: it seemed to demonstrate an awareness of the essence of a photograph. Light, shadow, color, intensity, and composition were integrated to unite images that were similar. These were images that shared a kind of visual DNA, the kind that is apparent at a glance. But the images were not at all related to each other in terms of content.

In Naples in 1868, Vittorio Imbriani published a pamphlet entitled "La quinta Promotrice." In this now almost forgotten text, he advanced a peculiar theory of art that centered on the color patch or, in Italian, the macchia (the word literally means stain or spot). According to Imbriani, the macchia is "the image of the first distant impression of an object or a scene, the first and characteristic effect, to imprint itself upon the eye of the artist." It is, in other words, the total compositional and coloristic effect of an image in the split second before the eye begins to parse it for meaning. Imbriani was writing against the academic idealists of his time, who were obsessed with categories of style and execution. "Every painting must contain an idea," Imbriani wrote, "but a pictorial idea, not just a poetical idea." And for him, this pictorial idea was a matter of "a particular organization of light and dark from which the work takes its character. And this organization of light and dark, this macchia, is what really moves the spectator. . . . Equally in music it is not the attached words, the libretto, but the character of the melody that produces emotion in the listener."

Imbriani's was an argument for the inner life of pictorial effect, not so much about the way in which visual organization transcended subject matter but the way in which it preceded subject matter. For Imbriani, a picture lived by its idea, by its melody. However, this wonderful and cogent theory gained little traction, and with the exception of a reconsideration by Benedetto Croce in 1929 and an adaptation by Hans Sedlmayr (who misunderstood Imbriani's main argument) in 1934, it never really entered the mainstream of art history.

In my years of struggle as a street photographer, I had stumbled across Imbriani's truth without knowing it: in each picture, I was building on a pictorial rather than a poetic idea. The same, I feel, is true of some of the color photographers I admire most. I love conceptual photography, but I also like to "run around taking pictures of things." I am now using Search by Image for my own personal color studies, for my own understanding of the color patch, and I don't know what might come of it. I'm watching to see what other photographers and artists can create using this latest manifestation of Big Data. As usual, they will have to navigate between the Scylla of copyright issues and the Charybdis of "that's bullshit, not art."

When I began to put some of my photographs into Google's Search by Image, it was like an arrival. This was work I had thought of in terms of a certain disregard for subject matter. I had a passion for light and shadow, a tendency toward ostinato patterns, and an almost fanatical interest in color distribution. In introducing images to one another (as I did in a previous project I called *Who's Got the Address?*) I was working with a notion of reuniting what had been shattered in some unseen pictorial prehistory. At other times, I had even organized some of my images by color kinship: the red and black ones in one group, the blue-green ones in another. But I did not understand fully that what I was after was macchie. This is what became clear when I gave myself over to Search by Image.

I fed a few of my photographs into the machine (there's a warning on the support page: "When you search by image, any images that you upload and any URLs that you submit will be stored by Google. Google uses those images and URLs solely to provide and improve our products and services"), and out of the "visually similar images" results, I selected the ones that best expressed the idea I had been after when I took the original picture. The photographer's task not only becomes curatorial, it has in fact always been curatorial. In each case I ended up with an assemblage of nine images, including my own original. I had arrived at Google's macchia and, beyond that, unantici-pated narratives. An out-of-focus picture of a woman with a hijab was now surrounded by her color patch relatives: a fighter jet, Bill Maher being conspiracy weary, President Obama in front of some computers, a lone rioter, a woman wearing a bi-kini, a policeman confronting what seemed to be, in the dis-tance, a group of women in black hijabs.

Another photo of mine, an adumbrated red image of the in-terior of the Musée d'Orsay, led to unexpected prodigies of vision: a fashion show, the new pope (seated like Don Corleone, flanked by consiglieri), North Korean acrobats, a New York City street, and a night raid. The pictorial idea of each picture told me what I knew but hadn't articulated about the pictorial idea of my own picture, its rhetoric of red and shadow and scat-ter. It was like hearing a familiar tune played on unfamiliar in-struments, with dramatic changes in the timbre but the pitches staying the same.

It was an uncomplicated experiment, not an attempt to create a new work of art. But I could see that there was potential there, perhaps not for me, but surely for others who might want to think through the capabilities of Google Image or Google Search by Image. Machine had once again met Mind, and Machine knew of Mind what Mind itself had not known. The Machine had its own ideas. But in the shards of light flashing off its silhouette were also, as usual, new possibilities for art, new light for the soul.

The Atlas of Affect

N EAR THE END of his life, Aby Warburg (1866–1929) found a form that began to answer his questions about images. The questions had centered on the relationship between memory and history. Somehow, the conventional practices of art history had left Warburg unsatisfied. There was a deeper logic, he believed, between certain classical images, and between classical images and the ones that came later.

This restless search led him to amass an idiosyncratic library on Renaissance scholarship (this library was transferred from Hamburg to London after his death, and became the core of the Warburg Institute). And it was also this search that propelled him to travel to the United States and live for several months in the mid-1890s among Hopi and Zuni people. The great insight happened many years later, in 1924, when Warburg set up large black cloth screens, and began to pin newspaper and magazine cuttings of paintings, prints, and photographs on them. Each screen was organized around an idea, a complex theme, and the sequence of images was a matter of reiteration as well as of imaginative leaps.

One panel was an exploration of the afterlife of classical gestures, organized around a painting by Ghirlandaio. Another looked at the iconological value of the figure of the hurrying nymph, and included paintings by Botticelli and Raphael, as well as a photograph of a young woman from Hamburg. The panels of Warburg's *Mnemosyne Atlas* owe something to the systematic imagination inherited from the eighteenth century and to the atlases of that time. But there is something else going on in the *Mnemosyne Atlas:* it is neither systematic nor complete. It borrows the form of the atlas for something more surreal, more suggestive, and more affective.

Scholars in the 1980s and 1990s began to pay more attention to Warburg in part because of Walter Benjamin's interest in him, but also because, like Benjamin's, his talent for montage-like effects was seen as emblematic of the twentieth century. In a way, the *Mnemosyne Atlas* had begun to do in images what Benjamin did a few years later in words with his *Arcades Project*. These projects, as Benjamin wrote, sought to "develop to the highest degree the art of citing without quotation marks." The use of images in conversation with other images (in other words, the use of dialectical images) became one of the standard gestures of the art of the twentieth century. It found powerful expression in works like Tarkovsky's *Mirror* and Gerhard Richter's incessant collection of cutouts, prints, photos, and fragments: the *Atlas Micromega* (1962–2013).

Richter's *Atlas Micromega* runs into hundreds of sheets, of faces, snapshots, mountains, cities, paintings, candles, nudes, landscapes: in short all the material that fed his large-scale pieces. But the *Atlas Micromega* exists also for its own sake: as a testament to what the artist saw, and what he collected, and how he sequenced it. I see a through-line here, from Warburg to Benjamin to Richter, and, finally, to Baltimore artist Dina Kelberman, who makes a long sequence of images and short films she has found on Google and on YouTube. But if one strand of the genealogy of Kelberman's *I'm Google* is indebted to this high-art lineage, another strand is about something else entirely: the kind of "atlasing" that only Google could make possible. This project is involved in the affective language of Warburg (Benjamin writes in the *Arcades Project:* "I needn't say anything. Merely show"). There's a satisfaction for the eye in wordlessly accounting for the link between one image and the one that follows it. It also contains, as in Benjamin, a critique of commodity culture. But Kelberman's project is, in addition, a visual world-building that explicitly sidesteps not only the language of antiquity and classicism but also any suggestion of "artistic" image making. Her choices are brightly colored, plasticky, almost naïve, and straightforwardly vernacular, less Warburg than Walmart.

Kelberman's images are related to each other by a more transparent and less obviously intellectualized logic. By contrast, the deadpan affect of Richter's *Atlas Micromega* is still freighted with a modernist melancholia. Kelberman's images are all found images, discovered by trawling through Google and YouTube, mostly by use of keyword searches, and her selection process excludes images with an intentional artistic intent. In a sense, she has arrived at a goal Richter stated in his *Notes 1964–65:* "I like everything that has no style: dictionaries, photographs, nature, myself and my paintings." But Richter has plenty of style; it is Kelberman whose hand-chosen images, with their impeccable timing and straight-faced absurdity, come close to being styleless.

Indeed, viewers have sometimes assumed that *I'm Google* is simply the result of a very clever computer program, a bot set free on Google Image Search and directed to Tumblr, rather than the selective record of countless hours of looking and sifting. As Kelberman said in an interview, "The blog came out of my natural tendency to spend long hours obsessing over Google Image searches, collecting photos I found beautiful and sorting them by theme." Anyone could do this. The deeper value here is in Kelberman's notion of the beautiful: "The images that interest me are of industrial or municipal materials or everyday photo snapshots." A more automated process—for instance, the one seen in Taryn Simon and Aaron Swartz's conceptually interesting Google-based *Image Atlas* (2012)—feels more limited and less suggestive, and more susceptible to distracting mistakes, in part because of the absence of a curatorial hand. It is worth pointing out that Kelberman's work exploits a strain in Internet art that challenges the viewer to assume it was made by a bot, not an artist: a kind of reverse Turing test.

I'm Google uses the possibilities of Google Image Search in a way quite distinct from what I considered in my essay on Google's Search by Image ("Google's Macchia"). Kelberman has said that she does not find Search by Image particularly helpful for this project. And yet, even in its styleless style, *I'm Google* does explore color patch (macchia) theory, the impact of first impressions. But it goes further, relying on visual as well as semantic similarities, in addition to very careful (and occasionally comic) timing. If classical macchia theory is about the nouns of things, and therefore just the appearances, then Kelberman builds similarities also on the basis of verbs: what sprays, what proliferates, what curls or curves or gleams or effloresces in a particular way. She holds the challenge of similarity to a more stringent standard, and yet out of this stringency, which explores static as well as kinetic interests, one feels she could end up just about anywhere.

The bright color palette, flat affect, shadowless lighting, and industrial obsessions in Kelberman's work—she also makes comic strips, animation, and GIFs, and writes plays—emerge in part from her fascination with Looney Tunes' Chuck Jones and the epiphenomena of *The Simpsons* (how clouds or furniture are rendered in the show; another Kelberman project consists of screenshots of such "nothing" moments from *The Simpsons*).

Kelberman's wonderfully named comic strips, *Important Comics,* are pared down in the extreme, often with simple shapes in place of people, but are emotionally anything but simple. In addition, she has an interest in synesthesia and in the ways that the mind makes links and meaning out of apparently unrelated things. And perhaps, for all the disavowal of classicism, there is also a strong classical idea at the heart of the *I'm Google* project: that of metamorphosis. As in the myths, there's a little jolt of pleasure (or even fascinated horror) at the moment when something begins to turn into something else. Kelberman accomplishes all this by means of a language that contains the gestures of taxonomy without being taxonomic. She builds an ark of "types."

In its list making, it is an update of the atlas of affect at the same time that it is a catalogue of what one might call catalogue realism, a sort of Sears, Roebuck catalogue stripped of labels and released into the wild, a sequence that includes logs, fencing, stadia, spray paint, colored paper, sponges, mugs, dirt, houses on fire, geysers, hoses, phone cords, construction sites, molds, paint, tomato sauce, batter, bread, plastic lids, jungle gyms, balloons, venetian blinds, table fans, scaffolding, greenhouses, kindergarten projects, messy bedrooms, televisions, explosions, liftoff, forest fires, forests, disabled-parking signs, auditoriums, soldering, car washes, surf, sand, powdered paint, string cheese, hair, wigs, clouds, foam, yards, roller coasters, blizzards, squalls, tornadoes, lightbulbs, computer screens, windows, booths, ski lifts, zip lines, watchtowers, waterslides, volcanic lakes, sand castles, team uniforms, group photographs, factory workers, crowds, balloons, mannequins, aquaria, window nets, mosquito nets, tents, canopies, piles, packing foam, gym mattresses, wildfire planes, desert rallies, dough, Play-Doh, hearing aids, earbuds, buoys, plastic bags, Ziploc bags, plastic gloves, palm prints, prosthetic hands, balloons, holders, painted bales of hay, silage wrapping, taffy machines, and more, because the world of things never ends.

Memories of Things Unseen

A T AN EXHIBITION at the FotoMuseum in Antwerp, I walked past a large color photograph of a forest. It was an exhibition about landscape in general, organized to give the visitor the feeling of a hike through mountainous terrain. The photograph of the forest was near the entrance of the exhibition, and I had walked past it without stopping because it seemed to be simply another big photo, of which there are so many in museums these days. But after going through the exhibition, I decided to double back. This time around, I took a good look at the large photograph, which was more than sixteen feet wide, and found that there was more to it than size. The leaves were odd, simplified. I read the caption. What the photograph (titled *Clearing*) showed was not a forest but a model of a forest. The German artist Thomas Demand had constructed this model from paper and set it in a steel frame fifty feet wide. Two hundred and seventy thousand leaves had been individually cut. The model was illuminated by a powerful lamp, to mimic shafts of sunlight falling through the trees.

The immense labor involved in creating *Clearing* was part of what made it now interesting to me. But more eerie was the knowledge that Demand had destroyed the model. All that remained was the photo. It was orphaned from its source, and that source would be remembered by only this one angle, this single point of view, under precisely these lighting conditions. The photograph gave us a memory of something we had never seen. Demand had done this intentionally, but *Clearing* reminded me of other photographs that were inadvertent records of artworks subsequently lost to war or fire. This was the fate, for instance, of Vincent van Gogh's *The Painter on the Road to Tarascon* (1888), which is believed to have been lost to Allied attacks on Magdeburg in 1945, late in the Second World War, and Gustave Courbet's *The Stone Breakers* (1849), which was incinerated during the firebombing of Dresden the same year. Each now exists only as a photograph.

Photography is inescapably a memorial art. It selects, out of the flow of time, a moment to be preserved, with the moments before and after falling away like sheer cliffs. At a dinner party earlier this year, I was in conversation with someone who asked me to define photography. I suggested that it is about retention: not only the ability to make an image directly out of the interaction between light and the tangible world but also the possibility of saving that image. A shadow thrown onto a wall is not photography. But if the wall is photosensitive and the shadow remains after the body has moved on, that is photography. Human creativity, since the beginning of art, has found ways to double the visible world. What photography did was to give the world a way to double its own appearance: the photograph results directly from what is, from the light that travels from a body through an aperture onto a surface.

But when the photograph outlives the body—when people die, scenes change, trees grow or are chopped down—it becomes a memorial. And when the thing photographed is a work of art or architecture that has been destroyed, this effect is amplified even further. A painting, sculpture, or temple, as a record of both human skill and emotion, is already a site of memory; when its only remaining trace is a photograph, that photograph becomes a memorial to a memory. Such a photograph is shadowed by its vanished ancestor.

I visited the Metropolitan Museum in early August 2015, at a time when the destruction of artifacts in Iraq and Syria was prominent in the news, to look at the museum's collection of works from the ancient Middle East. Next to a selection of second- and third-century Syrian gravestones (many of them fresh with the pain of loss and inscribed with the names of the dead and the word "Alas!"), there was an old photograph reproduced from a book of the Temple of Bel, an important archaeological complex in Palmyra. About a week later, the iconoclastic fanatics of ISIS blew up this very temple. The photograph was unchanged; it was still there on the wall of Room 406 at the Met, but it was now filled up with the loss of what it depicted. The Roman-era columns of the temple still stand in rows in the grainy image—ravaged by time, but standing. In life, they're gone.

The Institute for Digital Archaeology, a joint project of Harvard and Oxford Universities, uses sophisticated imaging techniques to aid conservation, epigraphy, archaeology, and art history. One of the institute's current efforts, the Million Image Database project, involves photographing artifacts that are at risk of being destroyed for military or religious reasons, a bleak necessity in a world in which the beauty or importance of an object does not guarantee its safety. The goal of the project is to distribute up to five thousand modified cameras, to professionals and to amateurs, and use them to capture a million 3-D images. Already, more than a thousand cameras have been distributed, and the 3-D data from them are being received (though the directors of the project, to protect their associates on the ground, are leaving a lag of several months before they make the images publicly available). In the event of some of the objects being destroyed, the detailed visual record could be enough to facilitate a reconstruction. Photography is used to ward off total oblivion, the way that the photographs of Courbet's *The Stone Breakers* and Van Gogh's *The Painter on the Road to Tarascon* accidentally made the lost paintings visible to future generations.

But memory has a menacing side. Our own appearances and faces are now stored and saved in hundreds, thousands, of photographs: photographs made by ourselves, photographs made by others. Our faces are becoming not only unforgettable but inescapable. There is so much documentation of each life, each scene and event, that the effect of this incessant visual notation becomes difficult to distinguish from surveillance. And in fact, much of the intent behind the collection of these images is indeed surveillance: the government retains our images in order to fight terrorism, and corporations harvest everything they can about us in order to sell us things.

Little wonder, then, that many people would like to be less visible or wish their visibility to be impermanent or impossible to archive. At the dinner party where I had been asked to define photography, I asked my interlocutor if Snapchat, the photo-sharing app that causes sent images to disappear after a set number of seconds, would technically be considered photography. The conclusion we jointly reached was that it certainly would: what was important was the possibility of retention, not actual retention itself. A technology that simply did not have the ability to save the images it was transmitting would be more revolutionary.

I sent a friend a photograph of my face on Snapchat. She sent me one of hers. I sent a photo of my hotel room, its furniture barely visible in the gloom. She sent me one of her hallway, with its piles of brightly colored shoes. We sent a few texts. Over a poor network connection, we video-chatted for about a minute, discussing Demand's *Clearing*. Afterward, the photographs, texts, and video were gone, leaving no evidence of who had done what, as in a meticulously executed heist. I am more familiar with Instagram, Facebook, and Twitter, where long-finished interactions can be retraced and relived, and the voiding of the record on Snapchat was startling. But it was also a relief. Our real selves remained, but the photographs were no longer there, and something about this felt like a sequence more preferable to the other way around, where the image lives on and the model is irretrievable.

But just as nothing can be permanently retained, nothing is ever really gone. Somewhere out there, perhaps in the Cloud or in some clandestine server, is the optical afterimage of our interaction: the faces, the shoes, the texts. In these all-seeing days, the traffic between memory and forgetting becomes untrackable. Photography is at the nerve center of our paradoxical memorial impulses: we need it there for how it helps us frame our losses, but we can also sense it crowding in on ongoing experience, imposing closure on what should still be open.

Death in the Browser Tab

————————

THERE YOU ARE watching another death on video. In the course of ordinary life—at lunch or in bed, in a car or in the park—you are suddenly plunged into someone else's crisis, someone else's horror. It arrives absurdly, in the midst of banal things. That is how, late one afternoon in April, I watched Walter Scott die. The footage of his death, taken by a passerby, had just been published online on the front page of *The New York Times*. I watched it, sitting at my desk in Brooklyn, and was stunned by it.

A video introduces new elements into the event it records. It can turn a private grief into a public spectacle, and set popular opinion at odds with expert analysis. Within the space of a year, I saw too many such videos. I watched the fatal shooting of twelve-year-old Tamir Rice, who was holding a toy gun in a Cleveland park. I watched a police officer choke a protesting Eric Garner to death. I watched Charly Leundeu Keunang tussle with police officers on a sidewalk in Los Angeles before one of them unloaded six bullets into him. And there was much I could have watched but opted not to: the ISIS beheading videos, the various other clips of deadly violence from around the world. Even so, just from the grim catalogue of what I'd seen, I felt that death had come within too-easy reach, as easy as open-ing up a browser and pressing play. I recognized the political importance of the videos I had seen, but it had also felt like an intrusion when I watched them: intruding on the sorrow of those for whom those deaths were much more significant, but intruding, too, on my own personal but unarticulated sense of right and wrong.

For most of human history, to see someone die, you had to be there. Depictions, if there were any, came later, at a certain remove of time and space. The day after I watched the video of Walter Scott's death, it so happened that I taught my students at Bard about a series of woodcuts by Hans Holbein the Younger. Holbein's woodcuts, designed around 1526 and entitled *Pictures of Death,* showed Death in the form of a skeleton arriving for each of his victims: a nun at prayer, a farmer plowing his field, a pope on his throne, a knight in full armor. Considering these prints made me understand something about videos like those of Walter Scott's death: they are part of a long line of images of the moment of death, an engagement with that mysterious in-stant in which a self becomes permanently unselved.

The first photographs about death did not capture the exact moment of death's arrival. They were postmortem pictures. The genre flowered in the nineteenth century, fostered in part by the technical limitations of photography: the dead don't move, and a portrait of a corpse was easier to make than one of a living person. This was at a time when death still happened at home. The bereaved propped up their beloved dead, dressed them in good clothes, and had them photographed as though they were still alive. But postmortem pictures, with their mel-ancholy grandeur and intimate setting, are different from im-ages that capture the rude shock of sudden death. Robert Capa's

1936 photograph of a Spanish militiaman purports to record such a moment: the militiaman falls backward on a sunlit battlefield, his body accelerating to meet its shadow. The photograph is contested now—was it staged, or was it truly caught, by serendipity and skill, in the heat of battle?—but it is an image that, for its time, is imaginable. It would have been difficult, if not impossible, to make a picture like it a half century earlier. And by thirty-two years later, in a world full of small cameras and quick-loading film, there is no longer any doubt that death can be photographed candidly. On a street in Saigon, the American photojournalist Eddie Adams clicks the shutter and captures the precise moment at which Nguyen Ngoc Loan, a South Vietnamese general, fatally shoots Nguyen Van Lem, a Viet Cong lieutenant, in the head. A second before the bullet hits Lem, his face is relaxed. Then the shot—the gunshot simultaneous with the snapshot—but there's no blood, no splatter, only Lem's face contorted in mortal agony. A second later he's on the ground, with blood gushing out of his head. We know these things because the execution was also captured on film, by Vo Suu, a cameraman for NBC. Suu's professional footage is invaluable, but Adams's picture, more striking and more iconic, earned him a Pulitzer Prize in 1969. The picture was remarkable for the rarity of its achievement in recording the unscripted last moment of someone's life. But when one sees death mediated in this way, pinned down with such dramatic flair, the star is likely to be death itself and not the human who dies. The idea that a photograph exists of a man being shot in the head in Vietnam is easier to remember than Nguyen Van Lem's biography, or even his name.

Having watched the video of Walter Scott's death once, I watched it a second time, in an effort to figure out where exactly it had been made. I was in Columbia, South Carolina, for work, and friends there had driven me to North Charleston. Michael Slager had stopped Scott in the parking lot of Advance Auto Parts on Remount Road, and had asked him some questions there. At some time during the interaction, Scott had fled. Where to? We found the parking lot. I went on foot, taking a left down Craig Road, following the route of the chase, a minute's walk, shorter if one were to run. Below a hand-painted sign for a Mega Pawn shop was a narrow, disused lot with a pale storage building on one side and a row of trees on the other, a scene both derelict and bucolic. At the entrance to the lot were a new chain secured by a new padlock and a bunch of flowers, now drooping, wrapped in plastic and wedged into the chain-link fence. This was the officer's point of view as he steadied himself, raised his .45-caliber Glock 21, and fired eight times at the man running away from him. In the near distance, just to the left of the paved track that bisected the grass, was a small memorial at the spot where Scott fell.

This was not only the scene of a crime. It also made visible certain things that were not apparent in the video: the last view Scott saw, the exit from the lot, the unnerving quietness of the area, the banality of dying in a small lot off a side street in an unremarkable town. But being there also revealed, in the negative, the peculiarities of the video, peculiarities common to many videos of this kind: the combination of a passive affect and a subjective gaze, irregular lighting and poor sound, the amateur videographer's unsteady grip and off-camera swearing. Taken by one person (or a single fixed camera) from one point of view, these videos establish the parameters of any subsequent spectatorship of the event. The information they present is, even when shocking, necessarily incomplete. They mediate, and being on the lot helped me remove that filter of mediation somewhat.

Later that day, back in Columbia, I had dinner with Tony Jarrells, a professor of English literature at the University of South Carolina. Jarrells suggested I read "The Two Drovers," a story by Sir Walter Scott (whose name had come up because of the coincidence). The story, first published in 1827, was about a pair of cattle herders, or drovers, working in the borderlands of England and Scotland. Harry, a Yorkshireman, and Robin, a Highlander, had a dispute about pasturage for their cattle. Harry challenged Robin to a fistfight and, when Robin refused, knocked him down. Robin, in response, walked "seven or eight English miles," got his dirk (a short knife), walked back, and stabbed Harry dead. This was the core of the story, Jarrells suggested to me: the stretch of time over which Robin intended his crime, those hours of premeditation. When there is premeditation—over hours or over a few seconds—the final moment is accompanied by the weight of the moments preceding it, moments necessary to establish that quantum of moral disregard out of which one person kills another. The video from North Charleston seemed to enact this disregard, this voiding of empathy, in seconds that felt like hours, seconds in which the shooter could have stopped and reconsidered, just as the murderous drover Robin could also have stopped and reconsidered, but didn't.

The videographic afterimage of any real event is peculiar. When the event is a homicide, that afterimage can cross over into the uncanny: the sudden, unjust, and irrevocable end of the long story of what one person was, who he loved, all she hoped, all he achieved, all she didn't, becomes available for viewing and reviewing. A month after I went to North Charleston, back in Brooklyn and writing about the shooting, I find a direct approach difficult. I write about Holbein's *Pictures of Death,* and about Robert Capa's photograph and Eddie Adams's. I write about "The Two Drovers," about Robin tramping through the borderlands intent on murder. I write about my morning in North Charleston, the gloomy drive there and back, the wilted flowers on the chain-link fence on Craig Road. If you set enough tangents around a circle, you begin to re-create the shape of the circle itself. Finally, I start to watch footage of Walter Scott's last moments. It's the third time, and it makes me uneasy and unhappy. The video begins with the man holding the camera racing toward the fence. A few seconds later, Walter Scott breaks away from Michael Slager. Slager plants his feet and raises his gun. There is still time. He shoots once, then thrice in quick succession. Scott continues to run. There is still time. That is when I stop the video and exit the browser.

The Unquiet Sky

MUSING OVER A fireplace in Avignon in 1782, the inventor Joseph-Michel Montgolfier had a brain wave. What if the force lifting the embers from the fire could somehow be controlled and used to carry heavier things, even people? It could be a way for Spanish troops to finally take the hitherto impregnable fortress of Gibraltar. Joseph and his brother Étienne immediately set to experimenting with hot air, which they believed had a special property called levity, and by late 1783 Étienne was able to ascend in the Montgolfier balloon.

Joseph's idea for airborne assaults proved impractical. The weight and limited efficacy of munitions in the late eighteenth century, not to mention the ease with which balloons could be downed, delayed that form of combat. But his instinct was correct: human-controlled flight is now inseparable from warfare. The Wright brothers flew their fragile, shaky, and miraculous biplane at Kitty Hawk in 1903. By 1911 an Italian plane was dropping bombs on a Turkish camp in Ain Zara, Libya. War from the air: until the enemy can retaliate, it is an insuperable advantage.

If aviation and militarism had a natural kinship at the beginning of the twentieth century, they entered an uncanny union at the start of the twenty-first. Until 2004 unmanned aerial vehicles (UAVs), or drones, as they're popularly known, were eyes in the sky; like fantastic periscopes, they ushered in new forms of farsightedness. Then, in June of that year, an American UAV fired a missile in South Waziristan. Two children were killed, as were several adults, one of them a mujahid called Nek Muhammad. More strikes followed the next year, and by 2008 the strikes were frequent and the death toll high, in the thousands. The results of the strikes followed the pattern established from the first one: many of the people killed were innocent of wrongdoing.

In the public mind, drones had rightly come to be seen as ominous machines tracking their hapless victims, harbingers of sudden death. But drones are gaining other, no less accurate meanings. They can be any size, and they can resemble planes or helicopters, or both, or neither. Someday they could deliver our packages or even come to play a role in commuter transportation. But the key expansion in the public understanding of drones is in the realm of popular photography.

A view from a great height is irresistible. It is twinned with the ancient dream of flight. For millennia, we have imaginatively soared above our material circumstances and dramatized this desire in tales from Icarus to Superman. Things look different from way up there. What was invisible before becomes visible: how one part of the landscape relates to another, how nature and infrastructure unfold. But with the acquisition of this panoptic view comes the loss of much that could be seen at close range. The face of the beloved is but one invisible detail among many.

When the French photographer Nadar leaned out of a hotair balloon in 1858 and made a series of images of Paris, it was the beginning of a new age. Our eyes were carried aloft. Cities began to appear in photographic portraits that echoed maps, but with all the latest and truest information included. In 1860 James Wallace Black and Samuel Archer King made *Boston, as the Eagle and Wild Goose See It*. And in 1906 George R. Lawrence, deploying a complicated rig of kites, created enormous photographic panoramas of San Francisco right after the earthquake. Lawrence's photographs gave the traumatized city a measure of its catastrophe. Three years later Wilbur Wright piloted the plane from which the first moving picture was shot. In the century that followed, aerial photography was used in archaeology, advertising, surveillance, and mapping. This precipitous rate of innovation also resulted in the technology that allows drones to fix their stares on those we deem enemies. And, higher up, satellites and geolocating devices have transformed our sense of the world itself.

My parents live in Lagos, Nigeria. Sometimes, when I miss them or miss home, I go to Google Maps and trace the highway that leads from Lagos Island to our family's house in the northern part of the city. I find our street amid the complicated jumble of brown lines just east of the bus terminal. I can make out the shape of the house, the tree in front of it, the surrounding fence. I hover there, "visiting" home.

The slippage between the domestic and the threatening aspects of aerial surveillance is something the photographer Tomas van Houtryve has explored in his powerful project *Blue Sky Days*. The title comes from the testimony of a thirteen-year-old Pakistani boy whose grandmother was killed in a drone strike. "I no longer love blue skies," the boy said, speaking before Congress. "In fact, I now prefer gray skies. The drones do not fly when the skies are gray." Houtryve attached a camera to a small drone and traveled around the United States, making aerial photographs of the sorts of events that have been associated with intentional or erroneous drone strikes: funerals, weddings, groups of people at play, in prayer, or during exercise. His images show Americans in the course of their daily lives, photographed from a great height, in bright sun that throws their distorted shadows far ahead of them, presenting them as unindividuated, vulnerable, and human. Houtryve makes it clear that the people in Yemen, Pakistan, Somalia, or Afghanistan who are killed by American drones are also just like this. With simple, vivid means, Houtryve brings the war home.

Houtryve's work has been published in magazines and, meticulously printed in large format, displayed in galleries. But there are other photographs made by or about drones that you encounter almost solely online. Two of these projects, very different from each other in effect and intent, happen to have settled on an identical name: Dronestagram. One, hosted at the website www.dronestagr.am, invites submissions from aerial-photography enthusiasts who are using small, commercially available or homemade drones to take photos or make videos. The site runs a photography contest, sponsored in part by *National Geographic,* and the winning images tend to be pretty, brightly colored landscapes of the kind that might end up on calendars or in tourist brochures. Photoshopped, wide-angled, and hectically spectacular, the photos are popular, garnering thousands of likes. But mostly they lack the element of formal provocation or conceptual rupture on which memorable images depend.

The other project that shares the name Dronestagram was created a little earlier, in 2012, by the computer artist James Bridle. He scours the news media for information about drone strikes and presents those events in capsule written form, accompanying them with a Google satellite image of the location or vicinity of the strike. In Bridle's project, which he presents on Twitter, Tumblr, and Instagram, we see a landscape directly from above, with buildings visible in plan form, set in brown or green surroundings. These are places where people died, whether they were suspected terrorists or bystanders. The images—sober, descriptive, clinical—are undramatic and sufficient. They make explicit the continuity between reconnaissance and attack and also embed the grim promise that it's not over. There are more strikes to come.

The two Dronestagrams, the sanguine and the melancholic, add to our ever-increasing archive of possible landscapes. Imagine all those pictures stitched together into a single image. In this ideal aerial view, neither the pervasive violence nor the sometimes cloying prettiness would be visible. Conquest and sentimentality would both be irrelevant. In other words, the image might be like the "blue marble" photograph of Earth, taken from the *Apollo 17* spacecraft in 1972. It is our world, serene and self-contained, seen in one glance. It is not a view that excites us into plans for bombing our enemies, for it includes us as well. It is a view that reminds us of how mighty we are, how fragile, how delicately connected, and how beautiful.

Against Neutrality

THE PHOTOGRAPH AND the words arrive simultaneously. They guarantee each other. You believe the words more because the photograph verifies them, and trust the photograph because you trust the words. Additionally, each puts further pressure on the interpretation: a war photograph can, for example, make a grim situation palatable, just as a story about a scandal can make the politician depicted look pathetic. But images, unlike words, are often presumed to be unbiased. The facticity of a photograph can conceal the craftiness of its content and selection.

This is why I noticed a tweet by John Edwin Mason, a historian of photography: "Another reminder that manipulation in photography isn't really about Photoshop or darkroom tricks." Embedded below this line was another tweet, which contained the photograph of a young woman. She was blond and wore a scoop-neck black sweater over a white blouse. Her eyes looked off to the side. The photograph was black and white, reminiscent of old Hollywood headshots. There was a link to an article at *Foreign Policy*'s website, and the subject of both the article and the photograph was Marion Maréchal–Le Pen, a twenty-six-year-old French politician and rising star of the far-right Front National. Maréchal–Le Pen is the granddaughter of the enthu-

siastically racist Jean-Marie Le Pen, co-founder of the Front
National. She has been careful not to sound too much like her
grandfather, but she remains closely associated with his nativist
priorities and xenophobic vision. She holds, for instance, the
charming view that Muslims in France should not be allowed to
have the same "rank" as Catholics. In a France gripped by anti-
immigrant fears in the wake of terrorist attacks, Maréchal–Le
Pen and the Front National have had obvious appeal and increased political success.

What kind of communication happens when a sympathetic
photograph is used to profile a figure like Maréchal–Le Pen? I
asked Mason what he meant by "manipulation" in his tweet.
"The style of photography is instantly recognizable as that of a
celebrity profile," he replied. "It's inviting us to identify with
the subject and see the subject as attractive and desirable. If you
wanted to glamorize young [Maréchal–]Le Pen, you'd pick precisely this photo." Benjamin Pauker, the executive editor of *Foreign Policy,* sees nothing untoward in the image (by the
photographer Joel Saget), and he objected to the idea that it
was in some way glamorous. But it was hard not to contrast
Saget's image, which appeared on the home page, with another,
by Patrick Aventurier, that accompanied the full text of the
piece. Aventurier's photograph is in color, and it shows
Maréchal–Le Pen on the podium, at a distance, with several
other people, and with French flags in the foreground and background. This photograph, by emphasizing Maréchal–Le Pen's
political role as well as her nationalism, sends a clearly different
message.

The right image to use with a written piece: it's an old worry,
relevant to portraiture, but argued about much more with regard to war photography. The question has been taken up again

by the writer David Shields, in his recent book *War Is Beautiful: The New York Times Pictorial Guide to the Glamour of Armed Conflict*. Shields believes that *The New York Times,* in particular, "glorified war through an unrelenting parade of beautiful images." He selected sixty-four photos from the thousands that ran on page A1 of the *Times* between 2002 and 2013 and arranged them into ten brief chapters under titles like "Playground," "Father," "God," and "Pietà."

The book includes a number of crepuscular or otherwise moodily colored scenes of choppers and trucks that could be outtakes from *Apocalypse Now*. But we also see a navy doctor cradling an Iraqi orphan, President George W. Bush meeting U.S. troops in Qatar, the blasted landscape of an Iraqi city, an imam blessing a newborn in Brooklyn, a grief-stricken Palestinian man carrying a boy killed during a protest, and a dead Iraqi soldier lying in the dust. Are these sixty-four photos, some of which are not war pictures at all, representative of *The New York Times'* coverage over the decade in question? Even on the evidence Shields presents, the *Times* has published some great images, some less great ones, some that could be read as antiwar and some that could be read as pro-war propaganda. Imagine looking at a pile of thousands of photographs taken over many years by a wide range of photojournalists: you would be able to select sixty-four to suit just about any argument.

An image depends radically on context, on how it is placed but also on who is looking at it. Susan Sontag observed: "The frankest representations of war, and of disaster-injured bodies, are of those who seem most foreign, therefore least likely to be known. With subjects closer to home, the photographer is expected to be more discreet." American journalism, *The New York Times* included, remains in thrall to this expectation, an expectation that is ripe for sustained and perceptive critique. But *War Is Beautiful* is not that critique. It feels instead like a missed opportunity, and it made me return to other recent projects that have addressed related questions more incisively.

Disco Night Sept. 11 (2014), by the photojournalist Peter van Agtmael, is not as high-concept as Shields's book. In fact, it is not conceptual at all. It is simply a courageous record of recent American wars by a photojournalist who made repeated trips to dangerous outposts in Afghanistan and Iraq, but who also visited injured and bewildered American veterans in places like Wisconsin and Texas. Van Agtmael captions most of the photos with a paragraph or so of reportage, and his captions are no less resonant than his uncannily crisp, dreamlike photos. A typical image is one taken in 2009 in Helmand Province, Afghanistan. Against a pale brown desertified landscape, seven soldiers are seen sweeping the ground for improvised explosive devices. Each man is separated from the others by a few paces. They are working together, but each is alone, and at this distance and from this height (it is hard to tell if the photographer is in a helicopter or on a rise), the men look like toy soldiers. They search, and they find nothing. Minutes later, there's an explosion. *Disco Night Sept. 11,* which presents many images from the moments just before something terrible happens or, even more vividly, from the years of aftermath, conveys the madness, confusion, theatricality, and ironies of war. It made me think what any book about war photography should: Just what the hell is going on here?

A very different project is *War Primer 2* (2011), by the artists Adam Broomberg and Oliver Chanarin. Like Shields, Broomberg and Chanarin make use of appropriated imagery. In their case, it is actually an appropriation of an appropriation: *War*

Primer 2 is based on Bertolt Brecht's *Kriegsfibel* (*War Primer,* 1955), a book of press photographs, largely culled from newspapers and magazines from the previous decades, that Brecht captioned with bitter, poetic quatrains.

For their update, Broomberg and Chanarin have pasted photographs associated with the Global War on Terrorism, downloaded from the Internet, into Brecht's book, layering them directly onto his original images. The new photos, as visceral, graphic, and sometimes plainly horrific as the old ones, include scenes of the tortures at Abu Ghraib, Saddam Hussein's execution, the White House during the mission to assassinate Osama bin Laden, and George W. Bush serving soldiers at Thanksgiving. Alongside Brecht's lines, the images become an uncanny indictment of American conduct in these recent wars, but also a lament about the evil of war in general.

The camera is an instrument of transformation. It can make what it sees more beautiful, more gruesome, milder, darker, all the while insisting on the plain reality of its depiction. This is what Brecht meant in 1931 when he wrote, "The camera is just as capable of lying as the typewriter." What then are we to do with this devious tool? One option is to resist the depiction of violence, to side with the reader who protests an unpleasant photograph and defends the bounds of good taste. But another—and to me, better—option is to understand that the problem is not one of too many unsettling images but of too few. When the tragedy or suffering of only certain people in certain places is made visible, the boundaries of good taste are not really transgressed at all. "We all have strength enough to bear the misfortunes of others," La Rochefoucauld wrote. What is hard is being vividly immersed in our own pain. We ought to see what actually happens to American bodies in situations of war or mass violence, whether at the moment they happen, as Broomberg and Chanarin show us, or in the wake of the violence, as presented in van Agtmael's book. We must not turn away from what that kind of suffering looks like when visited on "us." Photojournalism relating to war, prejudice, hatred, and violence pursues a blinkered neutrality at the expense of real fairness. (Domestically, this manifests as a tolerance for black suffering that would not be extended to white suffering; the proliferation of videos of black people being killed by police, for example.) All too often in our media, the words take us all the way there, but the photographs, habituated to a certain safety, hold back.

SECTION III

Being There

Far Away from Here

O NLY A FEW slender strings were attached: two public readings and a commitment to spend the majority of the six months in the country. Beyond that, I would be left to my own devices. An apartment would be provided, and a stipend. I didn't think about it for very long. I wrote back: yes.

The invitation had come from the Literaturhaus in Zürich, one of those wonderful arts institutions of which Europe seems to have so many. Every six months they selected one writer, from anywhere in the world, to stay in the apartment they ran with a foundation. When I received the invitation, I felt as though I'd won a raffle I didn't even know I had a ticket for.

Switzerland: the place comes with an easy set of mental associations. But I suspected there was more to it than its reputation for calendar-pretty landscapes, secretive bankers, and regular trains, and here was a chance to see for myself. Besides, I had a manuscript to work on, a nonfictional narrative of Lagos, Nigeria, the city in which I grew up. Where better to write about chaotic, relentless, overpopulated Lagos than in modest, quietly industrious Zürich? There would be so little else to do in Switzerland anyway (according to my less-than-enthusiastic friends) that I would be mainly absorbed in writing during my time there. Perhaps I might even continue my photographic exploration of landscape and memory, a project that comprised images from many countries I had visited over the past few years.

I arrived in June. The apartment was in a peaceful neighborhood of the compact and elegant city. The writing desk faced a row of windows, and there were mountains in the distance. I grew up mountainless, close to the lagoon and the sea, in a city where the only heights were high-rises. I was familiar with the extremes of city life: the crowds, the traffic, the energy, the crime. But nature's extremes, of violent weather or vertiginous terrain, were unknown to me. Those mountains, visible from my desk, were faint and blue in the distance, not particularly imposing. But already they beckoned.

I had taken a good camera to Zürich with me, a professional-grade Canon. There was a subtle problem with it that I often encounter in digital cameras: they are fine for bright landscapes, but they tend to struggle with highlights and the resulting images sometimes have a plastic sheen. The Canon had served me well on a recent trip to Palestine, but it wasn't working in Switzerland. I had also brought along a film camera, a beautiful Contax G2 range finder. But that wasn't working either: it didn't give me the focusing control I wanted, and I missed the momentary darkening of the visual field when I pressed the shutter, which is something you get with the flipped mirror of an SLR but not in a range finder. The iPhone 5 camera, meanwhile, which I don't rule out as a tool, wasn't going to give me the detail I needed for the prints I had in mind.

What I wanted was an SLR film camera. Sure, there was the cluttered cabinet in my New York City apartment with its eight cameras and their various lenses and filters: the Hasselblad, the Nikon, the Leica, a couple of other Canons, some cameras I hadn't touched in years. Each sat there, the physical evidence of some previous fervor. Nevertheless, the heart wants what it wants, and, about a week after arriving in Zürich, I bought an old Yashica and two lenses from a dealer near the Hauptbahnhof, for the very low and un-Swiss price of twenty-five Swiss francs, just a little over twenty-five dollars.

I loved that Yashica. During my six months in Zürich, I wrote a bit about Lagos and did a bit of other writing. But I stumbled into a surprise: the majority of my time went into traveling around Switzerland taking photographs, in all weather and at all elevations, thinking with my eyes about the country around me. The drama in these landscapes was real, and seemed almost to demand a response from the viewer.

August 2014. I'm on the Gemmipass, 2,770 meters above sea level and 670 meters above the town of Leukerbad. James Baldwin wintered in Leukerbad in the 1950s. Later he would write, "From all available evidence no black man had ever set foot in this tiny Swiss village before I came." The Gemmipass is a high mountain pass that connects mountains in the canton of Valais with those in the canton of Bern. I'm hunched over the tripod, pressing the shutter every few seconds. The weather has suddenly turned. Is this rain? Fog? I wipe the lens clean. Not only am I the only black man on the pass just now, I am the only human being of any kind. It's just me and the lake, the surrounding mountains, the rocks nearby, and some signs on the hiking trail. I have the wrong shoes on, and my jacket is not waterproof. I clamber over some hillocks so that I see the reverse of a yellow trail sign, the side on which there's no writing. The rocks on the mountain face are a beautiful scatter. The mist goes as it came, without warning. I put another roll of film in the Yashica and keep shooting.

A photo essay on London must have the Houses of Parliament or, at least, a red phone box, and one on Paris must include the Eiffel Tower. Rio de Janeiro is the statue of Cristo Redentor. Entire countries are reduced to their metonyms. Kenya is a safari, Norway is fjords. And Switzerland is mountains. This is an exaggeration, but the truth in it is worth thinking about: it is a country built largely in the lee of the Alps, the towns and cities formed from old human migrations that came to rest in valleys, on lakeshores, and, sometimes, in higher regions. I had a notion: if I could understand the mountains, I could understand the country.

The Alps, Europe's arching spine, have often been the obstacle to cross between one part of the continent and another. Hannibal's charge in 218 B.C. from Spain to Italy was celebrated even in antiquity and would later serve as a point of comparison for Charlemagne and Napoléon. During the Renaissance and Baroque periods, many Northern European artists went to Venice and Rome, via arduous Alpine crossings, returning home changed by the art they had seen. Dürer was obsessed by the canon of human proportions, Frans Floris took on a Michelangelesque vigor, Rubens imitated Titian, and, in the seventeenth century, the Dutch Caravaggisti plunged their styles into deep shadow and dramatic light.

But for Pieter Bruegel the Elder, who traveled to Italy in the 1550s, the major change in his art—which was unclassical before his trip to Rome and which remained unclassical after—was due to the Alps. He became a virtuoso of vertical landscapes, which were utterly alien to his native Brabant. His biographer, Karel van Mander, wrote, in 1604: "When Bruegel was in the Alps, he swallowed all the mountains and rocks and spat them out again, after his return, onto his canvases and panels." Bruegel's work was important for the development of independent landscapes: landscapes that did not need the pretext of a mythological or biblical event.

A few centuries later, the limitations of the daguerreotype meant that cityscapes and landscapes were among the earliest photographic subjects. In 1849 the great art critic and social reformer John Ruskin made what are believed to be the first photographs of the Alps. This was the age of firsts: the first photograph containing a human being, the first photographic self-portrait, the first aerial photograph, the first news photo (it showed a man being arrested). You couldn't have your photograph taken in 1825, but by 1845 there were thousands of photos, of people, things, and places. Light from the world could be fixed on a surface: it was possible to take the shadow away from the body and show it elsewhere.

There had been a powerful tradition of Alpine painting, connected both to the Romantic tradition and to scientific study. But photography made the Alps newly portable. For Ruskin, they were such a staggering geological fact that he visited Switzerland repeatedly, describing what he saw with intense drawings, photographs, and words: "There is indeed an appearance of action and united movement in these crested masses, nearly resembling that of sea waves; . . . they seem not to be heaped up, but to leap or toss themselves up; and in doing so, to wreathe and twist their summits into the most fantastic, yet harmonious, curves, governed by some grand under-sweep like that of a tide running through the whole body of the mountain chain."

Others took their enthusiasm for the Alps in a more athletic direction. Some well-known mountains had already been climbed, but from the nineteenth century onward, at a greater rate than ever, the first ascents of dozens of major peaks were recorded. The first ascent of the Dufourspitze was in 1855, the Eiger's in 1858, the Matterhorn's in 1865. The ascent of the Dom, on September 11, 1858, is typical in its details: the climber was the Reverend John Llewelyn-Davies, a Cambridge-educated classicist and prominent vicar, with the help of three Swiss guides. These were difficult undertakings, and the risk involved was sufficient, in the words of one commentator, to "lend climbing the dignity of danger."

Between 1863 and 1868, a photographer named William England produced a series of views of Switzerland and Savoy, showing lakes, roads, valleys, and mountains, work he carried out under the auspices of the Alpine Club of London. And the Italian photographer and mountaineer Vittorio Sella produced, in the 1880s and '90s, some of the most beautiful photographs ever made of the Alps, photos that later inspired in Ansel Adams "a definitely religious awe." Working near the end of the nineteenth century, with a heavy glass-plate camera, Sella captured the cold and awesome power of the Alps with an accuracy and descriptive sensitivity that has hardly been improved on.

All the while, leisure travel itself was changing. The publishing house established by Karl Baedeker in Germany issued *The Rhine,* one of its first travel books, in 1861. Not long after that came *Switzerland.* Informed about the best rails and trails, the most reliable hotels, and advice on local customs, an intrepid traveler could experience foreign lands without an entourage or local contacts. The Baedeker guides are tart and direct. Swiss hotels are praised: "Switzerland may be said to have a specialty for hotels; few better are to be met with in any part of the world." Swiss wine is condemned: "Wine is generally a source of much vexation. The ordinary table wines are often so bad that refuge has to be taken in those of a more expensive class, which is indeed the very aim and object of the landlord." But throughout Baedeker's *Switzerland,* over the hundreds of pages, what impresses is the attention to detail, the almost microscopic precision with which each itinerary, town, museum, mountain range, and hike is described.

Baedeker was already able to state, in that early guide to Switzerland, that places like the Rigi, the Brünig, and the Scheideck were on "beaten tracks." By the 1880s Switzerland was estimated to be receiving a million visitors a year. Travelers tend to go where other travelers have gone, and perhaps this is part of the reason travel photography remains in thrall to the typical. When you do visit Zürich or Cape Town or Bangkok, they are very much alike: the amusement parks have striking similarities, the cafés all play the same Brazilian music, the malls are interchangeable, kids on the school buses resemble one another, and the interiors of middle-class homes conform to the same parameters.

This doesn't mean the world is uninteresting. It only means that the world is more uniform than most photo essays acknowledge, and that a lot of travel photography relies on an easy essentialism. I like Italo Calvino's idea of "continuous cities," as described in the novel *Invisible Cities.* He suggests that there is actually just one big, continuous city that does not begin or end: "Only the name of the airport changes." What is then interesting is to find, in that continuity, the less obvious differences of texture: the signs, the markings, the assemblages, the things hiding in plain sight in each cityscape or landscape. This is what outstanding photographers are able to do, and it is the target the rest of us chase.

The question I confronted in Switzerland is similar to that

confronted by any camera-toting visitor in a great landscape: Can my photograph convey an experience that others have already captured so well? The answer is almost always no, but you try anyway. I might feel myself to be a singular traveler, but I am in fact part of a great endless horde. In the 1870s, Mark Twain was already complaining: "Now everybody goes everywhere; and Switzerland, and many other regions which were unvisited and unknown remotenesses a hundred years ago, are in our days a buzzing hive of restless strangers."

I went up many mountains in Switzerland, often jettisoning the dignity of danger for the luxury of cable cars, and took many pictures of slopes and summits. I suppose I knew, even then, that those photos would not necessarily play a central role in my project. I considered them, instead, small installments on a debt to beauty, a relief from having to be original. But beyond the mountains (this became gradually clear) lay smaller quarry: ordinary land, cityscapes, interiors. Having opened myself to the sublime experience of the Alps, it was to these I turned as I got deeper into my project. The Alps were the door, but what lay beyond, or below?

Switzerland isn't a huge country. It is about a third the size of Alabama. I traveled all over it, and I did not tire of it, was not bored even for a moment. I went to the Bernese Oberland and Interlaken, to Graubünden in the east, to Valais in the south, to Ticino in the southeast, to Geneva, Neuchâtel, Basel, Bern, Vals. I took trains, trams, funiculars, ferries, cable cars, buses. I walked and hiked, the camera always around my neck, the tripod on my shoulder. I went to crowded places and bare ones, to nightclubs and graveyards. The country is sane, clean, expensive, and saturated with a straightforward, unironic, and inexhaustible beauty. A couple of months into the residency, I was in a mesmerized state.

Lake Zürich, bigger than expected and as clean and graceful as the city whose name it shares, is described by Baedeker as follows: "Its scenery, though with slight pretensions to grandeur, is scarcely equaled in beauty by any other lake." But I found Lake Zürich's equal at Lake Brienz, which in summer is a turquoise color of hypnotic clarity and is ringed by steep green cliffs, which, in winter, threaten the small villages along the shore with avalanches. In fact, the problem I encountered was that each lake in Switzerland was the most beautiful, if it happened to be the one you were on.

Lake Geneva feels fully enfolded into civilization and has the air of the grand hotels from the 1950s. Lake Neuchâtel is compact, with fine vineyards nearby that make you think of France. Lake Lugano is warm and joyful, a page taken from the Mediterranean, and it slyly extends into Italy. Lake St. Moritz, Lake Silvaplana, and Lake Sils are pure and clear, the elongated splatter of the three of them visible from the mountains of the Upper Engadine as clearly as on a map. Lake Lucerne—the Vierwaldstättersee, the Four Forested-Cantons Lake—is the most mysterious of them all, a fjordlike lake, full of fog and silhouettes, inlets and outcroppings, and an extremely complicated coastline that spreads, as the name says, across four cantons. In the mountains and towns around all these lakes, days pass by like the hours of a dream. Travel, mountains, and photography lock together in dream logic.

But ambition always comes to darken your serenity. Technically proficient mountain pictures were good, but I also had to develop my own voice. In photography, as in writing, there's no shortcut to finding that voice. I could not decide ahead of time that I would take only ugly pictures or only beautiful ones, or that everything would be in focus or blurred, or that I would use only color or only black and white. I had been thinking about landscape, I had been exploring color film for a few years, I was drawn to abstraction, and a certain gentle surrealism to be found in the attitude of objects. But there then followed a situational focus, a sensitivity to what the environment gave me.

Out of this focus, many pictures emerged, most of which didn't quite work. But I also started to intuit my ley lines. As I shot more and more, I saw that I was drawn to signs, to mirrors in the landscapes (in Switzerland, there are rectangular mirrors at many street crossings, which frame the landscape behind you above the one you are facing), to maps and globes, to mountains as well as to pictures of the mountains on billboards and posters. I noticed—proof perhaps that we cannot help thinking of mountains photographically, the way we cannot help thinking of explosions cinematically—that some of my photographs of mountains looked like photographs of photographs of mountains. I was drawn to this shimmering partition between things and the images of things.

I became less interested in populating my images and more interested in traces of the human without human presence. I used deep shadows less frequently than I had in the past. I pretty much ceased nocturnal shooting. As the sequence began to take shape, I got a better sense of what belonged and what didn't. I was studying photographs constantly, but I also immersed myself in the rhythms of certain painters and collagists: Chardin, Matisse, Rauschenberg, Mehretu, Mutu. I let go of some "good" photos, the way you strike out pretty sentences from a draft, and I learned how a number of tightly argued photos should be followed by one or two that are simpler and more ventilated. Authorship, after all, is not only what is created but also what is selected.

Along the way, I felt the constant company of doubt: my lack of talent, my impostor's syndrome, my fear of boring others. Every once in a great while, there was finally a superb picture, but when I looked at it the following week, I would see that it actually wasn't very good: too obvious, too derivative. Three thousand photographs and three thousand doubts.

November 2014. Past the town of Paradiso, I come to Lugano proper and walk along the waterfront for a while. Then I see the cultural center, an angular building with a green wing cantilevered off a pair of red-brick walls. Behind are the windows of an off-white neoclassical building. In the middle distance is some construction material. On the lawn in the foreground are a bronze horse, a red bench, and a bush with orange flowers. Certain photographs contain notes that are unexpected but, brought together, poignant. I sense the tension created by the disparate elements of the scene before me. Fitting these unfamiliar notes into a single frame creates a strange new chord. But what does it mean? What it looks like is what it means.

The German word for homesickness is "heimweh." Legend has it that Swiss mercenaries from the fifteenth century onward, dispersed throughout Europe to fight foreign wars, were hardy soldiers susceptible to few weaknesses. But they missed home with a deranging intensity, longing for the high elevation of their cantons, their clear lakes, their protective peaks. This feeling they called, in their Swiss German, heimweh. The intense psychosomatic disorder was first treated in 1688 by a physician in Switzerland, Johannes Hofer, who also gave it the Greek name "nostalgia." It entered the English language in the late eighteenth century as "homesickness."

Heimweh, having been absorbed into standard German, acquired an antonym, fernweh. Fernweh is a longing to be away from home, a desire to be in faraway places. Fernweh is similar to wanderlust but, like heimweh, has a sickish, melancholy tinge. Wanderlust is rooted in the German Romantic tradition and is strongly tied to walking out in nature. Think of Caspar David Friedrich's paintings of a lone hiker in spectacular landscapes, communing with the overwhelming greatness and intricacy of nature. Fernweh is a bit more imprecise. One simply wishes to be far away. Fernweh: the syllables sigh.

"Think of the long trip home. / Should we have stayed at home and thought of here?" I've always loved Elizabeth Bishop's poem "Questions of Travel." With plain description, she presents the traveler's predicament. The poem continues: "What childishness is it that while there's a breath of life / in our bodies, we are determined to rush / to see the sun the other way around?"

I recognize myself in the childish rush that Bishop describes. It is connected to a willingness to reconsider what counts as home. The term "at home" describes both a location and a state of being. You can stay at home or feel at home, and often those two notions coincide. But what about when they don't?

I never felt Swiss. I never felt like moving to Switzerland. The appeal was all in the awayness of it, the estrangement that one could count on. And that's just the thing with fernweh: the cure and the disease are one and the same. Fernweh is the silver lining of melancholia around the cloud of happiness about being far from home. I wasn't homesick for Switzerland; I was homesick for the feeling of being far away that Switzerland elicited in me. While I was there, I didn't follow Swiss politics closely. I read some history but not a whole lot. My German remained poor, as did my French. My Italian was worse than poor, and I was not tempted to learn Romansch, Switzerland's fourth official language. Had I got into any trouble with the law, I wouldn't have known what to do. I was most at home in Switzerland precisely because I wasn't. It made me happy because it couldn't.

I remembered that James Salter, who was fond of Switzerland and its hotels, went to interview Vladimir Nabokov in 1975. Nabokov had by then been living for many years at the Montreux Palace Hotel, on the shore of Lake Geneva. I cherish both of these writers. One thing they have in common is a mastery in describing light in particular and optical phenomena in general; another is their inclination to evoke in-between states: drowsing, dreams, epiphanies, hallucinations. Both qualities, I think now, must be connected in some way with their appreciation of the in-betweenness of Switzerland. They loved this landlocked country of valleys and slopes, with its proliferation of odd hotels, its biggest languages shared with bigger neighbors, its neutral and independent international politics, its utopian but insular domestic politics, its extraordinary architects, its love of luxury and careful finishing. Switzerland is in-between but not average, a periphery in a central location, in this world but not of it.

"Should we have stayed at home and thought of here?" But to have merely thought of here would not have revealed its subtle peculiarities, the peculiarities that are not written in guidebooks. Only direct observation can reveal those. The way streetlights and traffic signs vary, the most common fonts, the slight variations in building codes, the fleeting culture of ads (different in each place, even when the company is a multinational), the noticeable shift in the range of hues that people wear in a given city, the visual melody of infrastructure as it interacts with terrain.

November 2014. The balletic glide of trams up and down Bahnhofstrasse, which connects the central train station with Paradeplatz, the elegant center of the Swiss banking industry. What terrible things are the bankers up to today? Don't ask, and no one will tell. At street level on Paradeplatz are fashion boutiques, luxury-watch dealers, and famous chocolatiers. I disembark from a tram. There is construction on a shop front. There is a man on a ladder and another holding it steady at the base. I'm taking pictures but I know I'm getting nothing. Then I turn around: the tram, the cutout ads for pralines and truffles along its top, and behind them, the rows of windows set into the pale-colored stone of what is probably a bank's building. Why do I like this picture? In part because of what it means, the way it compresses into one image three Swiss clichés: a bank, chocolates, and an efficient tram. But also because of how it looks: like a language that I simply don't know yet, a new cuneiform of the street.

By the time I leave at the end of November, I have shot and developed more than eighty rolls of film. Back in New York, I examine what I have: almost enough for a book, but not quite. I begin to plan a trip back to Switzerland: I want to revisit Basel and Zürich. And how can I leave out St. Moritz or Sils Maria? I long for these places as though I were a doppelgänger of those long-ago mercenaries. Just a few more days, a few hundred more photographs, and out of the whole pile of thousands, I'll be able to select the eighty that will go in my book. Fernweh: a sickness, a longing to swallow up the Alps or to be swallowed by them.

July 2015. Late afternoon. A hotel room in Zürich. I've been out shooting all day and have made no good pictures. I remove my lens cap. I'm shooting with a Canon Elan 7 now, a lovely lightweight film SLR from around 2000. I pivot the camera on its tripod. Covering the front of the freestanding wardrobe in the room is a picture of a ship on a lake, beyond which are mountains. You could wake up suddenly at night in this room and, seeing that lake dimly lit by a streetlight, imagine yourself afloat: the slightly vertiginous thrill of being nobody, poised in perfect balance with the satisfaction of having, for that moment, a room of your own.

I face the wardrobe. I open the windows behind me and increase the camera's exposure setting slightly. A black lamp, gray striped wallpaper, the wardrobe, a foldable luggage rack, black light switches, a brazen handle on a black door. Arrayed like that, they look like an illustration in a child's encyclopedia. This is a door. This is a ship. This is a lake. This is a mountain. This is a room to which you long to be away, a room redolent of fernweh. This is a man in a room, crouched behind the camera, readying his shot, far away from home, not completely happy, but happier perhaps than he would be elsewhere.

Home Strange Home

IN NOVEMBER 1975, when I was five months old, my mother took me home from America to Nigeria. My father completed his MBA and joined us a few months later. Growing up in Lagos, I began to invent memories of my place of birth, the small college town of Kalamazoo, Michigan. There was evidence in the form of photographs from those first months, and I had my American passport (pine green in color), a squeaky rubber puppy I'd played with in the cradle, and stories from my parents. I convinced myself that I could remember our one-bedroom apartment, on Howard Street. I even had a memory of the room at Borgess Hospital: it was just after five in the afternoon, and some Nigerian friends of my parents were there. I was born by cesarean section. The nurse pronounced me a "gorgeous Borgess baby."

In Lagos, I was a regular middle-class Nigerian kid. My first language was Yoruba, and I had Nigerian citizenship from birth. Yet I was also an American, the only one in the family—a fact and a privilege that my parents often alluded to. I didn't dwell on it. I tried to wear it as easily as I could, like someone who is third in line to the throne: aware of extravagant possibilities but not counting on any particular outcome. From the age of ten or eleven, when political arguments with other boys at school became a part of life, I took the side of America. When classmates insisted that the Russians had a superior nuclear arsenal, I pitied them their nonsense. During the Olympics, I rooted for the USA, Nigeria being unlikely to win anything anyway. And at home my father spoke of NASA and Silicon Valley as though they were natural future steps in my progress.

In the 1980s, Nigeria went from being the hope of Africa to being a poor and perpetually tense place. Inflation dragged most Nigerians into poverty. In 1990, in Liberia, the dictator Samuel Doe was tortured and killed, and a horrifying civil war began in that country. Who was to say that Nigeria wouldn't go the way of its West African neighbor? "If that happens," my parents said, almost in unison, "we'll just drop you off at the American Embassy. You will be airlifted from there. Americans never abandon their own."

My parents meant this seriously. I loved their insouciance about it, and rehearsed the scenario in my mind: Nigeria in flames, my parents handing me over through the embassy gates, me in a helicopter rising over Lagos. Later, I would find a way to return and save my trapped family. The American passport (renewed, and by this time a dark blue) was the ultimate get-out-of-jail card.

War never came. We faced a slower disaster: a corrupt ruling class, crumbling institutions, armed robberies, bad universities, despair. When I graduated from high school, my parents gathered up their savings and decided to send me to college in the United States. We considered various places, but I was destined to end up in the one town they knew and trusted: Kalamazoo. I arrived in the fall of 1992, and for the first two weeks I couldn't understand the language, which seemed to be an accelerated version of English, with bizarrely flattened vowels.

"Mop" was pronounced "map"; "map" was "mep." It was equally difficult to make myself understood. I did know about *The Cosby Show,* MTV, and baggy pants. I had anticipated something of the liberty and recklessness epitomized by sixteen-year-olds who drove their own cars (and I was soon to exercise my own liberty by choosing to be an art historian instead of an astronaut). But I was astonished by the Phil Donahue show, by how little sense of shame people seemed to have; and I was more than astonished by the black-white divide.

The journey to Kalamazoo seemed like a journey of return, the opposite of exile. A direct flight from Lagos to JFK, followed by a daylong train journey across the Midwest, had brought me to the town where my parents were married, the town where I was born and baptized. I had no anxiety about legal documents. Picking up my Social Security card was an afternoon's errand. I got a job at McDonald's, and banks gladly loaned me money for college. But, my first evening on campus, as I wandered around in what seemed like intolerable cold, it suddenly struck me that everyone I loved on this earth was almost six thousand miles away. I was flooded with panic, like a young boy in a helicopter being pulled away from all he'd ever known. Seventeen years of invented memories abandoned me. A sob ascended my spinal cord.

That evening, I began to invent new memories for myself. These new memories were all about the home I had left to come back home: what I had liked about that other life, and what part of it I was happy to be rid of.

The Reprint

IT WAS A small village in southern Germany. It was a summer's
day. From an old turreted tower, on the green hill that was
separated from the village by a sluggish river, the sound of bells
negotiated the afternoon. I was drowsy in that carillon sound,
looking out a window that framed the hill, and it seemed as
though the sound came from all the green hill and not just its
tower. Then the window suddenly shuttered, and I woke up in a
darkened room in Brooklyn. The bells continued a few seconds
more, until I reached across to the dresser and silenced them.
The clock said 5:00. I had gone to bed with my mind on James
Baldwin: somewhere, he tells the story of traveling into a small
Swiss village that had never seen a black man. In the strange
logic of dreams, Switzerland had become Germany, and Germany had dissolved into Brooklyn on the morning of November 4.

I padded around the house so as not to rouse my wife. I made
the last of the coffee her uncle, a kindhearted Jesuit in Pune,
had sent us, and prepared the things I was taking to the polling
place with me: ID card, camera, voter registration. I returned
to the bedroom and asked my wife for whom I should vote.
Flipping her pillow round to its cooler side, more or less still
asleep, she said I should return home immediately should

Obama lose. She feared riots; but it would be unlike me, she knew, to avoid one.

It was still dark when I stepped outside the house. The first faint pink traces of daylight were beginning to smudge the sky above the park opposite our place. I walked up to Sixth Avenue, then the six short blocks to Fiftieth Street. The neighborhood, through which I had walked countless times in daytime and at night, was different at first light. There was a light coating of frost on the cars, and the houses had a Georgian aspect, an air of Bloomsbury gentility. On each block, I saw one person or two, out early, sober and fitted for the yards of work. Two East Asian women rolled a cart across the street, fussing over its load: aluminum cans that they had spent the night collecting and sorting into large bags. The women were as habituated to the hour as I was a stranger to it.

The polling station, a high school, had just opened. There were five or ten people crowding at the door, but each showed a registration card and was swiftly ushered in by the uniformed police officers. I smiled when I saw the name tag of one of the officers. I said, "Florida. That's an auspicious name on a day like this, Officer." It was 6:10 A.M., and he was not in the mood. Voting was easy: antiquated-looking levers and knobs, which I soon figured out how to work. The poll workers outside argued in Chinese. I voted straight Democratic as planned, except for where I had the choice to select Working Families. I was done in five minutes: it felt like something accomplished, something weighty, and also like some stubborn pride finally released. I was part of the system now. I was moved to see the hall filled with my neighbors, at this hour, some of them with young children, pursuing that vague ideal called civic duty. When else, I tried to remember, would people willingly gather like this without the promise of entertainment, religion, or money? By the time I came out of the building, day had fallen fast, light had spread across the sky. I walked through the quiet streets, picked up some breakfast rolls at the Mexican panaderia, and headed back to the apartment.

I lay in bed and was soon asleep. A text from Siddhartha woke me up at 10:00: "It's a beautiful day. The ancestors are smiling." It felt true. I switched on the television, looked at early voting reports on MSNBC and CNN, but that all felt false, and I switched it off. I intended to head out later, and I decided to pass the next few hours in solitude and silence, bracing myself, trying not to admit to the nervousness I felt about the outcome of the election. Later, making lunch, I read some sections of Derek Walcott's long poem *The Arkansas Testament*. I heard in my mind's ear the troubled and beautiful rhythms, heard a meditation on being present to a place and unwelcome in it. I caught my breath especially sharply at some lines late in the poem, lines that seemed exact to the moment:

And afternoon sun will reprint
the bars of a flag whose cloth—
over motel, steeple and precinct—
must heal the stripes and the scars.

In the late afternoon, when I finally left the apartment again, my neighborhood in Brooklyn was quiet. There were no signs of the absorption and jitteriness that seemed to have seized hold of me and many of my friends. It was business as usual: the men lounging outside the minicab office, the Dominican restaurant, the Mexican remittance agency. The day, warm for the time of year, had been overcast and was now beginning to darken. I took the N train to Union Square, to pick up a lens for my camera. Walking down Eighteenth, sometime around 5:00, I felt the strangeness of time, the way one sometimes does. Soon, I knew, there would be some kind of permanent change in the collective psyche. And yet, at that precise moment, it was still hovering out of reach, this knowledge we all hungered for, like a cookie jar stashed on a high shelf. Time was like an expert card trick, a bait and switch invisible to the naked eye. I saw quiet anticipation in the faces that blurred past me in both directions. In the elevator of the camera store, a FedEx delivery-man was speaking to one of the employees. He said, "I just don't think that was necessary." The employee said, "It was funny though." The FedEx guy shook his head. "No, it was cruel. She already made a fool of herself, all by her own self. No need for prank calls."

He was muscular and short-statured. Outside, next to his truck, I asked him if he thought Governor Palin would return in 2012. "I don't think so," he said, "they'll use her and toss her away. Anyway, it's not my problem." But did the elections hold any special significance for him? "I'm thirty-seven years old," he said, "I've never voted before. I've been waiting my whole life for this, for the opportunity to vote the way I did today." A large statement, but more astonishing because of how common it was. It was true for me, too, in a way. I thought I had strong rational reasons for having opted out of all the elections for which I'd been eligible since 1992. But something not strictly rational was responsible for the pragmatic turn now in my thinking. Something had driven me to the polls that hadn't been there before. If I still prided myself on being skeptical of mass hysteria, I had added to it something else: the idea that participation, rational or otherwise, mattered. I had voted not because my doing so could change the outcome, but because voting would change me. Already, like a mutation that happens quietly on a genetic level and later completely alters the body's function, I could feel my relationship to other Americans changing. I had a sense—dubious to me for so long, and therefore avoided—of common cause. And not only with the millions of strangers who had pulled levers, filled in sheets, and touched screens that day, people like the black FedEx guy, but also with particular public figures, living and dead, like James Baldwin, John Coltrane, Philip Roth, and Carolyn Heilbrun, as well as with personal friends in the city and elsewhere. Assorted characters who had in common only the accident of citizenship. I was a part of what they were part of, in a new way.

This edifice threatens to collapse under its own weight. All these generalizations and self-contradictions are part of the empty rhetoric I hate about politics. Can those quickly flipped levers really mean so much? Don't I basically prefer things that have no meaning? The conflict was present in my mind as I got back on the train and headed midtown, to Rockefeller Center. My spiritual practice, to the extent that I have one, takes seriously the idea that one should avoid false refuge. The idea that change, in its most elemental form, could come from without was offensive to me. And yet, I felt different for having sullied my pristine record with partisanship. I felt healthier. That was the nub of the thing: I had been trying to stay pure, to have the correct idea, and had made the best the enemy of the good. Now voting for Obama, in spite of my strong objections both to some of his ideas and to much of the system in which he functioned, was a declaration, mostly to myself, that we participate in things not because they are ideal but because they are not.

Rockefeller Center was wretched. In the maze of underground passages leading up from the subway to Forty-Seventh Street, there was a large glass-fronted shoeshine place. I saw four pink-faced men seated in a row, and four red-jacketed brown-faced men stooped over cleaning the shoes on their feet. Then came the plaza itself, brilliantly lit, full of tourists and hawkers, and, in one section, television broadcasters. The ice rink was being prepared as a giant map of the country. Around its rectangular perimeter was an unbroken rank of American flags. Red and blue lights played over the flags, and onto the skyscrapers around, and the effect was like the toothache one gets from chewing ice. Mascots in donkey or elephant costumes mugged for photos, and workers on scaffolds put the names of the presidential candidates into place. What was it that was damaged in my brain, that reading a Caribbean poet on a grim journey made me feel more American, but a flag-filled fun-house of a city block provoked me to anger? I walked away from Forty-Seventh, onto the Avenue of the Americas, northward, alongside the solid and unblinking many-eyed bank buildings, until I came to Central Park South and Fifty-Ninth Street, then west to Columbus Circle, which was desolate and rather beautiful. I put Nayyara Noor's "Aaj bazaar mein," a ghazal written by Faiz Ahmed Faiz, into my iPod. I went into the subway and took the A train.

Harlem was where I would find whatever it was I was looking for tonight. In "The American Dream and the American Negro," an essay he published in 1965, Baldwin had noted the following:

> I remember when the ex–Attorney General, Mr. Robert Kennedy, said it was conceivable that in forty years in America we might have a Negro President. That sounded

like a very emancipated statement to white people. They
were not in Harlem when this statement was first heard.
They did not hear the laughter and bitterness and scorn
with which this statement was greeted. . . . We were here
for four hundred years and now he tells us that maybe in
forty years, if you are good, we may let you become President.

Forty years put us at 2005. This was year forty-three, around
8:00 in the evening, and the result was still in doubt. The
Harlem-bound A was peculiar. Never before, on countless trips
between 59th and 125th, had I seen so many white people on it.
It was one of the simplest anthropological gestures in the city:
entering a train and seeing who gets on and gets off where. The
A train, the D, the 7 to Queens: folks generally went with their
own kind. The mass exodus of Chinese at Grand Street, the Indians in Jackson Heights, the Poles and Russians in Bay Ridge.
On most days, there's nothing but black people at the 125th
Street stop. This evening I saw blond white boys in Obama
shirts, russet-haired, pale-skinned women with camera equipment, and Asian hipsters in skinny jeans. My disappointment
deepened, not on the bus across from St. Nicholas to Lenox,
which was all black, but at the Lenox Lounge, which, for the
evening, seemed to have been taken over by white people with
expensive-looking Canons and Nikons. A man with a large
video camera marked with a Reuters sticker wandered around,
getting footage of the few locals in attendance.

My mood soon improved, with the arrival of a Sugar Hill
lager, and my dinner: catfish stuffed with shrimp, and a side of
collard greens and yams. Some friends I had arranged to meet
soon arrived, as did more local color. These latter I searched for

signs of "laughter and bitterness and scorn," but things had perhaps changed since Kennedy's prediction. The dominant registers were deep seriousness and muted festivity. Before long, more than half of the people in the bar were African American, some dressed for the occasion in Afrocentric clothes. The man from Reuters had by then wandered off in search of blacker pastures. The television was set to CNN.

Soon, cheers began to ring out intermittently in the lounge, as polls closed and states were called. Throaty boos greeted McCain's predictable victories in southern states. The evening was long, like a cup final that lacked the fire and character of qualifying rounds. For the first few hours, there were no surprises. Blue stayed blue, and red remained red. Then, in the kind of flurry that seems disorienting at the time, and even more out of focus later on, Ohio and Pennsylvania were called. Big cheers. A gambler, by then, could have put everything on an Obama win. Still, it wasn't sinking in. Everyone was expecting dirty tricks, something untoward and unexpected, a Bradley effect for the ages. No one relaxed. At ten minutes to 11:00, Virginia was called. That was the biggest cheer of the evening. I immediately thought of my friend Peter, who had put in long hours canvasing for Obama in that state. The minutes that followed found me trying and failing to stay focused on the numbers on the screen as well as on the mental calculations of where the math now stood. Just as I was reaching the conclusion that, with surefire blue California added to the present tally, Obama would have 5 votes over the necessary 270, I saw CNN flash the graphic announcing, "Barack Obama, Projected Winner, President." That was it. It was all over.

Screams tore through the air. What does catharsis sound like? The shouts rose like a wave from us, and slammed down back on us, rose again, slammed down again. Instantly, several people began to weep. A middle-aged woman grabbed me in a tight embrace and cried, "Thank you Jesus, thank you Jesus." I forced my way outside. A pair of young women held each other's hands and jumped up and down. Shouts, as though they were signals thrown across a valley, bounced from one end of the night air to another. I began to run across Lenox Avenue, toward Adam Clayton Powell, and was almost hit by a speeding cab. The driver screeched to a halt and rolled down his window. He grinned and extended his hand. "We did it!" he said, "I don't know how, but we did it!"

What was not known a few hours before was now irrevocably known. Those ten minutes, between 11:00 and 11:10, were of a surreal intensity I will never forget as long as I live. Thousands of people, as though out of thin air, suddenly converged at 125th Street and Adam Clayton Powell. The TV screen that had been set up there earlier had been viewed by a sparse crowd. Now, the throng was tar-thick, and there was as exuberant and unscripted an outpouring of joy as I ever expect to see anywhere. Some people had brought out drums and were playing, and the crowd danced, and laughed, and jumped over and over. Over a PA, we heard "Signed, Sealed, Delivered." And then a brass band came through the densest part of the crowd, where there was hardly room to move, let alone dance, playing "When the Saints Go Marching In."

"The purification of the emotions by vicarious experience" is how the *OED* defines "catharsis." The word has a strong purgative association. The need for this cleansing is unquestionable, given the sheer quantity of impacted bullshit in politics. But, on that congested street corner, amid the music and happiness, my mind was already beginning to roam. I was experiencing catharsis, and running a skeptical mental commentary on it. To my own disgust, I thought of the Nuremberg rallies: a thought too far.

A makeshift stage had gone up below the giant screen, obscured from my view by the heroic statue of Adam Clayton Powell. Congressman Rangel was in attendance, as was Governor Patterson. While they spoke, laying claim in politicians' words to the moment—not entirely unfairly, since it was indeed a political moment—other claims were laid in segments of the crowd. Some people near me began to sing "We Shall Overcome," and it was taken up briefly by a larger group, but then abandoned. I had a sense that people were trying to find the right purchase on what was happening. Was it a civil rights moment? Was it a victory for partisan politics? Was it a racial affair?

Race loomed large. People took the stage and references were made to four hundred years of slavery, to lynchings and Jim Crow, and to the marches of the 1960s. Someone next to me called out, "Free at last, thank God almighty we are free at last." For some, the moment was experienced with pure extroversion. For others, there was a kind of sweet wonderment and solitude inside the pressing crowd. These faces seemed to possess a quietness that was all the more stark in comparison to the emotionalism around them. I suddenly saw the beatific face of a friend: the great documentary filmmaker Albert Maysles. I went to greet him, and promised to come visit him soon. Maysles had followed John F. Kennedy around with a video camera during the 1960 primaries. How wondrous that here he now was, in 2008, on his own two feet, watching the success of another callow genius. I watched him for a while: he radiated light.

At length, the president-elect, the black president to be, came on the screen. Everyone screamed. He gave a workman-like speech, "inspirational" by the numbers, full of the expected notes of unity, promises, and nationalistic nonsense. Black presidents were no novelty for me. About half my life, the half I lived in Nigeria, had been spent under their rule, and, in my mind, the color of the president was neither here nor there. But this was America. Race mattered. Not the facts: that Obama was not actually descended from slaves, that he was raised in a white household. The facts could be elided easily enough. Race was what mattered, race and the uses for which it was available; societal convention gave priority to his black roots over his white ones. This, I thought, was what was being misunderstood about the prospect of an Obama presidency. The argument could be made that he wasn't really "the first African American" to be voted into the office, because he was African American only in a special, and technical, sense, the same way I was African American: a black person who held American citizenship. But the history of most blacks in this country—the history of slavery, Reconstruction, systematic disenfranchisement, and the civil rights movement—was not my history. My history was one of emigration, adaptation, and a different flavor of exile. I was only a latter-day sharer in the sorrow and the glory of the African American experience.

The eagerness with which, minutes after he was declared winner of the elections, Obama was being narrated into the conventional African American story betrayed, I thought, an

American longing for simplicity. The country had a love of clear narratives and optimistic story arcs, hence "We Shall Overcome" on the heels of a massively well-funded and astute display of machine politics.

Obama, at the core of his experience, is hybrid. The significant achievement is not that, as a black man, he became president. It is that, as a certain kind of outsider American—of which the Kenyan father, Indonesian school, and biracial origin, not to mention the three non-Anglo names, are markers—he was able to work his way into the very center of American life. In other words, Obama is an avatar of a new American story, not one having to do with slave ships, or one relying on the *Mayflower,* or even the wave of poor Irish, Italian, and Jewish immigrants that the country welcomed (or at least tolerated) in the nineteenth and early twentieth centuries. The Obama story is the story of immigration in the age of air travel, the kind of Americanism that issues from exchange students and H-1B visas and lapsed work permits. This is a form of being American that has been invisible in plain sight. His victory, I would think, should resonate even more strongly with these out-of-place characters who have been toiling in the shadows of the American story: the graduate students with funny accents, the pizza-delivery guys with no papers, Americans, regardless of color, who remember a time when they were not Americans.

This was why my American friends who had Indian parents, or Nigerian parents, or who spoke foreign languages, or identified strongly, for whatever reasons, with more than one country, would feel this win on such an essential level. This was really their victory, that to be this new kind of American was no less valuable than to be one of the old canonized varieties. An inkling, on the part of the Republicans, about this argument about hybridity is what led to the kinds of attacks made during the campaign, all the nonsense about "pro-American" parts of the country, the talk about elitism, the insistence on mispronouncing the names of foreign countries, the pride in never having traveled. They knew, on a gut level, that it wasn't the white and black dichotomy that was being challenged, but the idea that to be American is to be white *or* black. Who knew what could follow on from this murky Kenyan-Indonesian-Hawaiian-Kansan mélange? They were right to be frantic. Obama had challenged the assumption that a person had to be from somewhere familiar, had to be from one place, and he had successfully smuggled that question into the center of American life. The hidden code in McCain and Palin's "Country First" was really "No hybrids please, we're American." It was "Old Ideas of Country First."

The message in the stunning electoral victory, then, was not that anyone could grow up to be president. It was that any hardworking, devilishly handsome, and absurdly gifted child of recent immigrants, regardless of color, might more easily negotiate the minefield of American racial politics than might perhaps an African American of longer standing. This was what the pundits' oft-repeated "he's not an angry black man" was all about. He did not come from slaves, and did not therefore carry the threatening rage of those who had been maimed by slavery. It was no coincidence that Barack Obama and Colin Powell, the two most popular black men in American political life, were both children of people who were not born American. Classifying them as "African American" gave whites an opportunity for self-congratulation, and no real risk of racial backlash.

I walked down Amsterdam Avenue toward Columbia University. "Change!" cried out Crazy Kev, still on the corner of 120th Street, where I first saw him eight years ago. I had no change, so I gave him five dollars. My ruminations did not displace my joy, even if the joy itself was a simple one: the joy of being with joyful humans. Walking down to Columbia's campus at around 12:30 A.M., slowly, as the crowd loosened, I saw white college students immersing themselves in the moment as well. They trooped en masse toward Harlem, a short walk away, but an area of town most of them had, until this night, avoided. One group passing me was singing "The Star-Spangled Banner." A few blocks up, another, smaller, group sang "America the Beautiful." Already on the first day in the life of the new thing, the narrative was bifurcating.

The crowd had cheered with a single voice, but interpretations varied. For some whites, it was all about America and America's greatness. For many blacks, it was a different story: a story about a racial triumph, one specifically tied to the enduring hurt of the slave trade. Yet, for all the assertion of a milestone reached, no one seemed worried that Obama's accession to the White House left the U.S. Senate without a single black senator among its hundred members: one signal among many of how dire the racial divide remains in the country. But I reminded myself that pragmatism had entered my life. I duly jumped into the swarm of emails and phone calls and text messages. I understood the shaking, the weeping, the trembling; I had a share in it. I remembered Faiz's words—"Let us go to the bazaar today in chains / let's go with hands waving / intoxicated and dancing / let's go with dust on our heads and blood on our sleeves"—and felt an immense gratitude that in some small symbolic way, I had participated in releasing the country from the rule of Bush and Cheney. These men had polluted the

world, and Obama's victory was a rebuke to them. It was a rebuke heard around the world, even if Obama's own political
ethos still remained beholden to aggressive consumerism and
militarism. Things would begin to get better a little bit at a
time. The healing of "the stripes and the scars" could com-
mence. The world would surely change. The bells were already
ringing.

No, no, the world would do no such thing: power would
eternally perpetuate itself. Greed would still ride roughshod
over everything, and money and ego would still poison brother
against brother. That was what reality actually looked like. The
world would not revise itself: I would. I had. Reading Walcott
against the basic sense of his poem, I told myself that November
4, 2008, had reprinted some part of me, and that was what
mattered. What is written over is less pure, less pristine. What
a wonderful sight, that the self as palimpsest, the unclear narrative, and the man from nowhere were now at the center of this
lineage-crazed nation. I got on the train from 116th Street for
the long journey back to Brooklyn, surrounded by curiously
sedate passengers, as though for them the celebrations above
ground were taking place on another planet. My wife, who was
sleeping when I got home, whom I'd last seen before I knew
what I now knew, was somehow able to murmur, when I slipped
into bed, "Welcome home, Mr. President." And that was true,
too.

A Reader's War

"THANKS TO LITERATURE, to the consciousness it shapes, the desires and longings it inspires . . . civilization is now less cruel than when storytellers began to humanize life with their fables." This defense, made by Mario Vargas Llosa when he received the Nobel Prize in Literature two years ago, could have come from any other writer. It is, in fact, allowing for some variety of expression, a cliché. But clichés, so the cliché goes, originate in truth. Vargas Llosa reiterated the point: "Without fictions, we would be less aware of the importance of freedom for life to be livable, the hell it turns into when it is trampled underfoot by a tyrant, an ideology, or a religion."

It would be hard to find writers who disagree with Vargas Llosa's general sense of literature's civilizing function. Toni Morrison, in her Nobel lecture, in 1993, said, "We die. That may be the meaning of life. But we do language. That may be the measure of our lives." This sense of literature's fortifying and essential quality has been evoked by countless other writers and readers. When Marilynne Robinson described fiction as "an exercise in the capacity for imaginative love, or sympathy, or identification," she was stating something almost everyone would agree with. We praise literature in self-evident terms: it is better to read than not to read, for reading civilizes us, makes us less cruel, and brings the imaginations of others into ours and vice versa. We persist in this belief regardless of what we know to the contrary: that the Nazis' affection for high culture did not prevent their crimes. It is simply not a true belief, but helplessly, at our most serious moments, we assert it again and again. But our attachment to this cliché is not harmless.

There was a feeling during the years of George W. Bush's presidency that his gracelessness as well as his appetite for war were linked to his impatience with complexity. He acted "from the gut," and was economical with the truth until it disappeared. Under his command, the United States launched a needless and unjust war in Iraq that resulted in terrible loss of life; at the same time, an unknown number of people were confined in secret prisons and tortured. That Bush was anti-intellectual, and often guilty of malapropisms and mispronunciations ("nucular"), formed part of the liberal aversion to him: he didn't know much about the wider world, and did not much care to learn.

His successor couldn't have been more different. Barack Obama is an elegant and literate man with a cosmopolitan sense of the world. He is widely read in philosophy, literature, and history—as befits a former law professor—and he has shown time and again a surprising interest in contemporary fiction. The books a president buys might be as influenced by political calculation as his "enjoyment" of lunch at a small-town diner or a round of skeet shooting. Nevertheless, a man who names among his favorite books Morrison's *Song of Solomon,* Robinson's *Gilead,* and Melville's *Moby-Dick* is playing the game pretty seriously. His own feel for language in his two books, his praise for authors as various as Philip Roth and Ward Just, as well as the circumstantial evidence of the books he's been seen holding (the *Collected Poems* of Derek Walcott, most strikingly), add up to a picture of a man for whom an imaginative engagement with literature is inseparable from life. It thrilled me, when he was elected, to think of the president's nightstand looking rather similar to mine (again, mindful of the cliché; again, unable to elude its grasp). We had, once again, a reader in chief, a man in the line of Jefferson and Lincoln.

Any president's gravest responsibilities are defending the Constitution and keeping the country safe. President Obama recognized that the image of the United States had been marred by the policies of the Bush years. By drawing down the troops in Iraq, banning torture, and directly and respectfully addressing the countries of Europe and the Middle East, Obama signaled that those of us on the left had not hoped in vain for change. When, in 2009, he was awarded the Nobel Peace Prize, we noted the absurdity of such premature plaudits but also saw the occasion as encouragement for the difficult work to come. From the optimistic perspective of those early days, Obama's foreign policy has lurched from disappointing to disastrous. Iraq endures a shaky peace and Afghanistan remains a mire, but these situations might have been the same regardless of who was president. More troubling has been his conduct in the other arenas of the Global War on Terrorism. The United States is now at war in all but name in Pakistan, Somalia, and Yemen. In pursuit of Al Qaeda, their allies, and a number of barely related militias, the president and his national security team now make extraordinarily frequent use of assassinations.

The White House, the CIA, and the Joint Special Operations Command have so far killed large numbers of people. Because of the secret nature of the strikes, the precise number is unknown, but estimates range from several hundred to over three thousand. These killings have happened without any attempt to arrest or detain their targets, and beyond the reach of any legal oversight. Many of the dead are women and children. Among the men, it is impossible to say how many are terrorists, how many are militants, and how many are simply, to use the administration's obscene designation, "young men of military age." The dependence on unmanned aerial vehicles for these killings, which began in 2002 and have increased under the Obama administration, is finally coming to wider attention.

We now have firsthand testimony from the pilots who remotely operate the drones, many of whom have suffered post-traumatic stress reactions to the work. There is also the testimony of the survivors of drone attacks: heartbreaking stories of mistaken identity, grisly tales of sudden death from a machine in the sky. In one such story reported by *The New York Times*, the relatives of a pair of dead cousins said, "We found eyes, but there were no faces left." The recently leaked Department of Justice white paper indicating guidelines for the president's assassination of his fellow Americans has shone a spotlight on these "dirty wars" (as the journalist Jeremy Scahill rightly calls them in his documentary film and book of the same title). The plain fact is that our leaders have been killing at will.

How on earth did this happen to the reader in chief? What became of literature's vaunted power to inspire empathy? (A power that we simultaneously disavow and perpetually cite.) Why was the candidate Obama, in word and in deed, so radically different from the president he became? In Andrei Tarkovsky's eerie 1979 masterpiece, *Stalker*, the landscape called the Zona has the power to grant people's deepest wishes, but it can also derange those who traverse it. I wonder if the presidency is like that: a psychoactive landscape that can madden whoever walks into it, be he inarticulate and incurious, or literary and cosmopolitan.

According to a report in *The New York Times*, the targets of drone strikes are selected for death at weekly meetings in the White House; no name is added to the list without the president's approval. Where land mines are indiscriminate, cheap, and brutal, drones are discriminate, expensive, and brutal. And yet they are insufficiently discriminate: the assassination of the Taliban chief Baitullah Mehsud in Pakistan in 2009 succeeded only on the seventeenth attempt. The sixteen near misses of the preceding year killed between 280 and 410 other people. Literature fails us here. What makes certain Somali, Pakistani, Yemeni, and American people of so little account that, even after killing them, the United States disavows all knowledge of their deaths? How much furious despair is generated from so much collateral damage?

Of late, riding the subway in Brooklyn, I have been having a waking dream, or rather a daytime nightmare, in which the subway car ahead of mine explodes. My fellow riders and I look at one another, then look again at the burning car ahead, certain of our deaths. The fire comes closer, and what I feel is bitterness and sorrow that it's all ending so soon: no more books, no more love, no more jokes, no more Schubert, no more Black Star. All this spins through my mind on tranquil mornings as the D train trundles between Thirty-Sixth Street and Atlantic Avenue and bored commuters check their phones. They just want to get to work. I sit rigid in my seat, thinking, I don't want to die, not here, not yet. I imagine those in northwest Pakistan or just outside Sana'a who go about their day thinking the same. The difference for some of them is that the plane is already hovering in the air, ready to strike.

I know language is unreliable, that it is not a vending machine of the desires, but the law seems to be getting us nowhere. And so I take helpless refuge in literature again, rewriting the opening lines of seven well-known books:

Mrs. Dalloway said she would buy the flowers herself. Pity. A signature strike leveled the florist's.

Call me Ishmael. I was a young man of military age. I was immolated at my wedding. My parents are inconsolable.

Stately, plump Buck Mulligan came from the stairhead bearing a bowl of lather. A bomb whistled in. Blood on the walls. Fire from heaven.

I am an invisible man. My name is unknown. My loves are a mystery. But an unmanned aerial vehicle from a secret location has come for me.

Someone must have slandered Josef K., for one morning, without having done anything truly wrong, he was killed by a Predator drone.

Okonkwo was well known throughout the nine villages and even beyond. His torso was found, not his head.

Mother died today. The program saves American lives.

I was in New York City on 9/11. Grief remains from that awful day, but not only grief. There is fear, too, a fear informed by the knowledge that whatever my worst nightmare is, there is someone out there embittered enough to carry it out. I know that something has to be done to secure the airports, waterways, infrastructure, and embassies of our country. I don't like war; no one does. But I also know that the world is exceedingly complex, and that our enemies are not all imaginary. I am not naïve about the incessant and unseen (by most of us) military activity that undergirds our ability to read, go to concerts, earn a living, and criticize the government in relative safety. I am grateful to those whose bravery keeps us safe.

This ominous, discomfiting, illegal, and immoral use of weaponized drones against defenseless strangers is done for our sakes. But more and more we are seeing a gap between the intention behind the president's clandestine brand of justice and the real-world effect of those killings. Martin Luther King, Jr.'s words against the Vietnam War in 1967 remain resonant today: "What do they think as we test our latest weapons on them?" We do know what they think: many of them have the normal human reaction to grief and injustice, and some of them take that reaction to a vengeful and murderous extreme. In the Arabian peninsula, East Africa, and Pakistan, thanks to the policies of Obama and Biden, we are acquiring more of the angriest young enemies money can buy. As a *New York Times* report put it, "Drones have replaced Guantánamo as the recruiting tool of choice for militants."

Assassinations should never have happened in our name. But now we see that they endanger us physically, endanger our democracy, and endanger our Constitution. I believe that when President Obama personally selects the next name to add to his "kill list," he does it because he is convinced that he is protecting the country. I trust that he makes the selections with great seriousness, bringing his rich sense of the lives of others to bear on his decisions. And yet we have been drawn into a war without end, and into cruelties that persist in the psychic atmosphere like ritual pollution.

Madmen and Specialists

R ELIGION IS CLOSE to theater; much of its power comes from the effects of staging and framing. And in a play about a preacher, theater easily becomes religion. The performance of Wole Soyinka's 1964 farce *The Trials of Brother Jero,* which I saw recently in Lagos, was not dissimilar to my experience at a Pentecostal church about two weeks later. *The Trials of Brother Jero* centers on a prophet, one of the many freelance Christian clerics of dubious authority that have proliferated in Nigeria. Charlatans are not charlatans all the way through: if they didn't believe at least a little in what they were selling, it would be difficult for them to persuade others. "In fact, there are eggs and there are eggs," Brother Jero proclaims in his first soliloquy of the play. "Same thing with prophets. I was born a prophet."

This element of make-believe is true of both prophets and actors, and so in a play like *Brother Jero* the point is doubled: both acting and religion have an imprecise relationship with the truth. The performance I saw was at a beautiful independent theater called Terra Kulture, on Victoria Island, an upscale neighborhood of the city. Brother Jero—"Velvet-hearted Jeroboam, Immaculate Jero, Articulate Hero of Christ's Crusade"—was played with slinky, mellifluous deviousness by Patrick Diabuah as equal parts Hamlet and Wile E. Coyote. The play was fast, funny, wordy, and physical, and it sent up deception for the two-way street that it was: an eyes-half-open transaction between the deceiver and the deceived. "Go and practice your fraudulences on another person of greater gullibility," says one of Jero's marks shortly before he, too, is flattered—drawn in with sweet words and gleefully defrauded.

Nigeria, too, is in a season of drama, and words are flying freely. In Rivers State, in the oil-rich Niger Delta, there is a power struggle. This struggle is entirely within the People's Democratic Party, which is the party of President Goodluck Jonathan, and it centers on the forthcoming elections, which the president is interested in contesting. The first lady, Dame Patience Jonathan, is from Rivers State, and she has been vocal on one side of the dispute, acting as the president's proxy. The governor of Rivers State, Rotimi Amaechi, widely liked and seen as an insurgent within the party, is on the other side. President Jonathan has been condemned by Nigerians for being ineffectual, for having a make-believe presidency that promises much and delivers little, but the Dame (as she is called) has been even more a figure of fun. Her command of English is unsteady: she once addressed a gathering of widows as "my fellow-widows." A cause for more sustained resentment has been her ostentatious personal style in what is still a desperately poor country.

In early July, a maneuver by the Dame's supporters to impeach the speaker of the Rivers State House of Assembly devolved into mayhem. In the ensuing brawl, one member of the House, Chidi Lloyd, attacked another, Michael Chinda, with a ceremonial mace, breaking his skull and critically wounding him in full view of television cameras. In the wake of this attack, Dame Patience made a conciliatory statement in which she described Governor Amaechi as her "son" (the difference in their age is seven years). Newspaper commentators found her appeal hypocritical, since she'd been widely credited with a major role in the state's crisis. After all, she had recently been in Rivers State on an eleven-day visit, with the full security apparatus of the presidency. Her visit was so disruptive and intimidating that the governor had been pinned down in his lodge, unable to move around his capital city, Port Harcourt. And in the House of Assembly there was a group of members so fanatically loyal to her that one of them, Evans Bipi, had declared to the press, "Why must [Governor Amaechi] be insulting my mother, my Jesus Christ on earth?"

Loudest among the voices of protest raised against the Dame was Wole Soyinka's. He took her to task for imposing herself on the people and for acting like a "parallel head of state." Soyinka called a press conference in Lagos and built his case against the president and his wife around an extended and unexpected metaphor: the twelfth-century persecution and murder of Thomas à Becket by the agents of Henry II. Speaking about the way a king might tacitly condone crimes and, thus, making pointed reference to the way Governor Amaechi was being stripped of power in Rivers State, Soyinka asked, "Are we not moving towards absolute monarchism? There are many worrying historical parallels." A written statement he gave to the press had a more ad hominem quality, ending with the line "You can extract a hippopotamus from the swamps, but you cannot take the swamp out of a hippopotamus." This was generally interpreted as an ungentle poke at the Dame, a woman of considerable size, and even some of Soyinka's supporters squirmed at the analogy.

Political activity has always been as central to Soyinka's work as theater has. He was uncensorable right from the start. He was imprisoned for twenty-two months in the late sixties, during Nigeria's civil war, for his attempt to negotiate a peace between the Federal and Biafran sides. He spent much of that time in solitary confinement, an experience that he wrote about in a memoir, *The Man Died*. In 1994 he fled Nigeria when the military regime of General Sani Abacha threatened his life. His passport had been seized, so he went across the land border into the Republic of Benin, and from there he made his way into exile in the United States. He agitated for a return to democratic rule and was charged with treason in absentia, in 1997. But he returned home after General Abacha died in 1998, and he lives in Nigeria now.

He remains one of the country's most fearless defenders of human rights, speaking out on issues from the Boko Haram insurgency to the aggressive legislation curtailing the rights of gays and lesbians. He is famous and respected, and perhaps better known to the ordinary Nigerian for his political activity than for the linguistically intricate and thematically complex plays—among them *Death and the King's Horseman* and *Madmen and Specialists*—that won him the Nobel Prize in Literature, in 1986.

Word of Soyinka's July press conference reached the Dame, and she was not amused. Three days later, she issued a statement in which she called Soyinka "an embarrassment" to Nigeria. And it was this unexpected turning of the tables, this swerve into the theater of the absurd, that I wished to ask Soyinka about. I got my chance a few days later, when I visited him in Abeokuta, about an hour north of Lagos, in his bucolic home at the edge of the woods. The house was cool, shadowed, and quiet. It had none of the ostentation that one expects from a Nigerian "big man"—no security fence or luxury cars or marble floors. Instead, there was indigo-dyed handwoven aso-oke cloth on the windows, and there were phalanxes of African sculpture, both Yoruba and otherwise, standing in watchful groups around the living room. It was a reassuring place, a suitable lair for a man whose name, soyinka, literally means "the daemons surround me." I was reminded of another one of the epithets for him: "child of the forest." He lived up to this designation as well, often going out hunting and bearing in himself a more congenial relationship with traditional religious belief than most Nigerians, converts to Islam or Christianity, would entertain. Soyinka is a devotee of Ogun—the god of iron and "the first symbol of the alliance of disparities"—and his *Myth, Literature and the African World* is a learned exploration of the links between epic theater, Yoruba ritual, aesthetics, and ethics.

My visit was about a week after his seventy-ninth birthday. He looked vigorous, effortlessly handsome. His famous Afro and beard, both a vivid white, looked less like signs of age than like evidence of some unending efflorescence. "So, what does it feel like to be an embarrassment?" His eyes closed with mirth.

"It is not only the end of farce. It is the end of all the genres." Then, still laughing, but with more fight in his voice, he added, "She was unelected—and it is irrelevant if she's a man or a woman—she is a mere appendage of power. If there's someone she doesn't find embarrassing, there must be something wrong with that person."

What It Is

Is Ebola the ISIS of biological agents? Is Ebola the Boko Haram of AIDS? Is Ebola the al-Shabaab of dengue fever? Some say Ebola is the Milošević of West Nile virus. Others say Ebola is the Ku Klux Klan of paper cuts. It's obvious that Ebola is the MH370 of MH17. But at some point the question must be asked whether Ebola isn't also the Narendra Modi of sleeping sickness. And I don't mean to offend anyone's sensitivities, but there's more and more reason to believe that Ebola is the Sani Abacha of having some trouble peeing. At first there was, understandably, the suspicion that Ebola was the Hitler of apartheid, but now it has become abundantly clear that Ebola is actually the George W. Bush of being forced to listen to someone's podcast. It's that serious. The World Health Organization calls it the Putin of Stalin. In layperson's terms, that's like saying it's the Stalin of U2. Now we are seeing the idea thrown around that it could be the Black Hand of the Black Death, not to mention the Red Peril of the Red Plague. If you don't want to go that far, you have to at least admit that Ebola is the Al Qaeda in the Islamic Maghreb of Stage IV brain cancer. At this point, it's very possible that Ebola could become airborne and turn into the Tea Party of extreme climate events. Throughout the country of Africa, Ebola is the Abu Ghraib of think pieces. Look, I'm not the politically correct type, so I'm just going to put this out there: Ebola is the neo-Nazism of niggling knee injuries. The kind of threat it poses to the American way of life essentially makes it the North Korea of peanut allergies. I'm not going to lie to you, and I don't care what color you are, you could be red, green, blue, purple, whatever; you need to understand that Ebola (the Obama of Osama, but don't quote me) is literally the "some of my best friends are black" of #NotAllMen. But the burning question no one has raised yet is whether Ebola is the *Newsweek* of halitosis. We'll go to the phones in a moment and get your take on this. But first let me open the discussion up to our panel and ask whether Ebola is merely the Fox News of explosive incontinence, or whether the situation is much worse than that and Ebola is, in fact, the CNN of CNN.

Kofi Awoonor

On Saturday, September 21, 2013, the Ghanaian poet
Kofi Awoonor was shot dead at Nairobi's Westgate mall by
terrorists. He was one of dozens of innocent victims of a massacre, for which the Somali group al-Shabaab claimed responsibility. I was about a mile away during the attack, giving a reading
at the National Museum. During the reading, as word of the
attack filtered in, people answered their phones and checked
their messages, but, onstage and oblivious, I continued taking
questions from the audience, including one about "the precari-
ousness of life in Africa."

The massacre did not end neatly. It became a siege that
lasted days. In my hotel room, about half a mile from the mall,
I was woken in the mornings that followed by the sounds of
gunfire, heavy artillery, attack helicopters, and military planes.
In counterpoint to these frightening sounds were others: incessant birdsong outside my window, the laughter of children from the daycare next door. In grief and shock, I read
Awoonor's poems, and watched a column of black smoke rise
from the mall in the distance. The poems' uncanny prophetic
force became inescapable. A section of "Hymn to My Dumb
Earth" reads:

What has not happened before?
An animal has caught me,
it has me in its claws
Someone, someone, save
Save me, someone,
for I die.

Just three days earlier, on Thursday, I'd sent an email from Nairobi to a friend in New York. "Kofi Awoonor, Mongane Wally Serote, and Kwame Dawes are here at the Storymoja Hay Festival. These are senior African boys!" He wrote back: "That's wonderful. It's important they be a full fledged part of all conversations, youth movements and Internet notwithstanding." I sat next to Awoonor at the press conference that opened the festival that day, excited to meet the man behind the books. Awoonor was a jovial man, dark-skinned and fine-featured, wearing a batakari, a striped tunic, which gave him a regal air. Coming in late, he had joked, "I apologize. When you said four P.M., I thought you meant four P.M. African time, which is five P.M."

Awoonor, widely considered Ghana's greatest contemporary poet, was a member of the literary generation that came of age in the fifties and sixties. Many of these writers were published in the Heinemann African Writers Series, the tan and orange spines of which could be seen on the bookshelves of homes across the continent. The series, under the editorship of Chinua Achebe, was the first flowering of African literature in English. Awoonor shared with many of his illustrious contemporaries an intense engagement with both African tradition and African modernity. The influence of T. S. Eliot was strong, and Awoonor's poems are often dense and mysterious. But, like Achebe, he also gave voice to a culture under rapid and destructive change from colonial influences, and he expressed a disillusionment with the violence that marred the postcolonial project. From "This Earth, My Brother":

The crackling report of brens
and the falling down;
a shout greeted them
tossing them into the darkness.

Like his late friend Christopher Okigbo, he was invested in the ritual and chthonic possibilities of African vernacular languages, in his case Ewe. From that Ewe tradition came the feeling for elegy, which he applied with seriousness and dark irony to the serial crises of post-independence Ghana. The Ewe language also gave his poetry strong musical cadences, so that even when the meaning was opaque, the lines were fluent.

On Monday, on the third day of what would prove to be a four-day siege, about 150 people made their way across uncharacteristically empty roads to Nairobi's National Museum. An impromptu memorial had been organized for Awoonor. Kwame Dawes, the Ghanaian Jamaican poet, spoke warmly about the man he considered an uncle. On Friday, Dawes had shown me the first volume in a new series on African poetry. That book (which Dawes edited for publication by the University of Nebraska Press in 2014) was an orange-colored, handsomely designed hardcover of Awoonor's *The Promise of Hope: New and Selected Poems*.

"It's got to be good," Dawes had said of the design. "It's got to be good because it's intended to last." His pride in the finished project was justified. Now, at the memorial, I asked Dawes if Awoonor had seen the volume he showed me.

"I showed it to him for the first time here in Nairobi. I told him, 'This is it.'"

"And what did he say?"

Dawes smiled. "He said, 'This is good.' That's what he said. 'This is good.'"

Awoonor's son Afetsi had accompanied his father to Nairobi, and we'd all been at the same hotel. Afetsi was injured in the attack—shot in the shoulder—but he came to the memorial, with a white bandage slung across his right arm. He had the same serene and easy smile as his father, and we embraced warmly. The Ghanaian high commissioner was there as well, as were three other members of Awoonor's family, who had flown in after the tragedy. (Awoonor had served as Ghana's permanent representative to the United Nations in the 1990s, and he'd come to the Storymoja Hay Festival at the behest of the Ghanaian government.) One of the authors at the festival, the young Ghanaian poet Nii Ayikwei Parkes, during his eulogy, referred to Awoonor in the present tense. As he corrected himself, replacing "is" with "was," grief took sudden hold, and his voice cracked.

After Parkes's eulogy, I read out Awoonor's short poem "The Journey Beyond":

The howling cry through door posts
carrying boiling pots
ready for the feasters.
Kutsiami the benevolent boatman;
when I come to the river shore

please ferry me across
I do not have tied in my cloth the
price of your stewardship.

The most resonant moment of the evening was the least anticipated: someone had made an audio recording from the master class that Awoonor had given at the festival on Friday. And so, in the silence of the auditorium, we listened to about a minute of his final lecture. And there he was, speaking to us in his own voice (how startling its clarity), as though nothing had changed: "And I have written about death also, particularly at this old age now. At seventy-nine, you must know—unless you're an idiot—that very soon, you should be moving on." Then he added, with both levity and seriousness, "An ancient poet from my tradition said, 'I have something to say. I will say it before death comes. And if I don't say it, let no one say it for me. I will be the one who will say it.'"

Captivity

THERE ARE VAST distances between the cities. The terrain is varied. Forest gives way to savanna with scattered trees (shea, locust bean), and then to drier Sahel landscape. On these journeys one forgets city life, enters into something more delicate and more fragile.

Girls walk by the side of the road, a cluster of bright patterns. Boys play in the dusty fields. Every now and again, a church flashes by, whitewashed or with a plain mud façade. Ways of life mix here in northern Nigeria; there are many Christians and Muslims, and many languages. "The Christian south," it is often written, "the Muslim north," but the country's truth is coexistence. This is true of the so-called Middle Belt, and in Kaduna, and Jos, and, continuing in the northeast direction, beyond my journey, in Borno.

In the town of Chibok, the girls, mostly sixteen or seventeen, had been cautious. They knew, as everyone did, that schools were being targeted. About forty boys had been killed at a school in Yobe last July. They'd been lined up in their dorms and shot. In the same state, twenty-nine others had died in February, their bodies burned, the culprits never found. And so the girls had come back to Chibok only for their exams—a quick, calculated risk before they returned home.

Where are they now? The shock of a sudden captivity will have given way to other fears. There are more than two hundred of them, Muslim and Christian. Nigeria's northeastern border is massive, porous. They don't know when they crossed the border, or if they crossed the border. They could be in Niger, or Chad, or Cameroon (these three neighboring countries are impoverished states with weak security). The girls know only what their captors say. They have lost track of time. But they feel, in their bodies, the distances covered by the rumbling trucks. They cannot imagine what the world is thinking about them, or if it is.

And what are they themselves thinking of, huddled in their dozens, warned to stay quiet? Not of the murders of Boko Haram's founder and some of his followers by Nigeria Police five years ago, which sparked the violent phase of the group's campaign of terror. Not of the thousands killed during that campaign, in suicide bombs, attacks on churches, and shootings at restaurants, a frightening catalogue of atrocities. Not of the Global War on Terrorism, or of America's strategic goals in that war. (Already, in Niger, a drone base is assembled; already American specialists are on their way to help the Nigerian government.) Not of Baga, some two hundred miles from Chibok, where last year government forces massacred two hundred civilians, or of Maiduguri, where, in mid-March this year, more than five hundred men were executed on suspicion of being terrorists. Not of Abuja, where bombs now explode with unnerving frequency. Not of next year's elections, which the president wants to win at all costs, or of the corruption fueling his reelection bid.

They are not thinking of Twitter, where the captivity is the cause of the day, or of the campaigns on the streets of Lagos for a more competent and less callous government, or of the rallies in front of Nigeria's embassies worldwide, or of the suddenly ramped-up coverage by international media, or of how this war will engulf even those who are only just beginning to hear about it, or of those who, free for now, will someday become captives.

They are perhaps thinking only that night is falling again, and that the men will come to each of them again, an unending horror.

In Alabama

WHEN I WENT down to Alabama, I listened repeatedly to John Coltrane's "Alabama." The introduction of the song has a discursive quality to it, like a black preacher's exhortations. And that, it turned out, was what it was: the keening saxophone line, built over rolling piano chords (like a congregation's murmuring), was a paraphrase of the eulogy Martin Luther King, Jr., gave after a bomb exploded at the Sixteenth Street Baptist Church in Birmingham in 1963, killing four girls.

Alabama's earth is red like West Africa's, dusty, unpromising. On this earth one expects nothing to grow, and on it everything grows. Kudzu and Virginia creeper run riot. This is fertile earth. William Christenberry likens it to brown sugar. James Baldwin wrote: "I could not suppress the thought that this earth had acquired its color from the blood that had dripped down from these trees."

I was sad all the way to Selma. We drove from Gadsden, where cattle prods had been used on protesters in 1964, down through the counties and across land that had known human love and life long before the white man's arrival. Selma's not much, a main drag, Broad Street, that chucks you out of town via the Edmund Pettus Bridge almost as soon as you arrive. The town is much smaller than those others in whose company it evokes the civil rights movement: Montgomery, Birmingham. In the hot sunshine of a Sunday, it was stunned and quiet, with the fable-like air of a crumbling movie set. Selma is named for an Ossianic poem; to my ear, it seems to meld "soul" and its Spanish cognate, "alma," into a single moody word. Selma's shops are closed that day. Pedestrians are few and drift about in the sun like people in Google's Street View. But if you take a left some crossings before the bridge, and a right, you come around to a housing project and, across the street from it, the clean and well-kept Brown Chapel A.M.E. Church, the starting point for those marches fifty years ago.

Long after history's active moment, do places retain some charge of what they witnessed, what they endured?

On Sunday, March 7, 1965, six hundred people, led by John Lewis, marched across the Edmund Pettus Bridge. Just after crossing the bridge, they were met by Alabama state troopers and local police. The men in uniform wore masks, and some of them were on horseback. They gave a brief warning, and then shot tear gas and charged into the crowd with billy clubs. They rolled through undefended people with a sickening carelessness for human safety that the corresponding scene in *Selma*—Ava DuVernay's necessary and otherwise fine film—failed to match. That's the point, perhaps: that what we watch from the safety of a movie theater cannot, and should not, relay to us the true horror of things. For how would we bear it?

But watch the original footage. These Americans brutally beat unarmed women and men, thorough in their merciless-ness, cheered on by other Americans, sending more than fifty Americans to hospital. The footage made the difference, and shocked the nation's conscience. It accelerated the passage of the Voting Rights Act. How not to link it all together? Selma and Ferguson, New York City and Cleveland, torture by the CIA and mass murder in Gaza, the police state and slave patrols: no generation is free of the demands of conscience, and no citizenry can shirk the responsibility of calling the state's abuse of power to account.

Selma was a small town then, and is a small town now. On Sunday, December 7, when I visited, the headline of *The Selma Times-Journal* was SURPRISE AT PARADE: FIRE DEPARTMENT MASCOT SPARKY MAKES RETURN AT CHRISTMAS PARADE. The lede: "Sparky the Fire Dog has returned and he made a grand entrance the morning of the Selma–Fallas County Christmas Parade. The dog costume was stolen from a vehicle parked at the Station 3 firehouse on Oct. 20 and found weather-damaged, dirty, torn and missing pieces behind the old Pancake House. . . ."

I walked down the Pettus Bridge alone. I thought not of Sparky but of John Lewis, whose face and whose spirit I like so much, his light brown trench coat, his backpack, the concentrated dignity in his small frame. I felt these things in my body, tried to honor with my solitary stride the bravery of those women and men, and, in the silence of my walk, the steep drop of the Alabama River to my left, the clear air ahead where there had been smoke and atrocity, I began to hear again Coltrane's "Alabama," not a melody but rather a recitation delivered with the saxophone.

Then the drive down to Montgomery, winter's dry bright landscape flicking by. This bitter earth, these crumbling signs, the things that may have happened in these woods: in this place, I touched on a fissure in America's unfinishable history. Selma to Montgomery on U.S. Route 80 is an hour's drive, some fifty-four miles. It was a walk of four days in 1965, and on that third and successful march, many thousands walked together, 25,000 of them by the time they surged into Montgomery and rallied at the Alabama State Capitol. Around those days, some died. Klan work.

"These children," sings Coltrane's line in 1963, "unoffending, innocent, and beautiful." McCoy Tyner weeping on piano. "Were the victims of one of the most vicious and tragic crimes ever perpetrated against humanity." Jimmy Garrison on bass and Elvin Jones on drums. After Montgomery, after the memorial to the many murdered during those years, the placid-looking Court Square where tens of thousands had been auctioned into slavery, Dr. King's church, the Rosa Parks museum and the woman who was so much more—so much smarter, so much wiser, so much more tactical—than her best-known act of refusal: after all this, we went to Birmingham. And Birmingham was heartbreak, too. At the Sixteenth Street Baptist Church, my soul took fright. How could humans?

History won't let go of us. We're pinned to it. Days later, after my return to New York and with "Alabama" still in my ear, I'm in the crowd of tens of thousands for a march that takes us some miles through lower Manhattan. The language is close in its keening, "I can't breathe," "Black lives matter." The raised voices echo down the caverns of the city's streets.

Bad Laws

NOT ALL VIOLENCE is hot. There's cold violence, too, which takes its time and finally gets its way. Children going to school and coming home are exposed to it. Fathers and mothers listen to politicians on television calling for their extermination. Grandmothers have no expectation that even their aged bodies are safe: any young man may lay a hand on them with no consequence. The police could arrive at night and drag a family out into the street. Putting a people into deep uncertainty about the fundamentals of life, over years and decades, is a form of cold violence. Through an accumulation of laws rather than by military means, a particular misery is intensified and entrenched. This slow violence, this cold violence, no less than the other kind, ought to be looked at and understood.

Near the slopes of Mount Scopus in East Jerusalem is the neighborhood of Sheikh Jarrah. Most of the people who live here are Palestinian Arabs, and the area itself has an ancient history that features both Jews and Arabs. The Palestinians of East Jerusalem are in a special legal category under modern Israeli law. Most of them are not Israeli citizens, nor are they classified the same way as people in Gaza or the West Bank; they are permanent residents. There are old Palestinian families here, but in a neighborhood like Sheikh Jarrah many of the people are refugees who were settled here after the nakba ("catastrophe") of 1948. They left their original homes behind, fleeing places such as Haifa and Sarafand al-Amar, and they came to Sheikh Jarrah, which then became their home. Many of them were given houses constructed on a previously uninhabited parcel of land by the Jordanian government and by the UN Relief and Works Agency. East Jerusalem came under Israeli control in 1967, and since then, but at an increasing tempo in recent years, these families are being rendered homeless a second or third time.

There are many things about Palestine that are not easily seen from a distance. The beauty of the land, for instance, is not at all obvious. Scripture and travelers' reports describe a harsh terrain of stone and rocks, a place in which it is difficult to find water or to shelter from the sun. Why would anyone want this land? But then you visit and you understand the attenuated intensity of what you see. You get the sense that there are no wasted gestures, that this is an economical landscape, and that there is great beauty in this economy. The sky is full of clouds that are like flecks of white paint. The olive trees, the leaves of which have silvered undersides, are like an apparition. And even the stones and rocks speak of history, of deep time, and of the consolation that comes with all old places. This is a land of tombs, mountains, and mysterious valleys. All this one can only really see at close range.

Another thing one sees, obscured by distance but vivid up close, is that the Israeli oppression of Palestinian people is not necessarily—or at least not always—as crude as Western media can make it seem. It is in fact extremely refined, and involves a dizzying assemblage of laws and bylaws, contracts, ancient documents, force, amendments, customs, religion, conventions, and sudden irrational moves, all mixed together and imposed with the greatest care.

The impression this insistence on legality confers, from the Israeli side, is of an infinitely patient due process that will eventually pacify the enemy and guarantee security. The reality, from the Palestinian side, is of a suffocating viciousness. The fate of Palestinian Arabs since the nakba has been to be scattered and oppressed by different means: in the West Bank, in Gaza, inside the 1948 borders, in Jerusalem, in refugee camps abroad, in Jordan, in the distant diaspora. In all these places, Palestinians experience restrictions on their freedom and on their movement. To be Palestinian is to be hemmed in. Much of this is done by brute military force from the Israel Defense Forces—killing for which no later accounting is possible. Some of it happens in the secret chambers of the Shin Bet. But a lot of it is done according to Israeli law, argued in and approved by Israeli courts, and technically legal, even when the laws in question are bad laws and in clear contravention of international standards and conventions.

The reality is that, as a Palestinian Arab, in order to defend yourself against the persecution you face, not only do you have to be an expert in Israeli law, you also have to be a Jewish Israeli and have the force of the Israeli state as your guarantor. You have to be what you are not, what it is not possible for you to be, in order not to be slowly strangled by the laws arrayed against you. In Israel, there is no pretense that the opposing parties in these cases are equal before the law; or, rather, such a pretense exists, but no one on either side takes it seriously. This has certainly been the reality for the Palestinian families living in Sheikh Jarrah whose homes, built mostly in 1956, inhabited by three or four generations of people, are being taken from them by legal means.

As in other neighborhoods in East Jerusalem—Har Homa, the Old City, Mount Scopus, Jaffa Gate—there is a policy at work in Sheikh Jarrah. This policy is twofold. The first is the systematic removal of Palestinian Arabs, either by banishing individuals on the basis of paperwork or by taking over or destroying their homes by court order. Thousands of people have had their residency revoked on a variety of flimsy pretexts: time spent living abroad, time spent living elsewhere in occupied Palestine, and so on. The permanent residency of a Palestinian in East Jerusalem is anything but permanent and, once it is revoked, is almost impossible to recover.

The second aspect of the policy is the systematic increase of the Jewish populations of these neighborhoods. This latter goal is driven by both national and municipal efforts (under the official rubric of "demographic balance") and is sponsored in part by wealthy Zionist activists who, unlike some of their defenders in the Western world, are proud to embrace the word "Zionist." However, it is not the wealthy Zionists who move into these homes or claim these lands: it is ideologically and religiously extreme Israeli Jews, some of whom are poor Jewish immigrants to the State of Israel. And when they move in—when they raise the Israeli flag over a house that, until yesterday, was someone else's ancestral home, or when they begin new constructions on the rubble of other people's homes—they act as anyone would who was above the law: callously, unfeelingly, unconcerned about the humiliation of their neighbors. This twofold policy, of pushing out Palestinian Arabs and filling the land with Israeli Jews, is recognized by all the parties involved.

And for such a policy, the term "ethnic cleansing" is not too strong: it is an alarming but accurate description.

Each Palestinian family that is evicted in Sheikh Jarrah is evicted for different reasons. But the fundamental principle at work is usually similar: an activist Jewish organization makes a claim that the land on which the house was built was in Jewish hands before 1948. There is sometimes paperwork that supports this claim (there is a lot of citation of nineteenth-century Ottoman land law), and sometimes the paperwork is forged, but the court will hear and, through eccentric interpretations of these old laws, often agree to the claim. The violence this legality contains is precisely that no Israeli court will hear a corresponding claim from a Palestinian family. What Israeli law supports, de facto, is the right of return for Jews into East Jerusalem. What it cannot countenance is the right of return of Palestinians into the innumerable towns, villages, and neighborhoods all over Palestine, from which war, violence, and law have expelled them.

History moves at great speed, as does politics, and Zionists understand this. The pressure to continue the ethnic cleansing of East Jerusalem is already met with pressure from the other side to stop this clear violation of international norms. So Zionist lawyers and lawmakers move with corresponding speed, making new laws, pushing through new interpretations, all in order to ethnically cleanse the land of Palestinian presence. And though Palestinians make their own case and though many young Jews, beginning to wake up to the crimes of their nation, have marched in support of the families evicted or under threat in Sheikh Jarrah—the law and its innovative interpretations evolve at a speed that makes self-defense all but impossible.

This cannot go on. The example of Sheikh Jarrah, the cold violence of it, is echoed all over Palestine. Side by side with this cold violence is, of course, the hot violence that dominates the news: Israel's periodic wars on Gaza, its blockades on places such as Nablus, the random unanswerable acts of murder in places such as Hebron. In no sane future of humanity should the deaths of hundreds of children continue to be accounted collateral damage, as Israel did in the summer of 2014.

In the world's assessment of the situation in Palestine, in coming to understand why the Palestinian situation is urgent, the viciousness of law must be taken as seriously as the cruelties of war. As in other instances in which world opinion forced a large-scale systemic oppression to come to an end, we must begin by calling things by their proper names. Israel uses an extremely complex legal and bureaucratic apparatus to dispossess Palestinians of their land, hoping perhaps to forestall accusations of a brutal land grab. No one is fooled by this. Nor is anyone fooled by the accusation, common to many of Israel's defenders, that any criticism of Israeli policies amounts to anti-Semitism. The historical suffering of Jewish people is real—it is in fact one of the most uncontroversially horrific instances of persecution in human experience—but it does not in any way justify the present oppression of Palestinians by Israeli Jews.

A neighborhood like Sheikh Jarrah is an X-ray of Israel at the present moment: a limited view showing a single set of features, but significant to the entire body politic. The case that is being made, and that must continue to be made to all people of conscience, is that Israel's occupation of Palestine is criminal. This case should also include the argument that the proliferation of bad laws by the legislature and courts of Israel is itself against the interests of Jewish people, to the extent that it fuels the ancient and wrongheaded calumnies against them. Nothing can justify either anti-Semitism or the racist persecution of Arabs, and the current use of the law in Israel is a part of the grave ongoing offense to the human dignity of both Palestinians and Jews.

Brazilian Earth

O N THE DRIVE in from the airport, I noticed the bridges and highways. For them to have been built, there must have been some kind of more or less efficient interaction between the economy and the national and metropolitan political structure. A similarly efficient interaction is necessary to keep the roads and bridges in good repair. Below the bridges, which are made of concrete, there is evidence of dredging. Beyond them, rock has been blasted to create tunnels through the mountains. In some neighborhoods, unpromising land was salvaged for construction, some of it shoddy. As is the case in most cities, what is rich and what is poor can be seen in the landscape. That journey in takes place in early-morning light, and the favelas hang on the sides of the mountains.

Long ago all we knew of other places was adventurers' reports and the material testimony of far-fetched goods. The other place was always wondrous order or wondrous disorder, and one has the feeling that Herodotus selected anecdotes only for their strangeness. The distant shore is a place for our dreams to rest, and foreign countries exist not for their own sake but for ours. "Long ago all we knew," and it remains so even now: India and Italy, Morocco and Brazil: each is summarized to answer in a different way the preset question of travel. At night the mountains of Rio look like hills. Seen from the bridge bringing us back into the city, a dense network of lights on each describes a dark shape. Each hill is like a chocolate cake covered in confectioners' sugar. This is the land of football, carnival, and samba, a joyous place, given to simple pleasures, unserious in all the best ways. Everybody fucks everybody, the races mix without anxiety, and the country is blended into shades of caramel, a preview in microcosm of what the world will look like someday. That is the story; but these are not the things I think about when I first enter the city. My thoughts are on first principles, that a city is a built thing, a made thing. To start with, the land is "discovered," won in a battle or in battles, and is tamed and ordered through the efforts of centuries so that its ports and its hinterlands are able to feed, serve, and entertain a large population. A city that manages to do those things well, grows until it becomes a megalopolis.

As cities go, Rio de Janeiro is not unusual. I note how similar the built environment is to that of every other great city I know: the overpasses and underpasses, the street vendors, the massive buildings in various states of newness or disrepair, the patient commuters crowding the bus stops, the evidence of things built by politicians, things built by consensus and on the back of a complex capitalist economy. Only later do I begin to note the dissimilarities: this is another city, an unusual city, and it is another country. It is, above all, on another continent and in another hemisphere, and there is a deep strangeness to a place in which the land and its water are related to each other in the usual way, but where the geological processes as well as the evolution of animals and plants have led to a different reality. At night, I see Venus in an unexpected part of the sky. When I run water down the sink, I look for the Coriolis effect. Within a few days, I have seen bays, inlets, birds, insects, leaves, and fruits unlike any I knew before, with variations in color, smell, cries, size, and scale. Only the humans are basically the same, their beauty, their elegance, their grouchy self-defense, their tiresome sentimentality, their needless cruelties. Only the humans need no special interpretation—or so I think—the humans and their dogs.

I see only one black person on my flight to Rio, the dry-skinned and skeptical man who peers at me from the mirror when I go to use the toilet on the plane. Everyone else on the flight is white, or just one or two Mediterranean shades south of white. But on disembarkation, I see two other black men, one about the color of the current American president, the other darker than me, older, and wearing a JAZZ NEW ORLEANS T-shirt. The darker man stands with me and a handful of others in the passport line for noncitizens. The Brazilian line is considerably longer and looks like the Brazilian neighborhood I visited in Astoria, Queens: a range from fair-skinned to very pale. But several of the baggage handlers and ground staff—I begin to look around now, and get into a mood, and begin to count—are black, some of them mulatto, some "slave-dark." There is an aggravating division noticeable, though I don't want to come to such conclusions so early in the journey. This is not the story the world tells itself about Brazil, or that Brazil advertises to the world about itself.

There are many more blacks on the streets. At a crossing, young black boys swarm the cars, selling cellphone chargers and newspapers. They look like Nigerians, like the boys who descend on cars at intersections in Lagos. But places are not transparent. I know that my understanding of divisions between the races is formed by American history and by my own experience in the United States and can only take me so far here. Would I come closer to the truth if I read a study on Brazilian race relations? I would come closer to *a* truth, I am sure; but there's a truth also in the immediacy of my own experience.

Later, I visit two beaches, whites-only beaches (or so the casual visitor would think) about two hours from Rio. One is for a richer clientele, the other less so, but almost all the blacks I see at both are vendors or workers. At the richer one, in Búzios, I enter a restaurant for lunch. The maître d' ignores my greeting, pretending not to see me. After a few awkward moments, I seat myself. Then I notice him whispering instructions to a black waiter, and it is this waiter alone who serves me and speaks to me while I am there. It is tempting to think the incident explains itself, but what one sees while traveling is rarely self-explanatory. Each place has its own worries, and there's a sense in which what is visible is the wake of a particular history, fleeting, active, but answering to a large and unseen thing. Each society deceives itself in particular ways. The forms of oppression that were practiced here for so long lead to specific pathologies in the society. In Rio there appears to be more socializing across the races than in the United States. But there also seems to be an elaborate and finely tuned colorism at work: among people who would all be considered black in the United States, there is a hierarchy of color. The northern European whites and the Mediterranean whites are more likely to socialize with fair-skinned blacks, and it isn't unusual to see groups of blacks in which everyone in the group is within a narrow range of color: very dark, brownish, yellow, and so on. It isn't the one-drop rule. The number of drops matters.

The guidebooks are full of warnings about the blacks, though of course the warnings are not expressed so baldly. One must not visit favelas alone, one must be careful in certain districts, and be alert on the metro, and avoid walking at night. It appears to be sensible advice, but there is a hysterical tone in the warnings. The warnings are intended for white tourists. I am a young black man, and my mode of dress and bodily attitude make me blend in easily with locals. I feel more welcome on the streets than in fine restaurants, where I am marked out more by my inability to speak Portuguese than by anything else. I hear the warnings from others, too, and they are the sorts of things that New Yorkers would say to visitors to their own city: the talk of "bad" neighborhoods, the kinds of people—whole classes of people—that one should avoid, the experiences the visitor couldn't possibly be interested in except from the safety of a tour bus going around the human zoo. But whether in reference to Harlem on a Sunday morning or to the favelas in an organized tour, "bad neighborhood" is a code term for other things, a rhetorical move that separates some imagined "us," rich enough to travel, white enough to see ourselves reflected in television melodramas and in advertising, from "them," whose presence at our travel destination is an inconvenience.

Rio is by some distance the most geographically spectacular city I have ever visited. Riding the cable car up to the Pão d'Açúcar adds something genuinely new to my experience of the world. The sea and its numerous inlets at the moment the sun is setting behind Corcovado, the streets and houses hundreds of meters below with their evening lights just coming on, and those lights seen all together nestled in the undulating land like so many fresh rivulets of lava, the massive monoliths scattered in the bay, and all of this viewed from the great height we crested in a nineteenth-century contraption: it was an awesome rush of sensation, an unanticipated seduction of the eye, fairy-tale stuff. The gneiss monoliths were extruded in ancient times when the continent that is now South America sheared itself away from Gondwanaland. How beautiful it all looks at dusk from the mountain named for the shape of the tins at sugar refineries. The shape of the coast created calm bays, calm bays are ideal ports, ports build great cities, and Rio de Janeiro became the entry and exit into one of the world's great expanses of wealth: sugar, mines for precious and semiprecious stones, and slaves.

In the Lapa district of the city, I meet a man who is selling "African" things at a street fair. He is Senegalese, short and with delicate features. I ask him how much some woven Islamic caps cost and see, in his bright eyes, a flicker of recognition: he responds in English, and immediately becomes curious about me, where I'm from, what my name is. His name is El Hadj, and he tells me he has been in Rio for twelve years. He speaks English well, with a considered tone. "It's a very difficult country," he says, unprompted. "They are very hard on blacks here. Things are difficult if you are black." For Brazilian blacks, or for Africans? "Both. But harder if you are Brazilian. I am an African. I know my rights"—I am struck by this usage of "rights," which sounds rather American to me—"but these Brazilians, it is so sad, you know. After five hundred years . . ." He taps his head.

El Hadj imports the goods from Dakar—trinkets, figurines, printed cloth, and handwoven material—for sale in Rio, but his real work, he says, is that he is a journalist. He is just trying to earn some money on the side to do his master's degree in Brazil. He has a calm and calming presence, with none of the tense energy or obvious fatigue of some of the brothers who do this street trade. He still writes, for French-language outlets, some of which are published in Senegal.

"The slavery is not over, you see. The blacks here try to be close to Africa. I think they are closer to Africa than those in America. In some ways, they are more connected to African culture. Because that is our problem as blacks, you see, we have surrendered our culture, the good things in our culture. Not all of it is good, but we should not give up the good things. This is our biggest problem. But Brazilian blacks . . ." Again, he taps his head. "And the whites in this country, forget it, they will give the blacks no chance."

"What about you? Do you move around freely?"

"Yes, sometimes, when I enter a nice mall, they really look at me strangely, you know. What is this guy doing here?" I tell him I have experienced the same. He says, "But it is a good country, a very good country. The food, the culture. I like Brazil, even though it is difficult. The women are beautiful."

He has to attend to one customer, then others come to join her, black Brazilians, dressed in white. Their affect is like that of the Afrocentric blacks in Brooklyn. The women begin to admire bales of El Hadj's wax-print cloth, and I leave him.

The place at which we arrive after crossing the world is a surprising version of home. It is home not in the far-fetched and marvelous view from the mountain, but in the street level, the bankers, the maids, the Internet service, the electrical grid, the supermarkets, the unctuous waiters, the videogames, the question marks over the cabdrivers, the schools and churches, the clean bathrooms, the dirty politics, the traffic jams, the little pockets of "authentic culture," the noise from kindergartens at midday, the translated American bestsellers, Celine Dion on the radio, *Who Wants to Be a Millionaire* on the television, the bored police officers with their brooding firearms, the indifferent water pressure from the showers, the sports pennants hanging from windows, the adults dressed like toddlers on game day, the beer, the wine, the graffiti, the transvestites, the auto repair shops, the gas stations, the cowboys, the cowhands, the hospitals, and the cemeteries.

What has us setting off to distant destinations in the first place? Perhaps "us" is wrong and travel writing, and travel thought, ought to begin in the singular, in some acknowledgment of the "I" that speaks. I am Yoruba, and in this country, of all the places outside Nigeria, the Yoruba heritage is visible. The orixás of the northeast of Brazil are the orishas of the southwest of Nigeria. Xangô is Shango, Exú is Esu, Yemanjá is Yemoja, Ogun is Ogu, and Obatalá is unchanged. The gods are all here, the language itself survives in ritual, and Yoruba drumming has found its way into the samba and, greatly decelerated, into bossa nova. Farofa is garri, the sweet-and-sour flour of the cassava plant, a staple food of Yorubas on both sides of the Atlantic. In the lifetime of my great-grandparents, slaves were still arriving in Brazil from Yorubaland. In the same generation and later, there were those who returned after slavery in Brazil. Names like Pereira, da Silva, and da Costa survive, and those families became important, particularly in Lagos. The architectural innovations the Afro-Brazilians brought back to Lagos, Abeokuta, and surrounding towns, the stucco façades, the two-story buildings, mark those places to this day. But none of this means an easy delight for me, a Yoruba man visiting Brazil. It suggests only that this country is the site of some trauma to which I am related, a trauma the memory of which catches me at sudden moments.

I'm writing these words in Tijuca, a working-class neighborhood of Rio, on a rainy afternoon, and there's a white cloud sitting on a green mountain in the distance. The cloud is so

densely white that it appears to be just as substantial as the for-
ested mountain itself. I am reading Machado de Assis's master-
piece *Epitaph of a Small Winner,* which is itself set in Tijuca, a
wry book, a funny and humane examination of cynicism in
Rio's upper classes, written by a black man when slavery was
still legal here. I remember—this is an overstatement, but it
feels right—I remember the things suffered here by Africans. It
is strange to think I would have understood the pleas at the
whipping post, that they would have been in my own language,
the language of my people—my people sold off into slavery by
my people. A blood knot ties each of us to ancient acts of violence. I am unhappy and at home.

But in writing all this, what I have managed to exclude is a
proper sense of the pleasure of travel, and the intense pleasure
of traveling to this particular place. I hate cheery travel writing,
but I feel I have overcorrected in the other direction, and already I begin to plan my return to Brazilian earth.

Angels in Winter

DEAR BETH,

Our first sight of land came from Lazio's farms, a green different from American green, less neon-bright, more troubled with brown. Later, on the express train into town, the impression was strengthened by the scattering of pines, palms, and cypresses along the tracks. I became aware for the first time of how plant life is part of the story of being in a foreign place. As the eye adjusts to different buildings and different uses of technology, as the ear begins to find its way into the local dialect, the flora, too, present a challenge to the senses. Here, the biome projected a certain obstinacy: these plants had struggled against both human culture and hot weather for a long time. It wasn't hot the day we arrived. It was cool, the fog interleaved with rain, spoiling visibility.

A woman from Verona, her ticket on her lap, sat across from us. She wore a business suit and sunglasses, and had the slight impatience of early morning work-related travel. On the other side of the aisle was a middle-aged couple, the man in a blue tracksuit (which at the belly strained to contain him). Facing them, a sharply dressed young man in dark blue suit, powder-blue shirt, and skinny black tie spoke loudly into the telephone—"Pronto! Sì, sì. Sì, sì, sì! Andiamo, ciao, ciao!"—

a clipped bare-bones negotiation. There was a performative busyness in his torrent of sì's; negotium, the negation of pleasure.

Italy is a Third World country. It has the ostentatious contrasts as well as the brittle pride. The greenery of Fiumicino quickly gave way to abandoned buildings with rusted roofs. We rumbled by a necropolis of wrecked cars in a wide yard, beyond which were muddy roads stretching back into the country and ceasing to be roads, become just muddy fields. On the culverts and walls, as those became more numerous, graffiti artists were indefatigable, covering every available surface. The tags were beautiful: they answered to the ancient ruins. The ruins themselves were as elaborate as stretches of aqueduct, or as simple as sections of broken wall. Their size as well as their integration into the landscape was the first real sign of the ubiquity of the past in Rome. In many places this past was elaborated and curated (as I would soon discover), but in others it was entirely untouched, the material relics simply remaining there, a testament to thousands of years of decay, an echo of the wealth and greatness of the people who lived here.

The suburban tenements soon appeared, festooned with washing, and increasingly small patches of open land on which flocks of tough-looking sheep grazed. By the time we arrived at Termini, the rain had begun again, this time heavily. We knew which bus we wanted, but there were no bus maps (everyone else seemed to know where to go). Finding the right embarkation point consisted of walking from one section of the parking lot to another, and we were drenched by the time we did find it. But time quickened, and we were soon inside Rome proper, in the Esquiline (one of the original seven hills), inside what felt like a gigantic Cinecittà set.

I was intoxicated by the visual impression of the place: the large well-laid-out squares, the dilapidated but elegant buildings, the Vespas, the mid-century modern feel of much of the signage, the ragged edges on everything (for some reason all this made me think of Julian Schnabel). It was alluring, even in winter, perhaps especially in winter, with the colors warm and bold (orange, red, and yellow), but somewhat desaturated. As we passed through Piazza Vittorio Emanuele, I noted the gargantuan scale of the built environment, and the profusion of ornament.

Both scale and ornament are related to history. "The classics" are not homogeneous. But what distinguishes Roman art from Greek art? I go with this impression: the Greeks were idealists, invested in the perfection of form, fixated on eternity. Isn't the way people die in the *Iliad,* sorrowfully but not without a certain dignity, part of the attraction? I thought of your love for the Greeks, Beth, which is related to this dignity. The Romans, who later adopted their forms with a startling exactness—much of what we know of Greek art is from Roman copies—were more grounded: they got more complicatedly into the preexisting questions of political advantage, obsequy, national honor, and, of course, empire. Propaganda became more vivid than ever. And so, the buildings got larger and more ornate, lurid even, ostensibly to honor the gods or the predecessor rulers (many of whom were deified), but in reality as guarantees of personal glory. The Greeks loved philosophy for its own sake, more or less, but the Romans loved it for what it could be used for, namely political power. This at least was the way I understood it—you'll forgive a traveler's generalizations.

Roman propaganda, the manipulation of images for political ends, hadn't begun with Augustus, Julius Caesar's successor and the first of the emperors, but he'd certainly brought it to a keen level. He'd enlisted architects and sculptors for the project of transforming him from violent claimant to the leadership— a position for which he was neither more nor less qualified than his main rival, Mark Antony—to Pater Patriae. The message, which got through, was that he was not merely fatherly but also avuncular. He was powerful, well loved, generous, and his leadership was inevitable.

Augustus's successful marshaling of art to the shaping of his image was the template for just about every emperor who came afterward. The skill and subtlety of Roman art, from the first-century emperors to Constantine in the fourth, was for the most part dedicated to dynastic and propagandistic goals. Was there after all, I asked myself, so great a leap between imperial Rome and the buffoonery of Mussolini? The misuse of piety was no new thing.

And so, on that first day, heading out in the late afternoon to the Capitoline Hill—the ancient site of an important temple to Jupiter, now a set of museums around a Michelangelo-designed piazza—I was braced for a mental separation between art and its public functions. I came up Michelangelo's broad, ramped staircase, past the monumental sculptures of Castor and Pollux, into the glistening egg-shaped piazza. The rain had ceased. Not many people were around. I had my arsenal of doubts at the ready.

But I want to set parentheses around this essay, Beth. It's no good pretending that, in going to Rome in 2009, one has gone to some exotic corner of the earth. Rome was as central a center of the world as there has been in this world. And now that there are many centers, it remains one of the important ones. So, I want to acknowledge not only that millions of other visitors do what I just did—visit Rome as tourists or pilgrims— but that this has been going on for a great long while. Those visitors have included many of the world's best writers, and, in addition, many of the world's great writers have been themselves Romans. I am unlikely to write anything new or penetrating about Rome. In writing about Rome, I am writing about art and history and politics, and how those things relate particularly to me, a solitary observer with a necessarily narrow, a necessarily shallow, view of the place. Rome is simply the pretext, and the font of specifics, for the discontinuous thoughts of a first-time traveler.

And while I'm at it, I also want to question the very possibility of writing anything about a people, in this particular case Romans. Is it possible, I wonder, to write a sentence that begins "Romans are . . . ," and have such a sentence be interesting and truthful at the same time? We are properly skeptical of generalizations, after a lifetime of "blacks are . . . ," "women are . . . ," "Indians are . . . ," "Pakistanis are . . ."

But an important part of the Roman enterprise, historically speaking, was the effort to characterize Rome and what it meant to be a Roman. This went beyond local pride, and also beyond imperial ambition. It was a certain relationship to fellow citizens and to the state, a relationship aided by war and by oratory. Principles were important, they were fought over if necessary, and any and all hypocrisies had to be practiced under the aegis of the principles. The motto SPQR (Senatus Populusque Romanus: a reminder that a given enterprise or monument was there at the pleasure of the senate and people of Rome) simply manifested the principles at stake.

Rome followed the example of Athens in this (think of Pericles's funeral oration, which had more sly jingoism than an American campaign speech) and would herself later serve as exemplum for the American experiment. Before American exceptionalism, there was Roman exceptionalism, to a much more severe degree. Our Capitol is named for the Capitoline Hill. Close parentheses.

Thus primed with my skepticism, a skepticism compounded with an anticolonial instinct, I entered the museums on the Capitoline Hill. Well: so much for preparation. I was floored. My theories simply had no chance against what I experienced—the finest collection of classical statuary I had ever seen. The strength of the collection was not limited to the famous pieces—the *Capitoline Venus,* the *Dying Gaul,* the *Colossus of Constantine*—wonderful though they were. There were countless other sculptures, including several, such as a standing Hermes, that would have been the proud centerpieces of lesser collections. The patron of boundaries wore his winged hat and winged sandals, held a caduceus in his hand—what a wonder to meet Hermes where Hermes meant so much. But what struck me most was the rooms full of marble portrait busts.

Ancient Roman marble portraiture rose to a very high degree of competence. It was an art that had been less thoroughly pursued by the Greeks, invested as they were in ideal forms. The fascination of Roman portraiture for me was twofold. First, I was struck by how subject to fashions it was, how, within the space of thirty or forty years, there were perceptible shifts in the sculptural style. The pendulum swung between "veristic" and "idealizing" techniques. A female portrait from the second century C.E., for instance, is rather easy to identify: the sculptors depicted the corkscrew hairstyle of the time in careful detail, and made extensive use of the drill (to poke holes in the marble, and give the hair an illusion of depth). Drills were used, too, in portraits of men during this period: after Hadrian's decision to wear one, beards were all the rage, and they were sculpted in marble with drills. By the time of Marcus Aurelius and his son Commodus (both bearded), portraiture had reached new levels of psychological acuity. To the realistic depiction of age and wrinkles, which was itself a conscious throwback to the portraiture of the Roman republic, there were now added indications of the subjects' frame of mind: melancholy, levity, exhaustion, fleeting states set in stone.

Among the many representations of the gods and emperors and senators were busts of ordinary citizens. What these portraits showed was that ordinary Romans participated intimately in this image economy. I was right to have been aware of the propagandistic aspect of image making, but not to the extent of forgetting how widespread and common images themselves were, and how generally sophisticated the ability to read them. One estimate puts the number of sculptures in Rome in the second century at 2 million. History tends to favor rulers and warriors, but the history that peered at me from the white marble faces on the Capitoline was closer to ground level: bakers, soldiers, courtesans, writers. It was a history of involvement and implication in the Roman project.

Whatever Rome was, or whatever it had been, it was so out of the enthusiasm of the people of Rome for Roman modes of being. The sculptures were one part of that. They were a way of expressing a desire to be honored and to be remembered. That the results were so visually arresting was no coincidence. The visual propaganda of the emperors would not have been so forceful had the populace not been already attuned to imagery.

So, "Romans are . . ." what? Romans are people who are part of Rome, and would rather be part of Rome. To be Roman was to participate in Rome. That was my inkling on the first day. But, of course, that inkling was not to last the week without revision.

"We are working hard. In fact we're just hustling. It's not easy at all," Moses said. He'd made little room for small talk or pleasantries. A certain bitterness was evident in his voice. Moses was a friend of Paula's, and she'd introduced him to me because he was a Nigerian, an Ibo. Before he came to the house, she'd told me that he was a building contractor. "He is in partnership with an Italian. You know why? If you have an employee, there are rules, you must pay a certain amount, of taxes, of benefits, a certain minimum salary. But if you are 'partners,' then there is no responsibility. And so this man cheats him by making him a partner; Italians cheat foreign employees this way. They painted this house, but I don't know who pocketed the money."

Moses's sober mien and sharp comments confirmed this picture. "Our problem is that when we go home, when we are there for a few days, we spend one thousand euros. And everyone thinks that life must be luxurious for us overseas. They think we live in palaces here. It is not so, but they don't know that. They get on the next flight and come. They meet a bad situation in Rome." I asked him about the Nigerian community in Rome. "There are many of us," he said, "not as many as Turin—you know, that's where our women are, mostly, doing, you know—but our people are always how they are. You know our people. No Nigerian helps you unless you help them first, unless you pay them money. Nothing is free. There is no help.

Teju Cole, *Zürich* (2015)

Teju Cole, *Lugano* (2014)

René Burri, *Men on a Rooftop* (1960)

Glenna Gordon, *Mass Abduction in Nigeria* (2014)

National Archives of South Africa, *A Prisoner Working in the Garden*
(Nelson Mandela) (1977)

Teju Cole, *Rome* (2008)

I've been in this country now nine years, and everything is still a struggle. Especially for those of us who don't have much education."

Moses spoke fluent Italian, and he wore a well-cut brown suit, a blush-colored tie, oxblood brogues. His mustache was meticulously trimmed to a slightly comical half-inch-thick strip on either side of his philtrum. There was no particular warmth in his interaction with me, confessional though it was. His presentation was smart, his manner courtly, a contractor dressed like a dandy; but the tone was all exhaustion. A miserable cry of exhaustion. "Our women" to describe the Nigerian prostitutes in Turin was, I thought, part of his resigned attitude. No activist he, just a brother trying to survive.

Paula was Italian, and separated from her husband. She ran the bed-and-breakfast with the help of a business partner. The husband, Carlo, helped when she needed it. We'd met him on the first day—an evasive, thin-faced man—and hadn't seen him since. Their split was recent. Paula herself was warm, an "accidental Italian" as she saw it, much more interested in Latin America, in salsa and tango, and in learning English.

One evening, at the kitchen table of her beautiful home, she said, "Have you read Saviano? Everyone here read this book. It's so sad, no? I feel such deep shame for my country." Roberto Saviano's exposé of the mafia, *Gomorrah,* had been a bestseller, and had been recently made into a film. But a number of threats on his life meant that he was now under round-the-clock police protection. It was a big story. For anyone who knew the ruthlessness and reach of the Naples organization known as the Camorra, the threats were credible, and chilling. Their tentacles reached into high levels of law enforcement and government. "I don't care about Berlusconi. Everyone hates him," Paula said, "but I care about the future of Italy. It means nothing to me, for myself, but I think always of my daughter. She is growing up here, she will maybe make her life here. We have a justice system so slow that it is like having no justice system. Mafia bosses are released on technicalities, but petty criminals get stiff sentences. Can you believe, in Naples, when the police comes to arrest a killer, the women get in the street and make a big scene, shouting, crying? The Camorra is like a cult; it controls them totally. I have such shame for this country. And our politicians, of course, they can do nothing. Berlusconi, he is the worst, just the worst. You say his name and people spit."

Perry Anderson, in a recent essay in the *London Review of Books,* wrote about the "invertebrate left" in Italy. From the engaged and partially successful interventions of Antonio Gramsci and Rodolfo Morandi there had now emerged . . . nothing. Italian politics was a mass of confusions, and within this confusion, rightist parties clung on to power.

Paula said, "We are excited for America. We love Obama. But we don't believe we can change things here. It's not possible, so we don't try. It's a great shame for us, though people don't talk much about it." Later, on television I watch Berlusconi speak rapidly and smugly, his hands gesturing at speed. The impunity that he and the Camorristi share is met with shrugs. He's made of money; he can outbid anyone.

Father Rafael said, "Italians are too interested in enjoying life to do anything about politics. Wine, fashion, that's what they care about. So people like Berlusconi face no opposition." Father Rafael was a Jesuit I had met through another priest in New York last summer. He now lived in Rome. He was easygoing, in his mid-forties, not at all ascetic. We'd first met over drinks and football matches. I was drawn to him then for his matter-of-fact style. "Most priests dislike this pope," he'd said to me, "he's old, his ideas are old. The sooner he dies off, the better. This is something we priests talk about openly. We loved John Paul, because he did a lot to move the church forward in the right ways. Now Benedict, among his other mistakes, has given a free pass to those who want to drop the vernacular and return to a Latin mass. What's the point?" Like many priests of his generation, he's not from Europe or America, not white. He's from Angola, though for many years he worked in Burundi, and considers it his home now. We met in a trattoria not far from the Colosseum. I ordered the pizza with prosciutto and fungi; he ordered the same, but without the ham; it was Lent.

"You won't have too much problem with racism here," he said, "especially if you speak the language. Italians love that, when someone from outside masters their language." He was doing advanced studies in biblical scholarship at the Society of Jesus. Italian, being only a half step away from Portuguese, had been easy for him to learn. "And you have to remember, there are racists everywhere."

But, I wanted to know, wasn't the situation of the Roma, the gypsies, especially bad? "That's true," he said, "people here have little patience with them. There is a belief that they are generally criminals and, well, they are. They raise their children up to be thieves." I had raised an eyebrow, so he softened his stance. "Out of every two crimes reported in the newspaper, one is committed by Roma. Is that the reality? Who knows? But that is what is reported. So, Romans don't view them as human beings, really. There is a big effort in the comune to push them out once and for all. There have been rapes and murders recently that they are blamed for. And that is why you haven't seen many of them: they're afraid! I think there's a real possibility of Roma men being lynched in this city now. The feeling about them is that hostile."

On the metro lines, there was a small set of videos that recycled endlessly on TV screens. One, a jaunty little cartoon, warned you against pickpockets. Another was a television blooper reel, most memorably featuring a fat man in a hurdle race who stumbled at every hurdle but kept going. And then there was the slickly produced spot that implored those who had been victims of racism to call the number provided. The "anti-razzismo" push was a serious public project. But privately? In many restaurants and museums, I was stared at, aggressively and repeatedly. In public interactions, I was treated either to the famous Mediterranean warmth (usually by the young) or to an almost shocking disdain. I had at least four incidents of speaking to people (in my few phrases of Italian) and being met with resolute silence, some transactions taking place entirely in that silence.

There were in any case many people of color in the city: Africans, Bangladeshis, Latin Americans. Around them was the inescapable air of being on the margins—the clergy seemed to be visitors, and the workers (newsagents, street florists, sellers of knockoff luxury goods) appeared to have scarcely more secure a hold. They were here only because Romans, for now, tolerated their presence. The comune was Roman, nativist. Not black, not brown, not Albanian, and definitely not Roma.

After Berlusconi's frothing performance, the RAI picture cut to a newscast. The newscaster was a middle-aged African man, much darker than I am, distinguished-looking, graying at the temples. He delivered the day's headlines in rapid Italian, and in the cloying, ingratiating style common to newscasters everywhere.

I used to hate angels. But even to put it that way gives them too much credence. It would be more accurate to say I don't believe in angels but I dislike the idea of angels, finding them silly, seeing none of the beauty, grace, or comfort that people seem to project on them. When I was more active in church life, I found angels actively embarrassing, as though comic book or fantasy novel characters had somehow lodged themselves into the center of the world's most serious narrative. Fairy tales should have no role in theology.

No feature of angels annoyed me more than their wings: impractical, unlikely, entirely incredible from a biological point of view. I always reasoned that for a man to fly with wings on his back, he would need back muscles as enormous as a bison's. Angels, in most depictions through the ages, looked like men with white toy wings tacked on. They were an infantile fantasy, made to bear a spiritual burden that they were, to my eyes at least, remarkably ill suited for. Angels were just about as relevant to my life as the preprocessed sentiment of Hallmark cards or Top 40 love songs: in other words, irrelevant.

Toward the end of my week in Rome, standing in the long gallery of the Museo Pio-Clementino in the Vatican, I saw another fine statue of Hermes. Nearby were two herms. I did not look at the herms for long, but—as is fitting to their function—they flashed through me memorably. You know I have been thinking about porous boundaries, shadow regions, ambiguities, and, lately, about the idea of embodied intermediaries. This is why I have become more interested in how these intermediaries have been narrated: Hermes, Mercury, Esu, and, in the case of the Christian religions, angels. But no, to say "interested" is insufficient. Better to call it "invested"—an investment in what, it now occurs to me, I might call a parenthetical mode of life.

I visited Rome in the waning of winter. The senses implicated me. The senses were key: in addition to the classical statuary, my most intense artistic experiences of Rome were the troubled architect Borromini and the troubled painter Caravaggio. Both freed my senses, caught my heart off guard, blew it open. Borromini's buildings—the small church of San Carlo alle Quattro Fontane in particular—seemed to be taking wing right before one's eyes. Caravaggio's paintings, meanwhile, were full of musicians, peasants, saints, and angels. His *St. John the Baptist* (at the Borghese Gallery), the young prophet with an inscrutable expression on his face, his body nestled next to a wild ram's, was a sensuous catalogue of subtle conflicts, as smoky and disturbing as anything by Leonardo da Vinci.

People, too, stood in as angels. Paula, the owner of the bed-and-breakfast, who declared that she did not believe in doing anything if she could not do it with amore, was one such. Another was Annie, a new friend, whose wisdom and intelligence steeped me in worlds entirely mine and entirely unknown to me. In stories of her friends and acquaintances, I caught glimpses of creativity and flexibility (hers, as well as theirs). Through her, I understood De Sica better, and Rossellini, and Visconti. I especially enjoyed her story about driving Fellini around—of his insatiable curiosity about everything around him. And through her, I met Judit, a Hungarian photographer, who, in the long low Roman light of a Sunday evening, showed me a quarter century of her work, pictures taken in Budapest and Rome. Our photographs—I shot a great deal in my brief time in the city—had uncanny areas of resonance. We were drawn to the same moments: reflections, ruins, motion, wings. I wondered if perhaps immigrants and visitors had certain insights into the heart of a place, insights denied the natives. My life and Judit's had been so different, she growing up in Communist Hungary, wrestling over a lifetime of creativity with the legacy of great Hungarian photographers—Kertész, Munkácsi, Capa, Brassaï— then moving to Italy, and raising a son in what still felt, to her, like a foreign country. I was grateful for the connection, of which Annie had been the intermediary. And for the connection with Annie, too, which had been brokered by her sister, Natalie. These avatars of Hermes who guided me from where I had been to where I was to be. And you also, Beth, through whom these words and images now enter the world in a new way.

At the Spanish Steps, where, even in winter, tourists swarm, there were lithe African men doing a brisk trade in Prada and Gucci bags. The men were young, personable as was required for sales, but at other moments full of melancholy. The bags were arranged on white cloths, not at all far from the luxury shops that sold the same goods for ten or twenty times more. It was late afternoon. Beautiful yellow light enfolded the city, and, from the top of the steps, the dome of St. Peter's was visible, as was the Janiculum Hill, on the other side of the Tiber. In that light, the city had an eternal aspect, an illumination seemed to come from the earth and glow up into the sky, not the other way around. Did I sense in myself, just then, a shift? A participation, however momentary, in what Rome was?

There was a sudden commotion: with a great whoosh the

African brothers raced up the steps, their white cloths now caught at the corners and converted into bulging sacks on their backs. One after the other, then in pairs, they fled upward, fleet of foot, past where I stood. Tourists shrank out of their way. I spun around and pressed the shutter. Far below, cars carrying carabinieri, the military police, arrived, but by then (all this was the action of less than half a minute) the brothers had gone.

Later, I looked at the image on my camera: the last of the angels vanishing up the long flight of steps, *a hurry through which known and strange things pass,* their white wings flashing in the setting sun.

Shadows in São Paulo

A RE THEY GANGSTERS? Are they bankers? There are certain photographs that seem to have been pulled out of the world of dreams. *Men on a Rooftop,* by the Swiss photographer René Burri (1933–2014), is one such picture. The photograph, taken in São Paulo in 1960, shows four men on a rooftop, seen from the vantage point of an even higher building. Far below them, stark in black and white, are tramlines and cars, and tiny pedestrians so perfectly matched with their long shadows that they look like miniaturized sculptures by Giacometti.

I'm not sure when my interest in *Men on a Rooftop* became an obsession. Through the years it gained a hold on my imagination until it came to stand as one of the handful of pictures that truly convey the oneiric possibilities of street photography. The celebrated Iranian photojournalist Abbas, who knew Burri well (they were both members of Magnum Photos), described *Men on a Rooftop* to me as "vintage René: superb form, no political or social dimension." Abbas zeros in on the formal perfection of the image, but I'm not sure I agree that it lacks a social dimension. To me, it literally portrays the levels of social stratification and the enormous gap between those above and those below.

A great photo comes about through a combination of readiness, chance, and mystery. Gabriel García Márquez, once asked whom the best reader of *One Hundred Years of Solitude* was, responded with a story: "A Russian friend met a lady, a very old lady, who was copying the whole book out by hand, right to the last line. My friend asked her why she was doing it, and the lady replied, 'Because I want to find out who is really mad, the author or me, and the only way to find out is to rewrite the book.' I find it hard to imagine a better reader than that lady." Like the lady in García Márquez's story, I thought some act of repetition would clarify things. And so I went to São Paulo in March 2015, looking for René Burri.

I was there once before, three years earlier, and I had been impressed by the city's thrumming energy, especially along the stateliest of its avenues, the Avenida Paulista. This was not the clichéd Brazil of soccer, sand, and samba. From a height in any central district of São Paulo, what you see is an incessancy of high-rises, as though someone had invented the high-rise and then forgotten to stop. This city of work and hard edges, I found, was the Brazil I preferred, and I somehow convinced myself that Burri's photograph, so keen in its evocation of capital, must have been taken on Avenida Paulista.

Shortly after arriving in the city, I went to visit a friend, the curator Thyago Nogueira, in his beautiful corner office on the fourteenth floor of a building on Paulista. There were great views of the avenue, but in neither direction could I see a correspondence with any aspect of Burri's picture. Where were the four silvery tram tracks glinting in the slanting sun? What about the steep canyon created by the tall buildings facing one another? And I couldn't find any building that matched the one on which the men were walking. Thyago began to mention other major roads in the city. Perhaps I wanted Rua da Consolação or Avenida da Liberdade? Or was Burri's view from the Martinelli

Building? As he threw out names, it dawned on me that I was lost: I'd come all this way, and all I had was a city, a year, a photographer's name.

In Magnum's New York office, there's a library print of *Men on a Rooftop*. On the reverse of the picture are stamps and scribbles: Burri's name, the words "Brazil" and "businessmen," and several five-digit numbers in different hands. It was a lovely artifact, but it told me nothing about exactly where in the city the picture had been made. Nor did an interview Burri gave late in life, in which he simply said, "Whenever there was a high-rise building, I was climbing up and knocked at the door and said, 'Can I take a picture?'" São Paulo is full of high-rises, and they all have doors. I tried a few. The view from the roof of the sinuous thirty-eight-floor Oscar Niemeyer–designed Copan building yielded no clues. The restaurant near the top of the forty-six-floor Edifício Itália offered a thrilling panorama, but I saw nothing that related to Burri's photograph.

There had been a terrible drought at the beginning of the year, but it was finally raining in São Paulo. I sat in my hotel room, brooding. During a brief lull in the downpour, a woman dressed in black and wearing high heels walked across the roof of the building on the other side of the street, smoking a cigarette.

Four days into my trip, Thyago emailed with news. A friend of his thought that Burri's picture was made from the top of a building that once belonged to the Bank of the State of São Paulo. That building, still informally called the Banespão, was completed in 1947, and was for a while the tallest in Brazil. I went up with a small group of tourists. It was mid-morning, the rain had stopped; we were limited to five minutes. From the viewing platform, thirty-six floors above the sprawling city, the vista was bright. I took photos in all directions and realized, with a sinking feeling, that I was again in the wrong place. Then the five minutes were up, and our small group had to descend.

A dead end. I wrote to thank Thyago anyway, and I asked other friends in the city about Burri's picture, but few of them knew it. The search had begun to take on some of the dream logic of the photograph itself. I was frustrated but also vaguely amused, as though I were suspended in the first half of an uncompleted joke. I asked the concierge. I asked the taxi drivers who took me around. None of them could recognize the photograph. It seemed that I would leave São Paulo empty-handed. In any case, the city had grown so fast and so hectically: perhaps the building the men walked on, or the one from which Burri took his picture, had been altered or demolished.

Then Thyago wrote back. His friend, he said, insisted that it had to be the Banespão. It could be no other. But I'd seen the view with my own eyes. What had I missed? It was a Friday, the day before the end of my vacation. And that was when I remembered a curious story that Burri told about the photograph. In those days, according to Burri, Henri Cartier-Bresson limited his fellow photographers to lenses from 35 millimeters to 90 millimeters. Burri had surreptitiously gone longer while shooting in São Paulo, to 180 millimeters. "I never told him!" he said. "At that point, I broke loose from my mentor." When you shoot at such an extended focal length, there's a great deal more compression between the middle and far distances. The canyons created by São Paulo's high-rises seem even more vertiginous. The angle of view is also severely narrowed, cutting out much of what the eye sees on the periphery of vision. Perhaps using the wrong lens was getting in my way? I'd taken a 50-millimeter lens with me. I now borrowed a longer lens from Thyago; it was only 85 millimeters, not ideal, but closer. Then I got in a taxi and went to the Banespão.

It was late afternoon, and by now the rains were torrential. The city was a gray blur. The buildings shone with wet. The time limit at the top of the building was the same as before, five minutes, and, in the open-air viewing platform, I got drenched. I set my eye to the camera's viewfinder and looked northwest. Suddenly, everything clicked into place, as in the final moves of a jigsaw. I saw Burri's view. To the right was the building the men had walked on. How could I have missed it before? It was (I later discovered) the Edifício do Banco do Brasil. What I hadn't seen in Burri's photo was that the "roof" the men were walking on was not the building's summit: the building had a stacked design, and a further set of floors rose just out of the shot. To my left and far below, meanwhile, was Avenida São João, slightly changed from 1960—the tramlines were gone—but certainly recognizable in its rain-slicked state. The avenue was full of cars, buses, and pedestrians. The rain kept coming down, and my five minutes were up. But the mission had been accomplished.

"The photograph isn't what was photographed, it's something else," Garry Winogrand once said. "It's about transformation." The photographic image is a fiction created by a combination of lenses, cameras, film, pixels, color (or its absence), time of day, season. When I'm moved by something, I want to literally put myself in its place, the better to understand what was transformed. This interests me as a writer and as a photographer: How do raw materials become something else, something worth keeping? "Those four guys just came from nowhere, and went to nowhere," Burri said of the men in his photograph. The photograph he made of them came from nowhere and went everywhere. My seeing his point of view and taking a picture from the same spot fifty-five years later did not solve the mystery. But in discovering all that can be known about a work of art, what cannot be known is honored even more. We come right up to the edge, and can go no farther.

Two Weeks

         ———————

S URELY IT'S A trick of time. But the facts are what they are: I
last visited Edinburgh eighteen years ago. This time round,
I'm here to give readings at the book festival. It goes well. After,
we have dinner at an Indian place with a friend whose new book
is just about to come out. I enjoy her excitement about it; we
talk about Virginia Woolf, and about how Woolf dealt with re-
views of her work (badly, from which we both take some comfort). I've time only for a little tourism. At the National Gallery
of Scotland, I'm drawn in by Titian, Rubens, and—a good
surprise—a large altarpiece by Hugo van der Goes, moodiest
of the Flemish primitives.

    When we leave Edinburgh, the light at Waverley railway sta-
tion, dappled and bright in the early morning sun, is like a photographer's paradise. But on this occasion, it's wasted on me: I
can't get into photographing mode. On the train to London, a
couple—he a tattooed middle-aged man in an England jersey,
she Chinese, and much younger—sit near us. The man insults
the "Scotch money" in his wallet. One senses he isn't joking.

    At King's Cross, the fine shock of suddenly seeing Wole So-
yinka as he's crossing the street. With his white hair and quick
gait, he's like an apparition. Shortly after, we check in to the *Roi*

des Belges, an art installation in the form of a one-room hotel in the shape of a boat. It is perched on the roof of the Queen Elizabeth Hall. I've been invited by Artangel, a London-based arts organization, to stay in the boat for four days, one of a year-long rotating cast of musicians, writers, artists, and idealists, all of whom are meant to produce some work in response to the installation and the view.

The boat is ugly from a distance—a jumble of styles—but it's also startlingly well designed and comfortable. What is most astonishing, though, is the view it affords. In one sweeping glance I take in the London Eye, Big Ben, Waterloo Bridge, St. Paul's Cathedral, and the Shard. Looking at the tiny people going about their business in the distance, I find it hard not to feel like a despot. Late at night, one or two voices drift up from the Southbank, echoes left over from the day.

WEDNESDAY

We wake up on the boat. The sky is white, wide. In bed I read *Heart of Darkness.* The *Roi des Belges* is named after the boat captained by Joseph Conrad when he was in the Congo in 1890. I toy with the idea that my essay for Artangel will begin with the words "What the fuck am I doing here?"

The view improves my mood. This is in the morning hour when everything is lit up but is as yet without shadow, as though each object, each building and structure, were its own source of light. Unless you live with such a spectacular view, you forget a certain peculiarity of weather: how small it is. I notice a squall over St. Paul's at the same moment that there is blue sky over the Houses of Parliament. Things happen quickly, and they happen all the time.

Thursday

I visit the Wallace Collection, which I find I don't especially like—with the exception of one stunning Velázquez—then it's on to Tate Britain for the exhibition *Another London,* a half century of photography about the city between 1930 and 1980. Disappointingly, there's no color photography in the show, but the photos that are there, some familiar, others rare, are very good. Strangely—I don't know why this should be strange, but it's strange—the best pictures are by exactly the photographers one would expect to have the best pictures: Robert Frank, Inge Morath, Henri Cartier-Bresson. I decide that, allowing for variations of style, it comes down to their impeccable sense of rhythm. I note sadly that the dates given for Martine Franck (whose images in the show are very fine, too) are 1938–2012. She died a few weeks ago; she was alive when the exhibition began. About death, as usual, one can only resort to the cliché: it is final.

It is an intense four days. I feel guilty about all the people I don't have time to see, my cousins especially. In Bloomsbury, I have drinks at my publishers Faber & Faber (Auden and Eliot frowning from their respective photographs in the entryway); I give a reading and book signing at the London Review Bookshop (readings are all different, this one was especially sober and intense); I meet various friends.

Friday

The novelist T and her husband have joined us for dessert. We suddenly realize that the man standing next to us is Tom Stoppard. Shortly after, some cooks at the outdoor market decide I look like Mos Def and, bizarrely, begin to clap.

I give a whole day over to writing the first draft of my essay. Rather than do another critique of *Heart of Darkness,* I decide to tell a more complicated story, the main strand of which is a recollection of an encounter with V. S. Naipaul. Writing such pieces feels like a descent. Writing as diving: an exhilaration, a compression, a depression. I get it done, and a recordist arrives to do a podcast of it.

SATURDAY

And, too soon, London ends. The taxi ride from the Southbank to Paddington Station is a march-past of empire: the Houses of Parliament, Westminster Abbey, Buckingham Palace and its enormous grounds. There are many statues of great men, including Abraham Lincoln. I notice for the first time the Memorial Gates at Hyde Park Corner. The gates carry the names of Bangladesh, India, Nepal, Sri Lanka, and Africa. "Africa"! You experience yourself in the particular, and are everywhere received as a broad generality.

SUNDAY

I'm in Brooklyn for just a single desultory, interregnal day. I do laundry, iron my shirts, and ignore my mail.

MONDAY

Then it's off to Moscow, Idaho, for the Hemingway Festival. I arrive around midnight, after an uncomfortable, longer-than-transatlantic flight. This is big-sky country, where the Pacific Northwest abuts the mountain region. The air is cold. I'm deranged by jet lag: exhausted but unable to sleep.

It is strange—this is my diary, and since only you and I are reading it, I can be confessional—it is strange to arrive in a town I had never even heard of, as the guest of honor at an event that is a highlight of the local calendar, to be met at the airport by enthusiastic strangers, to be deposited at a hotel. I open the curtains to a new view: the forlorn red neon of a twenty-four-hour pharmacy, the gloomy report of light from the dark asphalt of the parking lot. I half-suspect that, like Ryder in Kazuo Ishiguro's *The Unconsoled,* I have been invited here for no other reason than to undertake a series of cryptic errands across an unfamiliar landscape. I am so tired that, at moments, I find myself laughing helplessly. In the hotel restaurant early the next morning, I overhear snatches of conversation: "Saw one grouse. Hardly any turkeys this year." And, a little later, another man's voice: ". . . Caravaggio's secular paintings."

· · ·

Saturday

What I realize, during our five-hour wait at the King Hussein border crossing between Jordan and the West Bank, is that there is a fine art to wasting people's time. Everyone in our group of writers and artists invited to the Palestine Festival of Literature has the correct visas, correct passports, and letters of support from the British Council. But the point of this border is to make it difficult, mostly for Palestinians attempting to return home. There are forms to fill, and hours of sitting around. A young official emerges, walks toward one of the waiting groups, and hands out one or two stamped passports, or asks for more information, then vanishes for another twenty minutes. What should have been a two-hour journey from Amman to Ramallah takes seven. But we get there in the late afternoon. A beautiful town, in spite of its history of conflict. A resident tells us that, compared to other West Bank towns, it is a bit of a bubble.

SUNDAY

Nigerians are fond of titles, and to conventional ones like "Mr.," "Dr.," or "Alhaji" (a Muslim who has been to Mecca), we have added many others: "Engineer," "Architect," "Evangelist." A more recent one is "JP"—Jerusalem Pilgrim—which denotes someone who has gone on pilgrimage to the Holy Land. As I split off from my friends and follow a group of people I don't know around the Old City—there's the Via Dolorosa, there's the Church of the Holy Sepulchre—it occurs that, without quite intending to, I've become a JP. There is, of course, also the matter of faith, which I do not have.

Our group of writers is here to give readings and workshops. More important, I hope to better understand things I've only known by rumor. Earlier in the day, we came through the Qalandia checkpoint on foot. There was a crowd of people from the West Bank, let in at a trickle. There was the great wall, still under construction, but already extensive at the Jerusalem sector. And there was the guard ordering some members of our group to delete from their cameras the photos they had taken of the checkpoint.

MONDAY

How does one write about this place? Every sentence is open to dispute. Every place name objected to by someone. Every barely stated fact seems familiar already, at once tiresome and necessary. Whatever is written is examined not only for what it includes but for what it leaves out: Have we acknowledged the horror of the Holocaust? The perfidy of the Palestinian Authority? The callousness of Hamas? Under these conditions, the dispossessed—I will leave aside all caveats and plainly state that the Palestinians are the dispossessed—have to spend their entire lives negotiating what should not be matters for negotiation at all: freedom of movement, the right to self-determination, equal protection under the law.

The Augusta Victoria Hospital, on Mount Scopus, is one of the better hospitals available to Palestinians. It is easy for those in East Jerusalem to get to. For those living in the West Bank, a permit is needed, and usually one isn't issued unless there's urgent need: for radiation therapy, for instance, or dialysis. Dr. Tawfiq Nasser, who runs the hospital, tells us about a man from Gaza who had the wrong ID and thus for eight years couldn't see his son, whose ID was similarly restrictive. The man was diagnosed with cancer and finally got a permit to enter Jerusalem. He went to see his son in the West Bank, spent three weeks with him, came back to the hospital for one week of chemotherapy, and returned to Gaza and died.

TUESDAY

This is a pilgrimage after all, but in reverse. We find erasures and disheartening truths at every stop, evidence everywhere of who or what God abandoned. Our guide points out villages and towns that either are currently being encroached on by new settlements or were simply razed or depopulated in 1948 or in 1967 and renamed, rebuilt, and absorbed into Israel. We arrive in Hebron, the burial place of Abraham and the other patriarchs, a once beautiful city now strangled by aggressive new settlements (built in contravention of international law). The presence of the army, protecting these settlements, reminds me of what Lagos was like on mornings after coups: scowling men with heavy weapons and a wary manner. Parts of the city center are empty, ghostly, save for the soldiers. There are streets in which all doors and windows have been welded shut. How does this thing end? I see some Palestinian children playing in a side street. Their innocent game of blindfold, a block away from patrolling soldiers, suddenly seems sinister.

WEDNESDAY

The next morning we drive through beautiful country: Galilee and, briefly, the occupied Golan Heights. We stop at what is now the Bar'am National Park, which was established on what used to be the Maronite Christian village of Kfar Bir'im. The inhabitants of Kfar Bir'im were ordered to leave in 1949, and the Israeli Air Force destroyed the village in 1953, leaving only the church standing. The stony ruins of the village are still there. Now, more than sixty years later, some of the villagers come to the park for a daily sit-in. This has been going on for eleven months. They hope we will tell the world they want to return home.

I climb up a stone structure next to the church. Galilee: my inner JP remembers this is the landscape in which many of the events in the Gospels unfolded. I see two white doves nesting. A beautiful boy of about eight, whose wavy brown hair falls to his shoulders, looks, I think, like the young boy Jesus must have. Every mile of the journey dips into the vocabulary of parable: sheep, lakes, cliffs, vineyards, donkeys. I am lost in thought. Then I hear a cock's crow.

The Island

A CLEAR DAY IN the early 1980s, for example. A man drives
past the harbor of the city in which he lives. He sees docked
boats, restaurants, children at play, the island sleeping in the
distance. Without quite meaning to, he remembers that the island is a prison. And then, as he is a man of some imagination,
he imagines something worse: that people are tortured there. It
has been going on for a while.

Years pass. The rough sea of the crossing makes it feel far. The
swells are huge. The ferry could sink like a stone. Our tour
guide, used to it, sleeps on the journey. Soon, in less than half
an hour, the ferry arrives. The prison is now a museum. There
was and is a pitiful garden along a wall.

> *Obscene.* That is the word, a word of contested etymology,
> that she must hold on to as a talisman. She chooses to
> believe that *obscene* means *off-stage.* To save our humanity,
> certain things that we may want to see (*may want to see
> because we are human!*) must remain off-stage.*

* J. M. Coetzee, *Elizabeth Costello,* 2003.

A sunny afternoon, 1977. The torturers have arranged for some of the prisoners to be photographed. They lead them to an arid patch of land (away from their own tiny garden within the walls) and give them shovels. The press is told: This is a garden. A photographer takes a picture and captions it " 'n Gevangene werksaam in die tuin," "A prisoner working in the garden." The prisoner is not working. He stands erect, faces forward. He wears a floppy hat and dark glasses (when they let him go thirteen years later, he will be unable to shed tears: the limestone quarry will have ruined his eyes). He is a contained fury.

On the island, the tour guide mentions names. Each falls like a stroke of the cane. Sobukwe, Sisulu, Mbeki, Kathrada. The names raise memory's welts. On the other side of the island—the island that is surprisingly big, surprisingly wild—the waves break their heads against the rocks repeatedly, trying to forget. From time to time we see ruined ships.

Twenty-seven years later, the prisoner looks at the photograph. "I remember that day. The authorities brought these people to prove that we were still alive." Ambushed by memory, the prisoner becomes angry again. He begins to denounce one of the visitors from that day. A handler intervenes: "Khulu [Great One], you know you can't talk like that." He won't be corrected. "No, we must be honest about these things." The god of his youth is in his voice.

Blacks are allowed in the Company's gardens now. You can see them with their families on a warm day. Things have changed (but fewer are the blacks in the fine restaurants on Long Street, two blocks over; things are unchanged). Near the gardens is the Slave Lodge. In the heart of the gardens is the monumental statue of Rhodes, his arm raised toward the rest of the continent: CECIL JOHN RHODES, 1853–1902. YOUR HINTERLAND IS HERE. His gesture reads, through history's lens, like a Nazi salute.

White supremacy has its uses. Because of its great care and its thoughtful strategy, because of the tireless way it hoards its hatred, it is good at making heroes. Mohandas Gandhi, Martin Luther King, Jr., Desmond Tutu: What would our lives have meant without theirs? No wheel moves without friction. Without the obscenity of white supremacy to resist, they might have been mere happy family men. Nevertheless:

> Whoever was tortured, stays tortured. Torture is ineradicably burned into him, even when no clinically objective traces can be detected.*

The island migrates to other places and the torturers diversify. But the island is never far away. Occasionally, it leaps into the mind of a woman as she goes through her day during the twenty-first century. A man, somewhere, is jolted awake in the middle of the night by things he knows are true. If the island's physical distance is a little greater now, its moral distance is not.

Many many years later, the prisoner finally dies. The torturers take a moment to praise him (to praise themselves). Then they return to work.

---

* Jean Améry, *At the Mind's Limits: Contemplations by a Survivor on Auschwitz and Its Realities,* 1980.

Reconciliation

. . . DOWN DE VILLIERS GRAAFF MOTORWAY and talking about other things when my friend says, "Can you guess what this building is?"

It is my first day in the city. The building's looming presence tells me what I didn't know I knew. "They tortured people here?"

REPORT FOR FEBRUARY 1987
MISSING PEOPLE

Mrs. R was referred to us by the attorney acting on her behalf. Her husband was taken from their house in Old Crossroads by the "witdoekes" in June last year and they allegedly handed him over to a particular warrant officer and held him at Gugulethu Police Station. This police station (and all the others in the area) has no record of him ever being held there. The security police have no trace of him in detention. He has disappeared. It is difficult to know what to say to a wife in this position.*

---

* Catherine Taylor, *Apart*, 2012.

An alien visitor to our media environment this week might notice two things.

One: torturers and their assistants expressing how profoundly they forgive themselves. They love television, and they love newspapers, and their memories of what they did in the 1980s, what crimes they participated in or supported, are foggy. In fact, often, there is nothing to forgive. Everyone was on the side of the angels.

A second phenomenon, related to the first: torturers expressing their disappointment in the tortured. This disappointment quickly becomes anger. What is the matter with these blacks? The tortured act troubled, it is observed. They consistently fail to live up to the hopes the torturers have for them. Equality has not come, corruption is rampant, and the leadership is disgraceful. An alien visitor might note: the wounded are everywhere singled out for blame, the wounders almost never.

The one forgets to remember itself to its self. It keeps and erases the archive of this injustice that it is, of this violence that it does. The one makes itself violence, it violates and does violence to itself. It becomes what it is, the very violence that it does to itself.*

The torturer cannot forgive the tortured for having been tortured. And certainly not for having taken on some of the torturer's characteristics.

It is good to remember that for a brief moment (before reconciliation interrupted the work of mourning) the victims had a say:

* Jacques Derrida, *Archive Fever*, 1996.

After learning for the first time how her husband had died, she was asked if she could forgive the man who did it. Speaking slowly, in one of the native languages, her message came back through the interpreters: "No government can forgive." Pause. "No commission can forgive." Pause. "Only I can forgive." Pause. "And I am not ready to forgive."*

The second chapter of the fifth volume of the Truth and Reconciliation Commission of South Africa Report is entitled "Victims of Gross Violations of Human Rights." It contains a long list of names in alphabetical order. The document says there will be more names to come. But this, already, is a rich and representative sample. Take any section, and it could have come from a Johannesburg phone book:

MATISO, Peace
MATISO, Sithembele
MATITI, Zandisile
MATIWANA, Hombakazi
MATIWANA, Nontombi Beauty
MATIWANA, Siphiwe Headman
MATIWANE, David Ndumiso
MATIWANE, Lungisa Welcome
MATJEE, Lawrence

The names run into hundreds. Folded into the neat letters of each name is an invisible horror. We know a little more about

---

* Robert Rotberg and Dennis Thompson, eds., "Truth v. Justice: The Morality of Truth Commissions," 2000.

one of these names, Lawrence Matjee, because David Goldblatt took a photograph of him in 1985. No one in the history of photography ever captioned photographs more scrupulously than did Goldblatt.

"Yes, they tortured people here," my friend says. She points out the building. It has a façade of blue tile. This is John Vorster Square, headquarters of the security police. In the old days people went into this building and came out lessened, if they came out at all. It was an evil place.

The victim, by continuing to suffer, irritates the oppressor, who would rather be already past it.

We drive on in silence.

Will there someday be another Truth and Reconciliation Commission? One that features names like Faisal bin Ali Gaber, Nabila Rehman, and Zubair Rehman? Maybe. But should such a day ever come, if history's any guide, we won't be ready to forgive those people for what we did to them.

Break It Down

I N A DRY landscape, men work. With axes, hammers, and other tools, they break stones. It is hard work, from the looks of it, but they do it seriously. They are enthusiastic, and work as a team. Something is being cleared away, perhaps in preparation for something else to be built. A small walled house, made of hardened mud bricks and just a little taller than human height, comes crashing down. When the dust settles, the men, finding the large chunks of rubble unsatisfactory, reduce them further. With a pick, one man hits a flat concrete slab on which inscriptions are visible. At first, the pick glances, unequal to the task. But soon the slab is crossed by hairline cracks and begins to split. Two other men wander near the wall that has just come down. In the sand around their feet are large clay pots, and with effortless little kicks, like bored boys, they break the pots. Stone, mud, clay: patiently they break everything down. And a little distance away, behind the safety of a metal gate, some people watch the men at work. The watchers let the work continue undisturbed. They do nothing, are able to do nothing, about the demolition in process, the demolition of old Sufi shrines. Between the workers and their watchers, there is a difference in power. An automatic gun, resting on some stones, ignored but unignorable, indicates that difference.

In August 1566, an angry Calvinist crowd in the Flemish town of Steenvoorde attacked the pilgrimage church of Sint-Laurensklooster, destroying its art and architecture, and killing several of its priests. In the weeks that followed, the violence spread to the major Flemish cities of Antwerp and Ghent. And though there had been periodic outbreaks of iconoclasm all through European history—in Byzantine times, and then with renewed frequency in the age of Reformation—there had never been anything quite like the "Beeldenstorm," the Dutch "storm of statues" of the late sixteenth century. Sir Richard Clough, a Welsh merchant then living in Antwerp, was an eyewitness to the destruction, and, in a letter to London, he wrote of what he saw:

"All the churches, chapels and houses of religion utterly defaced, and no kind of thing left whole within them, but broken and utterly destroyed, being done after such order and by so few folks that it is to be marvelled at." He described the Church of Our Lady in Antwerp as looking "like hell with above 10,000 churches burning and such a noise as if heaven and earth had got together, with falling of images and beating down of costly works; in such sort, that the spoil was so great that a man could not well pass through the church."

Images are powerful. They can bring people into such a pitch of discomfort that violence ensues, and iconoclasm carries within itself two paradoxical traits: thoroughness and fury. The men (they are in Timbuktu), in their hardworking but boyish ways, and with their automatic weapons, are a good example of this thoroughness, and this cheerful, impish fury.

In early 2001, in the Bamiyan valley of central Afghanistan, a pair of monumental statues of the Buddha, intricately carved into the sandstone of a cliff in the sixth century, were dynamited and reduced to rubble. The larger of the statues was 180 feet high. The destruction was not easy: it took weeks. This act of straightforward iconoclasm was done at the direct order of Mullah Omar, leader of the Taliban. He had thought the Buddhas had some tourism value in 1999, but he changed his mind less than two years later, declaring them idols. And so the dynamite was laid, and where the Buddhas were, where they stood in their graceful embodiment of Gandhara art, in their fine blend of Greek and Buddhist artistic ideals, there now stands only silence, emptiness, a pair of monumental alcoves.

Iconoclasm is nominally about theology. Images that represent the wrong ideas must be expunged. But why be so furious about ideas? And, so, how are we to understand the destruction of Sufi shrines in the north of Mali? Ansar Dine, the rebel group that now controls Timbuktu, believes itself to be doing the will of God. The United Nations doesn't matter, Ansar Dine has said, UNESCO is irrelevant, only God's law matters. The locals are helpless, and horrified. Short of witnessing grievous bodily harm, few things are as astonishing as seeing the casual, physical destruction of what one holds sacred.

Surely, the Muslim piety of "the city of 333 saints" (as Timbuktu is known) should correspond to the Muslim piety of Ansar Dine, should it not? So far, eight mausoleums have been broken, many tombs destroyed, and the rebels are determined to continue the destruction. Their version of Islam—Salafist, fundamentalist—considers the syncretic practices of Malian Sufism, with its veneration of saints and incorporation of vernacular practices, haram. There is no direct Qur'anic proscription on image making, but the Traditions of the Prophet, the

Hadiths, object to using images to usurp God's creative power. From those Hadiths come such narratives as the one in the ninth-century Book of Idols:

> When on the day he conquered Mecca, the Apostle of God appeared before the Ka'bah, he found idols arrayed around it. Thereupon he started to pierce their eyes with the point of his arrow, saying, "Truth is come and falsehood vanished. Verily, falsehood is a thing that vanisheth [Qur'an 17:81]." He then ordered that they be knocked down, after which they were taken out and burned.

On French radio, Sanda Ould Bouamana, a spokesman for Ansar Dine, expressed their activity in strikingly similar terms: "When the Prophet entered Mecca he said that all the mausoleums should be destroyed. And that's what we're repeating." And that is why, more than a thousand years after he died, the tomb of the saint Sidi Mahmoudou has, in this past week, been destroyed and desecrated.

A peculiarity of the Timbuktu iconoclasm is that these shrines are architectural rather than representationally sculptural. They are generally modest in size, and usually made of mud. There is little of the opulence that might have maddened the sixteenth-century Flemish mob, and none of the lifelike mimesis of human form that offended sensibilities in the Bamiyan valley. In Timbuktu, a once vital trading city, in a place once fabled for both its riches and learning, now swallowed up by the Sahel, these mausoleums are expressions of local practice: simple and old beliefs in a land of griots and marabouts, the kind of syncretism common to all the big world religions, owing as much to universal edicts as to what works for the people in their land, in their language, and according to their preconversion customs of veneration.

There is in iconoclasm an emotional content that is directly linked to the iconoclasts' own psychology. The theological pretext for image destruction is that images are powerless, less than God, uneffective as a source of succor, and therefore disposable. But in reality, iconoclasm is motivated by the iconoclasts' profound belief in the power of the image being destroyed. The love iconoclasts have for icons is a love that dare not speak its name.

Iconoclastic hostility is complex. It expresses itself in different ways all through history. But what is generally true of iconoclastic movements is that they are never about theology alone. They include politics, struggles for power, the effort to humiliate an enemy, and a demonstration of iconoclasts' own neuroses. Behind iconoclastic bravado is a terror of magic, a belief in dead saints no less than that of iconophiles, and, crucially, a historical anxiety that, in the Timbuktu case, is about presenting the bona fides of Ansar Dine to its Wahhabi models in Saudi Arabia and to Al Qaeda in the Islamic Maghreb.

That which doesn't speak dumbfounds. After all, who can tell what such objects are thinking? Best to destroy the inscrutable, the ancient, if one is to truly usher in a pure new world. So, the invaders continue their work in Timbuktu with enthusiasm and good cheer, smashing pots, breaking bricks, rattling at the doors of the mosque. It takes a lot of work to silence silent objects. But already it is clear that not only the people watching from behind the gate are consumed with fear.

The White Savior Industrial Complex

A FTER I WATCHED the *Kony 2012* video, which in a short period of time had become a "viral" sensation, I wrote a brief
seven-part response to it, which I posted in sequence on my
Twitter account:

1- From Sachs to Kristof to Invisible Children to TED,
the fastest growth industry in the US is the White Savior
Industrial Complex.
2- The white savior supports brutal policies in the
morning, founds charities in the afternoon, and receives
awards in the evening.
3- The banality of evil transmutes into the banality of
sentimentality. The world is nothing but a problem to be
solved by enthusiasm.
4- This world exists simply to satisfy the needs—
including, importantly, the sentimental needs—of white
people and Oprah.
5- The White Savior Industrial Complex is not about
justice. It is about having a big emotional experience that
validates privilege.
6- Feverish worry over that awful African warlord. But

close to 1.5 million Iraqis died from an American war of
choice. Worry about that.

7- I deeply respect American sentimentality, the way one
respects a wounded hippo. You must keep an eye on it,
for you know it is deadly.

These tweets were retweeted, forwarded, and widely shared
by readers. They migrated beyond Twitter to blogs, Tumblr,
Facebook, and other sites; they generated fierce arguments. As
the days went by, the tweets were reproduced in their entirety
on the websites of *The Atlantic* and *The New York Times,* and they
showed up on German, Spanish, and Portuguese sites. A friend
emailed to tell me that the fourth tweet, which cheekily name-
checks Oprah, was mentioned on Fox television.

These sentences of mine, written without much premeditation, had touched a nerve. I heard back from many people who
were grateful to have read them. I heard back from many others
who were disappointed or furious. Many people, too many to
count, called me a racist. One person spoke of me Mau-Mauing.
The *Atlantic* writer who'd reproduced them, while agreeing
with my broader points, described the language in which they
were expressed as "resentment."

Not long after, I listened to a radio interview given by the
Pulitzer Prize–winning journalist Nicholas Kristof. Kristof is
best known for his regular column in *The New York Times,* in
which he often gives accounts of his activism or that of other
Westerners. When I saw the *Kony 2012* video, I found it tonally
similar to Kristof's approach, and that was why I mentioned
him in the first of my seven tweets.

Those tweets, though unpremeditated, were intentional in

their irony and seriousness. I did not write them to score cheap points, much less to hurt anyone's feelings. I believed that a certain kind of language is too infrequently seen in our public discourse. I am a novelist, and my goal in writing a novel is to leave the reader not knowing what to think. A good novel shouldn't have a point.

But there's a place in the political sphere for direct speech, and, in the past few years in the United States, there has been a chilling effect on a certain kind of direct speech pertaining to rights. The president is wary of being seen as the "angry black man." People of color, women, and gays—who now have greater access to the centers of influence than ever before—are under pressure to be well behaved when talking about their struggles. There is an expectation that we can talk about sins but no one must be identified as a sinner: newspapers love to describe words or deeds as "racially charged" even in those cases when it would be more honest to say "racist"; we agree that there is rampant misogyny, but misogynists are nowhere to be found; homophobia is a problem, but no one is homophobic. One cumulative effect of this policed language is that when someone dares to point out something as obvious as white privilege, it is seen as unduly provocative. Marginalized voices in America have fewer and fewer avenues to speak plainly about what they suffer; the effect of this enforced civility is that those voices are falsified or blocked entirely from the discourse.

It's only in the context of this neutered language that my rather tame tweets can be seen as extreme. The interviewer on the radio show I listened to asked Kristof if he had heard of me. "Of course," he said. She asked him what he made of my criticisms. His answer was considered and genial, but what he said worried me more than an angry outburst would have:

There has been a real discomfort and backlash among middle-class educated Africans, Ugandans in particular in this case, but people more broadly, about having Africa as they see it defined by a warlord who does particularly brutal things, and about the perception that Americans are going to ride in on a white horse and resolve it. To me though, it seems even more uncomfortable to think that we as white Americans should not intervene in a humanitarian disaster because the victims are of a different skin color.

Here are some of the "middle-class educated Africans" Kristof, whether he is familiar with all of them and their work or not, chose to take issue with: Ugandan journalist Rosebell Kagumire, who covered the Lord's Resistance Army in 2005 and made an eloquent video response to *Kony 2012;* Ugandan scholar Mahmood Mamdani, one of the world's leading specialists on Uganda and the author of a thorough riposte to the political wrongheadedness of Invisible Children; and Ethiopian American novelist Dinaw Mengestu, who sought out Joseph Kony, met his lieutenants, and recently wrote a brilliant essay about how *Kony 2012* gets the issues wrong. They have a different take on what Kristof calls a "humanitarian disaster," and this may be because they see the larger disasters behind it: militarization of poorer countries, shortsighted agricultural policies, resource extraction, the propping up of corrupt governments, and the astonishing complexity of long-running violent conflicts over a wide and varied terrain.

I do not accuse Kristof of racism, nor do I believe he is in any way racist. I have no doubt that he has a good heart. Listening to him on the radio, I began to think we could iron the whole thing out over a couple of beers. But that, precisely, is what worries me. That is what made me compare American sentimentality to a "wounded hippo." His good heart does not always allow him to think constellationally. He does not connect the dots or see the patterns of power behind the isolated "disasters." All he sees is hungry mouths, and he, in his own advocacy-by-journalism way, is putting food in those mouths as fast as he can. All he sees is need, and he sees no need to reason out the need for the need.

But I disagree with the approach taken by Invisible Children in particular, and by the White Savior Industrial Complex in general, because there is much more to doing good work than "making a difference." There is the principle of first do no harm, and the idea that those who are being helped ought to be consulted over the matters that concern them.

I write all this from multiple positions. I write as an African, a black man living in America. I am every day subject to the many microaggressions of American racism. I also write this as an American, enjoying the many privileges that the American passport affords and that residence in this country makes possible. I involve myself in this critique of privilege: my own privileges of class, gender, and sexuality are insufficiently examined. My cellphone was likely manufactured by poorly treated workers in a Chinese factory. The coltan in the phone can probably be traced to the conflict-riven Congo. I don't fool myself that I am not implicated in these transnational networks of oppressive practices.

And I also write all this as a novelist and story writer: I am sensitive to the power of narratives. When Jason Russell, narrator of the *Kony 2012* video, showed his cheerful blond toddler a photo of Joseph Kony as the embodiment of evil (a glowering dark man), and of his friend Jacob as the representative of help-lessness (a sweet-faced African), I wondered how Russell's little boy would develop a nuanced sense of the lives of others, particularly others of a different race from his own. How would that little boy come to understand that others have autonomy; that their right to life is not exclusive of a right to self-respect? In a different context, John Berger once wrote, "A singer may be innocent; never the song."

One song we hear too often is the one in which Africa serves as a backdrop for white fantasies of conquest and heroism. From the colonial project to *Out of Africa* to *The Constant Gardener* and *Kony 2012,* Africa has provided a space onto which white egos can conveniently be projected. It is a liberated space in which the usual rules do not apply: a nobody from America or Europe can go to Africa and become a godlike savior or, at the very least, have his or her emotional needs satisfied. Many have done it under the banner of "making a difference." To state this obvious and well-attested truth does not make me a racist. It does give me away as a "middle-class educated African," and I plead guilty as charged. (It is also worth noting that there are other middle-class educated Africans who see this matter differently from me. That is what people, educated and otherwise, do: they assess information and sometimes disagree with each other.)

In any case, Kristof and I are in agreement about one thing: there is much happening in many parts of the African continent that is not as it ought to be. I have been fortunate in life, but that doesn't mean I haven't seen or experienced African poverty firsthand. I grew up in a land of military coups and economically devastating, IMF-imposed "structural adjustment" programs. The genuine hurt of Africa is no fiction.

And we also agree on something else: that there is an internal ethical urge that demands that each of us serve justice as much as he or she can. But beyond the immediate attention that he rightly pays hungry mouths, child soldiers, or raped civilians, there are more complex and more widespread problems. There are serious problems of governance, of infrastructure, of democracy, and of law and order. These problems are neither simple in themselves nor reducible to slogans. Such problems are both intricate and intensely local.

How, for example, could a well-meaning American "help" a place like Uganda today? It begins, I believe, with some humility with regard to the people in those places. It begins with some respect for the agency of the people of Uganda in their own lives. A great deal of work had been done, and continues to be done, by Ugandans to improve their own country, and ignorant comments (I've seen many) about how "we have to save them because they can't save themselves" can't change that fact.

Let me draw into this discussion an example from an African country I know very well. Earlier in 2012, hundreds of thousands of Nigerians took to their country's streets to protest the government's decision to remove a subsidy on petrol. This subsidy was widely seen as one of the few blessings of the country's otherwise catastrophic oil wealth. But what made these protests so heartening was that they were about more than the subsidy removal. Nigeria has one of the most corrupt governments in the world, and protesters clearly demanded that something be done about this. The protests went on for days, at considerable personal risk to the protesters. Several young people were shot dead, and the movement was eventually doused when union leaders capitulated and the army deployed on the streets. The movement did not "succeed" in conventional terms. But something important had changed in the political conscious-ness of the Nigerian populace. For me and for a number of people I know, the protests gave us an opportunity to be proud of Nigeria, many of us for the first time in our lives.

This is not the sort of story that is easy to summarize in an article, much less make a viral video about. After all, there is no simple demand to be made and—since corruption is endemic—no single villain to topple. There is certainly no "bridge character," Kristof's euphemism for white saviors in Third World narratives who make the story more palatable to American viewers. And yet, the story of Nigeria's protest movement is one of the most important from sub-Saharan Af-rica so far this year. Men and women, of all classes and ages, stood up for what they felt was right; they marched peacefully; they defended one another, and gave one another food and drink; Christians stood guard while Muslims prayed and vice versa; and they spoke without fear to their leaders about the kind of country they wanted to see. All of it happened with no cool American twenty-something heroes in sight.

Joseph Kony is no longer in Uganda and he is no longer the threat he was, but he is a convenient villain for those who need a convenient villain. What Africa needs more pressingly than Kony's indictment is a more equitable civil society, a more ro-bust democracy, and a fairer system of justice. This is the scaf-folding from which infrastructure, security, healthcare, and education can be built. How do we encourage voices like those of the Nigerian masses who marched this January, or those who are engaged in the struggle to develop Ugandan democracy?

If Americans want to care about Africa, maybe they should consider evaluating American foreign policy, which they al-ready play a direct role in through elections, before they im-

pose themselves on Africa itself. The fact of the matter is that
Nigeria is one of the top five oil suppliers to the United States,
and American policy is interested first and foremost in the flow
of that oil. The American government did not see fit to support
the Nigeria protests. (Though the State Department issued a
supportive statement—"our view on that is that the Nigerian
people have the right to peaceful protest, we want to see them
protest peacefully, and we're also urging the Nigerian security
services to respect the right of popular protest and conduct
themselves professionally in dealing with the strikes"—it
reeked of boilerplate rhetoric and, unsurprisingly, nothing tangible came of it.) This was as expected; under the banner of
"American interests," the oil comes first. Under that same banner, the livelihood of corn farmers in Mexico has been destroyed by NAFTA. Haitian rice farmers have suffered appalling
losses due to Haiti being flooded with subsidized American
rice. A nightmare has been playing out in Honduras in the past
three years: an American-backed coup and American militarization of that country have contributed to a conflict in which
hundreds of activists and journalists have already been murdered. The Egyptian military, which is now suppressing the
country's once-hopeful movement for democracy and killing
dozens of activists in the process, subsists on $1.3 billion in an-
nual U.S. aid. This is a litany that will be familiar to some. To
others, it will be news. But, familiar or not, it has a bearing on
our notions of innocence as well as the ways in which we offer
help.

Let us begin our activism right here: with the money-driven
villainy at the heart of American foreign policy. To do this would
be to give up the illusion that the sentimental need to "make a
difference" trumps all other considerations. What innocent he-

roes don't always understand is that they play a useful role for people who have much more cynical motives. The White Savior Industrial Complex is a valve for releasing the unbearable pressures that build in a system developed on pillage. We can participate in the economic destruction of Haiti over long years, but when the earthquake strikes it feels good to send ten dollars each to the rescue fund. I have no opposition, in principle, to such donations (I frequently make them myself, and I believe in the necessity of emergency aid), but we must do such things only with awareness of what else is involved. If we are going to interfere in the lives of others, a little due diligence is a minimum requirement.

Success for *Kony 2012* would mean increased militarization of the antidemocratic Yoweri Museveni government, which has been in power in Uganda since 1986 and has played a major role in the world's deadliest ongoing conflict, the war in the Congo. But those whom privilege allows to deny constellational thinking would enjoy ignoring this fact. There are other troubling connections, not least of them being that Museveni appears to be a proxy of the United States in its shadowy battles against militants in Sudan and, especially, in Somalia. Who sanctions these conflicts? Under whose authority and oversight are they conducted? Who is being killed and why?

All of this takes us rather far afield from fresh-faced young Americans using the power of YouTube, Facebook, and pure enthusiasm to change the world. A singer may be innocent; never the song.

"Perplexed . . . Perplexed"

O N FRIDAY, OCTOBER 5, 2012, four students at the University of Port Harcourt, in southern Nigeria, went to the nearby village of Aluu. They had gone to collect a debt from a man named Coxson Lucky. The students were young men, all in their teens or early twenties. At Aluu, they tried to shake down Lucky (how aggressively, no one really knows); it seems they also seized some items belonging to him. Lucky raised an alarm, a crowd gathered, and the students found themselves accused of stealing laptops and phones. They were immediately set upon by the mob, stripped, paraded through town, and beaten with sticks. They began to plead for their lives and, even as they did so, were weighed down with tires and set alight. All four of them—Chiadika Biringa, Ugonna Obuzor, Lloyd Toku, and Tekena Elkanah—died there, in the mud of Aluu village.

Lynching is common in Nigeria. Extrajudicial killing is often the fate of those accused of kidnapping and armed robbery, but also of those suspected of minor crimes like pickpocketing. These incidents, if reported at all, get one or two paragraphs in the newspapers and are forgotten. Nevertheless, the killings of the Aluu 4, as they have come to be known, touched a nerve in Nigeria. This was in large part because the murders were filmed and uploaded to YouTube and, soon after, seen by many among

Nigeria's huge population of Internet-savvy youths. In the days that followed, there was a pained and horrified discussion across Nigerian social media. How could this happen? What sort of society had we become? Would the guilty be caught and punished?

I could not watch the video. I was still haunted by a clip I saw years ago of another lynching. Two men had been set on fire, and were being whipped. The skin came off their bodies in oily red strips, and their tormentors urged one another to slow down and let them suffer. I could bear only to look at the stills from this new video. But I found the response to the incident among the Nigerian public interesting. The outrage was loud and long. It was as though this were the first time such a thing had ever happened, as though Nigerian society were not already mired in frequent and almost orgiastic spates of violence. Somehow, this incident had differentiated itself from the terrorist attacks by Boko Haram, the endless killings by "unknown gunmen," the carnage on the roads, the armed robberies, the dispiriting catalogue of crimes in places high and low.

What was the cause of this soul-searching? What made the Aluu 4 different from dozens of others killed by mobs in the past few years? What innocence had been destroyed by this particular spontaneous instance of murder?

One evening in September 2010, the lawyer and poet Tade Ipadeola was driving home in Dugbe, Ibadan, in southwestern Nigeria. It was a drizzly night. Visibility was poor. From his car, a white sedan, he saw a speeding motorcyclist ahead of him collide with another motorcyclist. The motorcycle that was hit wobbled slightly and went on its way. The one that caused the collision was slewed across the road. The male motorcyclist and his female passenger lay prone on the asphalt. The man wore no helmet, and blood from his cracked skull pooled on the road. The woman writhed in pain. Ipadeola parked some fifteen meters from the scene of the crime, left his engine idling, his beams on, and hurried to help the accident victims. He was the first on the scene, but, very soon after, other cars had parked, and so had other motorcycles. Someone from the gathering crowd said, "The white car hit them." At this announcement, a sudden fear coursed through Ipadeola. That was his car that had been mentioned. His guilt was established by his mere presence at the scene.

"It takes ten seconds, more or less, for the mob to decide whether to administer their brand of justice," Ipadeola said, in recounting the incident to me. "The diabolical compression of time was the most frightening part." Everyone looked at him menacingly. Especially dangerous was the assembled brotherhood of motorcyclists, who are always to be found defending their own in such situations. There were only two possible outcomes once guilt was established: either they burned the car or they burned the car and its driver. But on this night, another voice spoke out of the crowd claiming that, no, it was the man bleeding on the road who had hit another motorcycle. Some section of the crowd seemed to believe this, and Ipadeola walked back to his car, shaking, hoping that the tide, which had suddenly turned in his favor, wouldn't suddenly turn again. He made it home alive that night. He lived to tell the tale.

One of the chief characteristics of a mob is its quickness. It is sudden. It pounces. In Ikeja, Lagos, in 2011, two men, Alaba and Samuel, were severely beaten and very nearly killed for eating human flesh. Closer investigation showed that what they'd been chewing on was, in fact, beef. By this time, their punishers had long dispersed into the city. In Nigeria we sometimes call these mob actions "jungle justice." Most people are not opposed to them on principle. As a sweet-natured aunt of mine said a few years ago, referring to my question about thieves who had been killed by vigilantes, "Why do we need such people in the society anyway? It's better to just get rid of them." She was expressing the pain that many feel about the violent crimes, and their desire for instant restitution.

"Jungle justice": the term is uncomfortable in the way it seems to confirm the worst prejudices that outsiders might have about daily life in Nigeria. Won't the expression make people think that Nigeria is a savage place? Certainly, from the experience of the people I know who barely escaped being lynched by an irate mob, who encountered that sudden, startling, and almost fatal diminishment of self that occurs when hostile strangers close in on you, no term is too strong or too angry to characterize what mobs do. Jungle justice is not the half of it. But we should be fair enough to set Nigerian street justice in its various contexts.

Mob rule—or to give it its technical name, "ochlocracy"—was not invented in Nigeria. Theories of the mob predate ancient Rome. Extrajudicial murders litter the post–Civil War history of the American South, all the way to, and beyond, the story of James Byrd, Jr., in 1998. Punitive murder by the police and by vigilantes has existed in all societies at some point, and probably still exists in most. In cosmopolitan centers like New York and Paris, until at least the early years of the twentieth century, lynchings were reported in the newspapers. Félix Fénéon, writing faits divers—brief news items, usually of a peculiar or violent nature—in *Le Matin* in 1906, recorded several instances of people being set upon by mobs. For instance one reads (in a translation by Luc Sante): "Near Brioude, a bear was smothering a child. Some peasants shot the beast and nearly lynched its exhibitor."

While working on a project I call *small fates,* modeled closely on Fénéon's faits divers, I found several similar instances in the New York of a hundred years ago. Lynching in the United States is so closely tied to racial violence that we forget that it often featured in incidents where race was not at issue. In one story, a man on East Houston Street, who had attacked his lover with a razor, nearly lost his life to a mob. There were other incidents of lynchings or near lynchings: after a jailbreak, when people attacked a driver who hit a child, and so on. More recently, there has been a rise in such spontaneous acts of violence in places such as Jamaica, Pakistan, and Kenya.

What many of these societies have in common is a crisis of modernity. People, finding themselves surrounded by newly complex circumstances, and finding themselves sharing space with neighbors whom they do not know and with whom they don't necessarily share traditions, defend themselves in terrible new ways. The old customs have passed away, and the new, less reassuring, less traditional modes of life are struggling to be born. Mobs arise out of this crisis. They are a form of impatience.

The investiture of legal power in the hands of the state evolved as a way to stem endless vendettas, blood feuds, and unauthorized violence. In countries with properly functioning legal systems, the mob continues to exist, but it is rarely called upon to mete out capital punishment. The right to take human life belongs to the state. Not so in societies where weak courts and poor law enforcement are combined with intractable structural injustices. The mob flows into that vacuum, and looks for whom to kill. A mob is not, as is so often said, mindless. A mob is single-minded.

In 2011, in Gusau, a town in the northern state of Zamfara, Saminu Ibrahim, a journalist, went to a local branch of Skye Bank to withdraw some money. While he was there, one of the bank staff, Idowu Olatunji, suddenly experienced a hysterical episode in which he felt his penis had vanished. This peculiar form of anxiety, which happens with some regularity in public places in Nigeria, is usually followed by the accusation that someone nearby "stole" the penis. A crowd gathers, and rarely is there any kind of examination of the accuser's body. His word is simply taken for it, and a beating of the accused, sometimes fatal, follows.

Within its highly particularized context, this bizarre sequence of events makes a perverse sort of sense. It might even be interpreted as no more perverse than some things that pass for the normal abnormality in other societies, such as those in American culture, "alcohol and drug abuse, major depression, dysthymia, mania, hypomania, panic disorder, social and specific phobia, and generalized anxiety disorder," a list presented by Frank Bures in his extraordinarily nuanced *Harper's* essay on penis theft in Nigeria, "A Mind Dismembered." Bures, struggling to understand the psychological context for this kind of anxiety, notes that "every culture has its own logic, its own beliefs, its own stresses."

That day in Gusau, the banker Olatunji accused the journalist Ibrahim of penis theft. All of a sudden, Ibrahim found himself in mortal danger from a crowd. They closed in on him with murderous intent, and only the presence of quick-thinking policemen saved him from a grisly death. But what made this case truly unusual, and makes it a textbook case of Nigeria's neuroses and its perplexed modernity, was that Ibrahim later sued Olatunji in a court of law for defamation and false accusation. His response to this intolerable threat to his life was the formalized idea of the law guaranteed by the state. He answered jungle justice with civil justice. And it was at this point that the story dropped out of the public view.

Crowds are attractive because of their egalitarian promise. The mob is a form of utopia. Justice arrives now, to right what has for too long been wrong with the world. As Elias Canetti wrote in his masterful psychological study, *Crowds and Power,* "All who belong to the crowd get rid of their differences and feel equal." In this sudden equality is part of the appeal of a lynching. But it is a spurious appeal. As Canetti says of the equality that mobs feel, "It is based on an illusion; the people who suddenly feel equal have not really become equal; nor will they feel equal forever."

When I asked my Nigerian friends to tell me about their own close calls with mob violence, I was surprised, and a little dismayed, by how many of them actually had stories to tell. Eghosa Imasuen, a sharp-minded and witty novelist, told me about his experience at Alaba, the main electronics market in Lagos. This was in 2003, and the salesboy, who had opened the cardboard box of a television, wishing to force a sale, began to loudly allege theft. It was a hustle. He had done it before. As Imasuen put it, "An expletive-filled denial saved me. It was scary. I had received a few slaps before the crowd noticed that my friend and I were too angry to be thieves." The crowd turned on the accuser instead, and gave him a severe beating before taking him to the chairman of the market, who in turn handed him to police.

In the case of Akin Ajayi, who writes on arts and culture for Nigerian and international publications, it happened one day when he was fifteen, playing truant from the elite boys' boarding school King's College. He had snuck off campus, in Obalende, on Lagos Island, to buy some suya, the spicy grilled meat popular all over the country. A misunderstanding over change, or perhaps, again, a deliberate hustle, from the suya seller, led to Ajayi being suddenly surrounded by violent merchants. He felt the danger, and broke into a run. For a hundred yards, he was pursued by them. It frightens him still, to think of that day.

Elnathan John, who is also a journalist and satirist for Nigerian newspapers, had been taking photos of a government raid on an illegal market in Abuja. The government officers, though armed, were beaten back; the situation became dangerous all of a sudden, even for onlookers. One man, a black-marketer of petroleum products, objected to John's camera, and tried to chase him down and hand him over to the angry crowd of traders. John was just barely able to run around a corner, jump into his car, and speed off. The memories are fresh in his mind: it happened just this year.

Those of us who have lived a long time in Nigeria have heard, in the marketplaces, the cries of "Thief, thief!" We have seen chases that won't end well for the person being chased. We have all seen, at the very least, in some market square or busy inter-section, the charred remains of what used to be a human being, what used to be some mother's son, some child's hapless father. Many of us remember hearing of how a boy of eleven, accused of kidnapping a baby, was burned alive near the National Sta-dium in Lagos in 2005. In that case, as in the case of the Aluu 4, a video recording was made of the incident and circulated; part of it was broadcast on television. There can be little doubt that before the current year is through, several more people will be lynched in Nigeria, for petty crimes or on the basis of false ac-cusations.

When I'm in Nigeria, I find myself looking at the passive, placid faces of the people standing at the bus stops. They are tired after a day's work, and thinking perhaps of the long com-mute back home, or of what to make for dinner. I wonder to myself how these people, who surely love life, who surely love their own families, their own children, could be ready in an instant to exact a fatal violence on strangers. And even though I know that lynchings would largely disappear in a Nigeria with rule of law and strong institutions—just as they have largely disappeared in other places where they were once common— I still wonder what extreme traumas have brought us to this peculiar pass. I suppose it must be a blood knot, one that in-volves all the restless ghosts of our history-maddened country: the gap between rich and poor, the current corruption of the ruling class, the recent military dictatorships, the butchery of the civil war in the late sixties, the humiliations of British colo-nialism, the internecine battles of the nineteenth century, and the horrors of the slaving past. We have, by means of a long steeping, been dyed all the way through with callousness.

. . .

I was frightened out of my skin one Sunday morning in Su-
rulere, near the National Stadium in Lagos—in other words,
close to where the eleven-year-old boy was lynched in 2005. I
saw a van accidentally hit a motorcycle. Neither the motorcyclist nor his passenger appeared to be seriously injured, but the
driver of the van, possessed by a sudden panic, didn't stop. He
drove off in an attempt to escape. A cadre of motorcycles gave
immediate chase, and there was no doubt that they would bring
him to a rough form of justice. "They'll catch him," a man said
loudly. "They'll certainly catch him." Already, I could see that
the driver would soon run into traffic and have to face his tormentors. I was appalled, but not especially surprised. I understood well that this was part of what passed for normal in the
troubled street life of present-day Nigeria.

The inspector general of police made a statement vowing to
capture the culprits in the murder of the University of Port
Harcourt students. A heavy police presence descended on Aluu,
and a large number of people have now been arrested, including the traditional ruler of Aluu and a police sergeant who apparently helped the crowd. A manhunt is under way for Lucky,
the debtor who is believed to have incited the violence and is
now being called, in a bit of wishful thinking, the "mastermind"
of the murders.

It's hard to escape the conclusion that, in addition to the
shock of actually seeing the murders on video, the concern
being expressed here by the government—in response to a
public outcry that began online—has other, unspoken, elements. These young men are "us" in a way that is not comfort-

able to confront, in ways that might seem trivial. The contrast between the photos released by their friends—polo shirts, sunshades, jeans, clear skin, jaunty caps worn just so—and the awful sight of their bloodied and naked bodies in the mud is sickening. They are, or were, close to the world of many other cool young Nigerians. Their presence on social media brings them even closer: Ugonna was active on Twitter, and was nicknamed Tipsy. With Lloyd, a.k.a. Big L, he was a hip-hop enthusiast. They had recorded a track together, and this song was widely shared on Nigerian networks. In this sense, they were in the same class as many of the young Nigerian people on Twitter, somewhere along the imprecise continuum that constitutes the Nigerian middle class. They had some access to material resources; they had educated and somewhat well-to-do parents; one or more of them had been overseas; they were technologically savvy; and they had a sense of the world beyond Nigeria. The Aluu 4 are in all these ways just like the young Nigerians who lamented them on Twitter and other social networks, the ones who helped push the police response to the killings, and began a petition to have a bill passed criminalizing mob violence. The Aluu 4 were also, in this material and cultural sense, more like us than they were like the poor villagers who killed them; the violence was probably not disconnected from the terrible income gaps that are a fact of Nigerian life, and the explosive resentments those gaps can create.

It is startling to consider that another atrocity had occurred in northeastern Nigeria four days earlier, at the Federal Polytechnic Mubi, when gunmen had lined up and shot no fewer than twenty-six college students. Some reports put the number of dead as high as forty. The response to the Mubi killings was stunned, but much quieter. That incident has essentially dropped out of the public discussion now. We do not know the names of the dead students, nor do we know if they recorded hip-hop music in their spare time, or had Twitter accounts, or traveled overseas. They seem to have been from more modest backgrounds than the Port Harcourt students. The Mubi killings also seem to have some element of the incessant religious conflict that is ripping the north of the country apart. Boko Haram might have been involved. The conflict in the north frightens many privileged southern Nigerians, but rarely touches them directly. Places like Borno, Bauchi, and Adamawa are far away from the world inhabited by most educated, cosmopolitan Nigerians. The Boko Haram conflict and the various incidents of religious violence in the north are exceedingly complex, and have come with a shockingly high death toll. Nevertheless, many who heard the news of the Mubi massacre would simply have surmised that, although the dead were our fellow citizens, they were not really "us," not in the discomfiting way the Aluu 4 were.

But even if it is true that there is an element of class loyalty and regional identity in the attention being paid to the murders in Aluu, Nigerians now have a chance to think about a subject too long considered just a part of life. The outrage could lead to legislation. The very slow process of making Nigerians understand that ochlocracy is murder might gain some traction.

Tade Ipadeola, the lawyer who described mob action as a "diabolical compression of time," had added: "And to think that we all complain that normal court proceedings are inordinately long in Nigeria." In a country where the rich commit crimes with impunity, and where the majority of the people in prison are awaiting trial, it is sad, but no great wonder, that citizens so often opt for the false utopia of the mob. But no Nigerian can now shake the feeling that it could be any of us falling afoul of the hive mind. No one really believes that there's just one mastermind in the case of a mob killing. It was always our problem, but, in a destabilizing new way, it really is our problem now.

I took a look at eighteen-year-old Ugonna Obuzor's Twitter account (@tipsy_tipsy), which he last updated on October 3, two days before he was lynched alongside his three friends. His time line isn't wordy, but it's fairly opaque, written mostly in the terse, quasi-American argot familiar to anyone who reads young Nigerians. There are a few messages in which he seems distressed about some unexplained event. Perhaps he was going through a romantic breakup (some of his retweets support this reading) or some other personal disappointment, but in light of his sudden death, the messages have taken on a decidedly different cast. On September 14, he wrote, "Its a shame buh it is wat it is . . . its real as this," and, six days later, on the twentieth of September, "It breaks my heart evrytym I tink abt it . . . still can't beliv it." I scrolled farther down. On August 21, Ugonna had written, simply: "Perplexed." And on the day following, on August 22, 2012, the same single, haunting word again: "Perplexed."

A Piece of the Wall

I HEAR THE SOUND of faint bells in the distance. It is like a sound in a dream, or the jingling at the beginning of a Christmas song. Jingle, jingle, jingle. The sound comes closer. Jingle, jingle, jingle. And then they come in, seventy of them, all men, chained together, bound wrist and waist and foot. They shuffle bright-sounding into the courtroom, a large bright room that is, for them, a chasm of hopelessness.

What you think is true of the country in which you have arrived is often true only of where in it you are. I immigrated to small towns in Michigan. Later on, I went to New York City. These places became my America, and their landscapes and ways of life became natural to me. Other Americas—Salt Lake City, Anchorage, Honolulu—I knew by name only, and considered part of my America only through the imagination. If I traveled to one of these distant Americas, I had to reimagine them. I only slowly understood how I was connected to life there. This was my experience of Tucson, and of the Sonoran desert in Arizona, which goes all the way up to and beyond the border with Mexico. This dry and severely beautiful region, alive with traces of the old Spanish missions, is the home of the Tohono O'odham. Their land preceded Mexico or the United States and stretches across the current border. And the border is incessantly crossed, by various people for various reasons, a matter of commerce, culture, law, and unhappiness.

The program, called Operation Streamline, is about to jail and then deport these men. Most of them are indigenous people from Mexico or farther south, here in search of work, arrested in the desert or in town. Seventy small dark men. For most of them, Spanish is a second language.

The brightness of the courtroom is like an assault. They have been coached to say yes, to say no. They are charged with illegal entry, reentry, or false claim to citizenship. Soon—each gets less than a minute in front of the judge—they'll be taken back to detention. They will be imprisoned for weeks or months, then put on a bus or plane to Mexico City, hundreds of miles away from home. For now, as I watch them in the courtroom, they are like animals in a pen, fastened to one another, a shimmer of sound each time one moves. The security officers are imposing, white, and impassive. The judge is named Bernie. After, I speak with him.

"Are you, yourself, from a Mexican family?"

"My father didn't fight for this country in World War Two so that people could call me Mexican."

"But the chains: these men are not dangerous. Why the chains?"

"It's more convenient."

I'm writing in the restaurant of the lodge. The server asks me about my computer. She's thinking of buying a similar one, but not right away. She has just bought a mobile phone. She paid quite a lot for it, six hundred dollars. Well, it's because she didn't want to be tied to a contract, her boyfriend paid, she isn't ready to buy a computer yet. The drift of talk.

Her name is Aurora. She is Peruvian, and in her thirties. She has been in Tucson for nine years.

"What are you doing here, vacation?"

"No, I'm a writer. Here to find out more about the border and immigration."

It has been a season of trouble, and it has gotten worse since 9/11. This is why I've come. This grief, this unsteadiness, is everywhere.

"Do you know anyone who got into trouble?"

"Many. I was working in a hotel about six years ago. The owners were Indian. In one morning, twelve Mexican girls, maids, were taken away. They never returned."

"You were a maid?"

"Me? No, I've always worked in banquets."

She glances at the counter. It's mid-morning. The restaurant is quiet.

"But I've had trouble. I get stopped all the time while driving. Two years ago, a policeman stopped me, and I didn't have my resident card. I'm not afraid, but the policeman is so angry. He starts to shout. I look at him directly"—she raises her hand to her face and makes a V with her fingers, pointing at each eye—"I look at him and say, 'I'm not afraid of you. I'm legal. I have all my papers at home.' I know if he arrests me, he will be in trouble, because I have done nothing wrong." She speaks low but with holy intensity. "But now I carry my card with me all the time."

Drive an hour directly south of Tucson, and you come to the small town of Nogales, Arizona, at which there is a wall eighteen feet high. On the other side of the wall is the town of Nogales, Sonora. The wall goes on, with gaps, for more than six hundred miles, in California, Arizona, New Mexico, and Texas. Most of it is in Arizona. Like a river, it takes different forms along its course. More closely guarded here, lower there, deadlier elsewhere. In Nogales, it is great vertiginous rust-colored iron bars spaced just close enough to prevent even a child's head from getting through.

Looking through the fence, I see two kids in white and green school uniforms waiting for the bus. They are standing in front of a freshly painted house. Nogales, Sonora, looks, if not prosperous, not desperately poor. The bus arrives. They get on. It leaves. At my feet is a small bar of rusted iron, a heavy rectangular ingot about a half inch square and seven inches long: a piece of the wall. I pick it up and put it in my bag. The wall is not extensive in Texas, and it stops short of the most inhospitable parts of the desert in Arizona. Those who wish to cross on foot are compelled to walk around the wall. Many do. It's a quick two- or three-day trek in ideal circumstances. It is much longer for those who get lost. Hundreds of people each year die attempting to cross, killed by heatstroke, cold, dehydration, Border Patrol agents, or wild animals. Some of the lost, the "lucky" ones, are found alive. If they are not arrested, they are simply dropped off, with neither money nor help, on the Mexican side of the border.

In Nogales, Sonora, in a simple shedlike building close to the checkpoint, Father Martin talks about his organization, the Samaritans. The Samaritans provide shoes and some emergency care for those who have been brought in from the desert. Father Martin speaks of the sorrow of the rescued, and of their wounds (terrible pictures of blistered and burned feet have been put up). Some of the rescued migrants, particularly those who have been separated from their families, will attempt to cross again.

One of the volunteers at Samaritans is Peggy, a blond American woman in her late fifties or early sixties. She drives down from her ranch in Arizona weekly to work here. She is a retiree and had worked as a nurse in Oregon. She more closely fits the profile of those who fear undocumented immigrants: white people, old people, retired people. What she says when I ask her to describe Arizona's situation surprises me.

"It's a race war. They just don't like the Mexicans."

"Is that true? Most people would hesitate to say that."

"What else could it be?"

Through narrow darkness, through scrub forests and rocky cliffs, our Elder Brother brought us across, his name was I'itio. On our setting out from the other side, he turned us into ants. He brought us through narrow darkness and out at Baboquivari Peak into this land. Here we became human again, and our Elder Brother rested in a cave on Baboquivari, and there he rests till this day, helping us.

The land is a maze. You have to be guided through, right from the beginning you had to be guided. The first story in the world is about safe passage.

This, too, is my America: people wandering in the desert in fear of their lives. At this very moment they are there. There are people in the desert, a never-ending migration. They die out there because the policy is to let them die (the wall is strategically incomplete) to discourage others from crossing. In their thousands they have died, for the crime of wishing to be in America or the crime of wishing to return. In Tucson I go out to dinner with Roberto Bedoya, an eloquent and thoughtful man who runs the city's arts council. "There are three ways of making a space," he says. "Through systems, through arguments, and through poetics."

After dinner, he drives me out to the parking lot of the Casas Adobes supermarket. Here, less than a year earlier, a young man had shot eighteen people and killed six. The U.S. Representative Gabrielle Giffords had been shot in the head, and reported dead, but she had lived. The parking lot is quiet. What do we miss unless we are told? What do we fail to see? Roberto drives me back across the city to the lodge. In spite of the city's lights, I can see the stars near the horizon.

If you go down from Tucson by a southwesterly route, you come to the border at Sasabe. To our right is Tohono O'odham land. The sacred peak of Baboquivari has a changing profile with each passing minute as we go down the narrow road. I am with a group of artists brought down by an organization called CultureStrike. The land is dry, covered with small hardy trees, shrubs, brown grass, and the saguaro cactus. (The saguaro, which is native to the Sonoran Desert, has always been for me a shorthand for the Southwest.) There is an element of "come and see what is being done in your name" in this journey.

At Sasabe, under the high brown wall that rises and falls with the variegated terrain, officers have set up targets for shooting practice. Their M16s shatter the air of the quiet crossing point. We present our passports, and cross the border from Sasabe into the small Mexican community of El Sasabe. There are kids playing here (the gunfire of the M16s from the American side still audible), and a pair of thin horses graze in a field. We are taken to a small bungalow to listen to Grupos Beta give a presentation. Grupos Beta is a sort of Mexican cognate of the U.S. Border Patrol: a federally funded uniformed service mandated to work along the border. But Grupos Beta does not prevent people from migrating; it aims only to help them. It provides medical help, search and rescue services, water stations on the Mexican side, and up to three days of temporary housing. And this is what they talk about during the presentation, sidestepping any questions about the drug trade. In the office is a large map of the border and the Sonoran Desert. One red dot for each death, the officer says. The map is a field of proliferating color, like something growing out of control in a petri dish.

When we return to the border point, the shooting has stopped. The wall spins away into the distance like an unspooling length of ribbon. In the grass near the inspection post, on the Mexican side, someone has planted two white crosses. The large one lists at a forty-five-degree angle. On the smaller one, I can make out the word "mujeres." The tag of the man who takes my passport says OFFICER BAXTER. I ask him about the work of the Border Patrol. He has a ready answer: "The Mexican government doesn't care. They are not doing their share of enforcement. They need to make their country good so that people don't need to come over here."

The majority of migrant deaths happen in the Tucson sector, around two hundred each year. Arizona's legislature and its law enforcement are notorious—or, to some, admirable—for their aggression toward recent immigrants. Racial profiling is legal, and there are initiatives to expunge Mexican American studies from public high schools. This aggression is also there on the federal level. President Obama has deported people at a greater rate than any of his predecessors. The deportation rate has been kept up, even after the president offered amnesty to undocumented residents who came to the United States as children. The horror of sudden familial division is something experienced by thousands of people in the United States every month. Human rights activists in Tucson organize on several fronts.

The organization Coalición de Derechos Humanos serves as a local gathering point for some of these acts of resistance. They work on gathering information, organizing protests, documenting abuse, doing legal work, and offering direct aid to migrants. They also work in partnership with other organizations. CultureStrike, which involves creative people in immigration policy, is one. The faith-based group No More Deaths, which provides humanitarian assistance, is another. I attend a meeting of No More Deaths one evening in the basement of Tucson's St. Mark's Presbyterian Church. It is a welcoming group of about fifteen, most of them white, and most middle-aged or older. It feels like a classic church missions group. After a moment of silence in memory of the dead, they discuss a strategy to replenish drinking stations on the American side of the border.

At the Tucson office of Coalición de Derechos Humanos, I speak with Kat Rodriguez and Isabel Garcia, two of its leaders. Isabel is also a Pima County public defender, and has been prominent for several decades in the fight against inhumane immigration policies. She tells me about one of the men who died in the desert, a man named René Torres Carvajal, a father of five. His body was never found. Many of those most desperate to return after deportation are people whose lives are here, whose entire families are here. Kat shows me the storeroom, with a large pile of white crosses made by volunteers, for use in a memorial procession on Día de los Muertos. The crosses are marked either with the name of someone who died or "desconocida," "desconocido," unknown. Desconocido, desconocido, desconocida, desconocido, desconocida, desconocida, desconocido, desconocido, desconocido: to infinity, it seems.

"The visibility of groups like No More Deaths is important for our work," Isabel says. "In 2005 two young white men were arrested for rescuing a migrant, and it was a big story. Because they look like the people who consider themselves the real Americans. We need a lot of education in this country. People have opinions, but they are ignorant of what's going on."

"Ignorant and maybe also desensitized?" I ask.

"People have to be desensitized," Kat says, "to allow the kind of horrible death that happens to someone like René. If you really confronted it, it would be unbearable. If a dog died like that, there would be an uproar."

"Our friends—the unions, the churches, the politicians—have let us down, they're the ones who make this happen," Isabel says. "They are afraid and don't want to deal with root cause. They don't want to deal with the six million jobs NAFTA took. They don't want to think about American intervention in Central America and all the refugees that caused. We paid for that army to be persecuting its own people. And our 'war on drugs' is going to cause more refugees."

I ask them to tell me about the penalties for those who are arrested.

Kat says, "Illegal entry is up to a hundred and eighty days, and they are the more fortunate ones."

Isabel says, "It's two to twenty years in prison for reentry: reentry is a felony. All these people are relabeled as criminals. Definition of criminal: drug dealers, violent offenders, and 'repeat immigration offenders.' So they sweep them up with a few actual criminals, send them to prison, and the prisons make money. Obama gives this speech in El Paso: 'We have to enforce the law.' How come they don't enforce the law on Wall Street?"

"And once you get branded as a criminal," Kat says, "no one is going to want to defend you. The American people just think: well, they are drug barons and rapists. They don't know 'criminal' more often means someone who committed immigration offenses."

I wonder if, for the 11 million who are undocumented now, amnesty would be the answer.

"It wouldn't be the answer," Kat says. "It would be a start. People want to go home: those conditions have to be addressed."

"These neoliberal trade agreements that are creating poverty have to stop," Isabel says. "What we want is comprehensive reform. We've got to address root cause, and we have to recognize these people who are already working in this country. And a third thing, just as important: we have to demilitarize the border."

"And the bodies that are found in the desert: can you tell me your role in getting those bodies identified?"

"Kat gets these calls. 'My brother crossed here five weeks ago, can you help me find him?' "

"And I have to ask them difficult questions," Kat says, nodding. "Did he have any broken bones? Birthmarks? When he laughed, did you notice metals? A silver filling? And I can feel them imagining their lost brother laughing. When I speak to people, I never use the past tense. I say, 'What color are his eyes?' not 'What color were his eyes?' "

The Pima County Medical Examiner's Office depends on the information Coalición de Derechos Humanos provides. They have a relationship of trust with the community. The government doesn't. Kat shows me René's cross and tells me that his sister comes here to visit it.

"You said some of these crosses are for people of unknown gender. How come?"

"Sometimes the remains are too dispersed," she says. "The men can be small. In the absence of a pelvis, it's hard to tell man from woman."

"But people keep looking."

"Who do you know who would ever stop looking for their loved ones? Nobody would."

As I leave, a woman in a green shirt comes into the office, and Kat says: "That is René's sister." A woman returning again and again to the only place she can, worrying a grief bare.

Later that day, I make a wasted visit to the Tucson Sector Border Patrol headquarters. It is a complex of new buildings on Swan Road, just outside the city. After I put in my request and after a short wait at the Public Information office, Officer Escalante comes out. "Everybody is interested in what we do here," he says. "We get a lot of requests."

"There's no one I could talk to, even briefly?"

"No."

The taxi driver who takes me back into town from Swan Road is named Al. He is jovial and bearded, and looks like Dumbledore.

"We didn't cross the border. The border crossed us. We've always been here. This business of trying to keep people out: in the end it's futile."

"What do you think the government should do?"

"I think every border in the world should be knocked down, and let people go wherever the hell they want. If people want to come here and be respectful of our ways, then we should be welcoming. It's not poor people coming through the border. You have to pay the coyote, what, six thousand dollars? I don't know about you, but I don't have six thousand dollars in my pocket I can pay somebody."

"We are talking about extremely courageous, extremely hardworking people here."

"People say: they're taking our jobs. Let me see: the non-English-speaking, undereducated person came here and took your job? Don't be telling people that. It's embarrassing."

"In your view, what's really going on here?"

"Our policies that have created the narco situation down there. Our policies have created the poverty."

Citizenship is an act of the imagination. I was born American, but I also had to learn to become American. I have had to think for myself about "the systems, the arguments, and the poetics" of this complicated country. These thoughts took me deep into the history of the Black Atlantic. My understanding of American experience has mostly been from the point of view of a recent African immigrant. I tried to understand the interconnected networks of trade and atrocities that formed the histories of the cities I've known and visited. I've brooded on New York City and Lagos, but also New Orleans, Ouidah, Cape Town, Port of Spain, and Rio de Janeiro. In Tucson, witnessing the ongoing crisis in the borderlands, I have to revise my understanding of my country to include this, too.

We wander out to the intake area. It is like an emergency room's loading bay, but simpler. Inside is a small morgue unit; outside, a larger one. Dr. Hess says, "This can take up to one hundred forty-two bodies."

Dr. Greg Hess is the chief medical examiner for Pima County. He is about forty years old, with sandy hair and a friendly face that makes him look about ten years younger than he is. The larger morgue unit contains rows of body bags in metal shelving, stacked in a regular array like a card catalogue, five levels high.

Oh, Death.

"They are mostly John Does. It's worse in summer. Border Patrol brings them in, and we work with the folks at Derechos Humanos to try to identify them. We do our best, whether we think the person is American or not. We try to treat them as we would our own family. We mostly fail. People cross the desert without identification, or their personal effects are scattered by coyotes or birds."

He takes me into the property room, where unclaimed personal effects are kept. The clear plastic bag I examine has typical contents: a red comb, pesos, dollars, a bank card, a damaged birth certificate. Hess points to a locked metal cabinet. It is empty for now, set aside for next year's unknowns. These deaths will continue.

On my way out, he shows me the anthropology department of the County Medical Examiner's Office. There are skeletal remains on the table.

But this is not a migrant from the desert. It's from a murder in Pima County itself. There is a bullet hole in the skull, and parts of the skeleton are charred black where someone tried to burn it. The remains of some argument.

"What happens to the unknowns," I ask, "after every effort to identify them is exhausted?"

"Cremation, and then interment at the county cemetery."

On the table on which I write this is the piece of iron I took from the base of the wall at Nogales more than two years ago. The officers at Tucson Airport gave me trouble (it was in my hand luggage, and came up strange and solid on the X-ray). I told them it was a memento. They took it out of the bag and examined it, puzzled. Then they let me go, with my piece of the wall.

Tucson's Evergreen Mortuary and Cemetery is a good example of what Elysium might look like. Its quiet lawns and abundant shade, provided by twelve varieties of evergreens, are a tranquil setting for the beloved dead. That much green speaks of repose. But drive a little bit past the serene atmosphere of Evergreen, past some construction work, perhaps stopping to ask for directions. Leave the green behind, drive on into the dusty back section. You have come to quite a different view of the afterlife. This dusty field is the Pima County Cemetery. There is no grass here, a couple of young trees but no shade, and there are no visitors. All there is is dirt. Here and there are plastic flowers swallowed by the dust.

The headstones are sunken, overruled by dirt. There are two columbaria for urns. The wind blows trash across the graves. Some of the grave markers, particularly the older ones, have names and dates on them. Many others are simply marked JOHN DOE, JANE DOE, or UNKNOWN, though each, to someone somewhere, must once have meant the world, and more.

SECTION IV

Epilogue

Blind Spot

ONE NIGHT IN April 2011, I stayed up late, reading the final pages of Virginia Woolf's diaries. Those pages, written in late 1940 and early 1941, were about the loss of her London home in the war, her terrible nervousness about the ongoing air raids, the unexpected death of Joyce, her love for Leonard, her engagement with literature, and, above all, her losing battle against depression. But the pages held a radiance, too, because of Woolf's prose, the intensity of her attention to life, and the epiphanic moments that intermittently illuminated the gloom. I went to sleep in the glare of her words. It was late, around three. I slept dreamlessly. When I woke up, there was a gray veil right across the visual field of my left eye. The blindness wasn't total—I could see around the lacelike edges of the obstruction—and there was no pain. At the bathroom sink, splashing cold water into the eye, I wondered if this was simply my subconscious at work. Was I like those highly suggestible people who, out of sympathy with something written, drift into an area of darkness?

I have always had weak eyes. From the age of eleven I wore glasses for myopia, and over the years the prescriptions got stronger. My brothers and my mother are severely myopic, as was my grandfather. Glasses, inconvenient as they are, are also an occasion for gratitude at not having to live life in an impressionistic blur. But blindness was another matter. Blindness happened in literature and films, it happened to blues musicians, to mythical figures, to those unfortunates one encounters on the streets of Lagos or on the subways of New York. I leaned over the sink and splashed cold water into my eye once again. But the gray veil remained, and, try as I might, I saw almost nothing out of my left eye.

I felt concern, not panic. Why should I suddenly lose my vision, without warning and with no apparent cause, one fine morning in my mid-thirties? There was nothing to worry about. At the beautiful and remote writers' residency where I was staying in upstate New York, with several other people, I went down to the communal kitchen and told them what was happening. Quickly, a car was organized to take me down to hospital in the small town of Hudson, some twenty minutes away. If it is a detached retina, one of them said, which is what it looks like, you should have it looked at right away. It can be fixed, but only if it's done quickly. And when I heard those words, which were meant to be reassuring, I worried.

After my colleague dropped me off at Columbia Memorial Hospital, I did my insurance paperwork and was asked to wait on a bed in an emergency triage area. From the other side of the screen, I heard a family discussing the kidney problems of the man on that bed. They spoke in troubled tones, and I could hear that the man, whom I couldn't see, was in some pain. At length, a doctor arrived and examined me. He asked a few questions and, puzzled, wrote me a referral to a private ophthalmologist nearby. And so I picked my way gingerly down to the Union Street address he had given me, about four blocks away.

It was a bright day, hot for April. The ophthalmology practice was set back from the street, a low brown building at the end of a tarred lot. There, too, the first order of business was about my insurance bona fides—the sense of relief at having insurance, or the distress at not having it, is part of any medical procedure in the United States—and then I sat in the ophthalmologist's chair in a darkened room, and she leaned over me in that solicitous way that medical practitioners share with barbers and flight attendants, and that I have always liked. She tested my vision on the alphabet charts, irrelevantly, I thought, since I wasn't there to have new glasses made, and then, dilating both pupils with mydriatic drops, examined each eye with a powerful lamp. She looked closely. In the vision-canceling intensity of the lamp, my gray veil became a thick red cloud of pure vision, and I imagined I could see my own optic nerve. The doctor asked questions. Had I had the problem before? Had I carried anything heavy lately? No, not that I could think of. I did not mention Mrs. Woolf's diaries. I can tell you it isn't a detached retina, the doctor said. You'd better see a specialist, in Albany or in New York City. As I stepped out of the office, I made an appointment at the New York Eye and Ear Infirmary for that evening. It was mid-afternoon, a Thursday. I had begun to feel the curiously woolly effect of dilation on my eyes. Darkness encroached by degrees, and, in the afternoon sun, I could hardly see out of my right eye, and not at all out of the left. I had become almost completely blind. I began to walk down Union Street in the direction of the train station, glaring and squinting, trying, and mostly failing, to see what was ahead of me.

Hudson is old and elegant, settled by the Dutch in the seventeenth century, and retaining much of its nineteenth-century built environment. One uncertain step at a time I began the walk past the old houses, to the station, which was a little more than a mile away. Is this real? Am I stumbling alone and almost blind down a quiet street in an unfamiliar town? The sun was as strong as a hallucination. The houses were brightly painted, crisp against the sky, making of the whole street a collage, foggy in parts, clear in others, grainy in the distance, so that, all of a sudden, I was no longer in the present at all but back in the era of the earliest photographs.

I heard faint noises, the occasional car going down another street, a voice lightly thrown from its unseen body, the hum of distant machines, and the sound of my own breathing as I put one foot in front of another. My body made its way down the bright street, mystified and almost inadvertent. The journey took a long time, twice as long as it should have taken, and I was afraid I'd get knocked down at one of the intersections. Each house looked much the same as the next, polygonal, almost flat, neither more nor less substantial than the sky above, each successive block glowing like the built landscape in the very first street photograph, the view from Niépce's country house in Le Gras in 1826. The view seemed on the perpetual verge of vanishing. I myself felt like a cutout: diminished and simplified because the sense of sight on which I was so dependent flickered with each step.

At long last I reached Front Street. As I had eaten nothing all day, I went into a diner. It wasn't particularly full, but I sat at the counter because it was near the door, and I was given a menu that I couldn't read. I blinked and squinted, but the words refused to resolve in the meaningless hieroglyphics of my right eye and in the total darkness of the left. As I handed the menu back to the waitress, explaining to her that my pupils were dilated, I was ambushed by a sudden shame: that she would think me illiterate and a liar. The thought, foolish as it was, caught me by surprise. At the far end of the counter was a party of four, all young, two blond women and two men, also fair-haired. Their laughter tinkled around the diner, then ceased, and they went back to talking in hushed tones. I distinctly heard one of the women say: Disfarmer. But I could make out nothing else of the conversation. I was afraid.

When we write fiction, we write within what we know. But we also write in the hope that what we have written will somehow outdistance us. We hope, through the spooky art of writing, to trick ourselves into divulging truths that we do not know we know. *Open City,* published two months before my eye troubles began, is in part an examination of the limits of sensitivity and of knowledge. One passage, narrated by Julius, the young psychiatrist at the center of the story, reads as follows:

Ophthalmic science describes an area at the back of the bulb of the eye, the optic disk, where the million or so ganglia of the optic nerve exit the eye. It is precisely there, where too many of the neurons associated with vision are clustered, that the vision goes dead. For so long, I recall explaining to my friend that day, I have felt that most of the work of psychiatrists in particular, and mental health professionals in general, was a blind spot so broad that it had taken over most of the eye. What we knew, I said to him, was so much less than what remained in darkness, and in this great limitation lay the appeal and frustration of the profession.

I arrived in Manhattan that evening. My pupils had gone back to normal size, and I could see out of my right eye again. The left remained obscure. That night was the first of more than half a dozen visits to the New York Eye and Ear Infirmary. Not until the following Monday, after several exams by several doctors, after contrast scans and high-resolution photographs of my retinas, in which they billowed like mysterious red planets, after sitting in waiting rooms with the sad, quiet blind, many of whom were elderly, after overhearing those who had been told that nothing further could be done for them, only after this unguided tour of misery did I receive a diagnosis. By then the gray veil had retreated and my eyesight had come back. The scans had been alarming: my left retina was strewn with exploded blood vessels, which showed up in the photographs as wiry black tangles against the red field. Where those vessels had bled over the retina, the vision was obscured. That accounted for the field of gray: I had been trying to look through a hemorrhage. You have papillophlebitis, said Dr. L, who had a thick Russian accent and a laconic manner. He was friendly, and a little impatient, as all specialists are. It is idiopathic, he said, so I can't tell you what caused it. It just happens, it begins on its own, something occludes your retinal veins. It's also called big blind spot syndrome. It's a young man's disease, and, as far as we can tell, it has nothing to do with diet, or genetics, or anything we can trace. But don't worry, it probably won't happen again. We'll just cauterize some of these damaged vessels with a laser. Simple procedure. Big blind spot is benign. He smiled, like a matador who'd just wrestled down a calf, like a man who hadn't gotten quite the challenge he'd hoped.

On my next visit, Dr. L did the laser surgery, and I returned to normal life, to regular myopia. But of course big blind spot did happen again. That insurgent area of darkness took over my eye, and I returned to the hospital later in the year, and again it cleared up. And I expect that it will happen again, and again, until it is supplanted by something worse, as it was written.

Acknowledgments

I WOULD LIKE to thank the family, friends, commissioning editors, and colleagues with whose help I wrote the essays contained in these pages. My heartfelt appreciation goes in particular to Susan Aberth, Beth Adams, Oye Akisanya, Svetlana Alpers, Katie Assef, Jin Auh, David Bajo, Elise Blackwell, Tracy Bohan, Chris Boot, Leon Botstein, Lee Brackstone, Finn Canonica, Wah-Ming Chang, Ken Chen, Amy Conchie, Kwame Dawes, Sonali Deraniyagala, David Ebershoff, Kay Eldrege, Max Fisher, John Freeman, Glenn Greenwald, Susan D. Gubar, Gioia Guerzoni, Malcolm Harris, Miriam Hefti, Aleksandar Hemon, Richard Herold, Ana Paula Hisayama, Florian Höllerer, Andy Hsiao, Vijay Iyer, Maria Koliopoulou, Karsten Kredel, Glenn Kurtz, Alexis Madrigal, John Edwin Mason, Jennifer McDonald, Joel Meyerowitz, Beatrice Monti, Michael Morris, Christine Mykityshyn, Christine Richter-Nilsson, Thyago Nogueira, Adewunmi Nuga, Ore Nuga, Afolake Oguntuyo, Akin Omotoso, Abimbola Onafuwa, Dimeji Onafuwa, Beth Pearson, David Remnick, Kornel Ringli, Rachel Rosenfelt, Ebisse Rouw, Kathy Ryan, John Ryle, Jonathan Sa'adah, James Salter, Gesa Schneider, Parul Sehgal, James Shapiro, Lola Shoneyin, Stephen Shore, Jake Silverstein, Ahdaf Soueif, Linda Spalding, Nanda Sugandhi, Monika Tranströmer, Tomas Tranströmer, Pauline

Vermare, Roel Veyt, Binyavanga Wainaina, Bill Wasik, Alex Webb, Rebecca Norris Webb, and Andrew Wylie.

I am grateful to various residencies and institutions that have facilitated the work in this book, in particular Ledig House, A Room for London, the Literaturhaus Zürich, the Literarisches Colloquium Berlin, the Windham Campbell Prize, the Laudinella, and the team at *The New York Times Magazine*. I would like to thank my father and mother especially. I would like to thank Angela Chen for advice, research help, and invaluable assistance in assembling the book, and Sasha Weiss, without whose editorial acuity many of these essays would have been much poorer. Caitlin McKenna edited the book with tremendous grace, faith, and patience. My debt to Karen remains inexpressible.

This book is dedicated to three extraordinary writers who read and encourage me: Michael Ondaatje, Amitava Kumar, and Siddhartha Mitter.

Art Permission Credits

INSERT I

WANGECHI MUTU
Even, 2014
Collage painting on vinyl
203.04 × 173.2 × 8.9 cm
80 × 68¼ × 3½ inches
© Wangechi Mutu. Photography: Bill Orcutt. Courtesy of the artist and Victoria Miro, London.

MALICK SIDIBÉ
Je veux être seule, 1979
Vintage gelatin silver print, glass, cardboard, tape, string
7¼ × 5¼ inches
© Malick Sidibé. Courtesy of the artist and Jack Shainman Gallery, New York.

ALEX WEBB
Bombardopolis, Haiti, 1986
© Alex Webb/Magnum Photos

ROY DECARAVA
Mississippi Freedom Marcher, Washington, D.C., 1963 (1963)
Silver gelatin photograph
© Estate of Roy DeCarava 2016. All rights reserved.

GUEORGUI PINKHASSOV
Parc des Buttes-Chaumont, Paris, 2012
© Gueorgui Pinkhassov/Magnum Photos

RICHARD RENALDI
Nathan and Robyn, 2012, Provincetown, MA
© Richard Renaldi

PENELOPE UMBRICO
541,795 Suns from Sunsets from Flickr (Partial) 1/26/06, 2006–ongoing
Detail of 2,500 4-inch × 6-inch machine C-prints
© Penelope Umbrico

INSERT II

RENÉ BURRI
Men on a Rooftop, 1960
© René Burri/Magnum Photos

GLENNA GORDON
Mass Abduction in Nigeria, 2014
Courtesy of Glenna Gordon

PHOTOGRAPHER UNKNOWN (NELSON MANDELA)
A Prisoner Working in the Garden, 1977
Courtesy of the National Archives of South Africa

Text Permission Credits

TEJU COLE was born in the United States in 1975 and raised in Nigeria. He is the author of *Known and Strange Things, Every Day Is for the Thief,* and *Open City.* He has won the PEN/ Hemingway Award, the Internationaler Literaturpreis, the Rosenthal Family Foundation Award for Fiction from the American Academy of Arts and Letters, and the New York City Book Award. He has been short-listed for the PEN/ Open Book Award and the National Book Critics Circle Award. In 2015, he won the Windham Campbell Prize. His photography has been exhibited in India, Iceland, Italy, and the United States. He is the photography critic of *The New York Times Magazine,* where his "On Photography" column was a finalist for a 2016 National Magazine Award.

tejucole.com

@tejucole

ABOUT THE TYPE

This book was set in Perpetua, a typeface designed by the English artist Eric Gill (1882–1940), and cut by the Monotype Corporation between 1928 and 1930. Perpetua is a contemporary face of original design, without any direct historical antecedents. The shapes of the roman letters are derived from the techniques of stonecutting. The larger display sizes are extremely elegant and form a most distinguished series of inscriptional letters.